Making Waves

The People and Places of Iowa Broadcasting

WDG Publishing

Making Waves

THE PEOPLE AND PLACES OF IOWA BROADCASTING

Jeff Stein

Foreword by Grant Price
Preface by Jack Shelley

Frontispiece: R. J. McElroy during a live "Voice of Iowa" radio broadcast in Waterloo in the 1940s.

PUBLISHED BY WDG PUBLISHING

Making Waves

The People and Places of Iowa Broadcasting

Editor   Elinor Day
Editorial Coordination   Jennifer Van Dyke
Design/Art Direction/Production   Duane Wood, Sam Otis, Sharon Boyle

First published in the United States of America by
WDG Communications Inc.
3500 F Avenue NW
Post Office Box 9573
Cedar Rapids, Iowa 52409-9573
Telephone (319) 396-1401
Facsimile (319) 396-1647

Library of Congress Cataloging-in-Publication Data

Stein, Jeff, 1963-
  Making waves : the people and places of Iowa broadcasting / Jeff Stein ; foreword by Grant Price ; preface by Jack Shelley.
      p. cm.
  Includes bibliographical references.
  ISBN 0-9718323-1-5
  1. Broadcasting--Iowa--History. I. Title.
  PN1990.6.U5S74 2004
  384.54'09777--dc22

                        2004006915

Printed in the United States of America

10 9 8 7 6 5 4 3 2 1

Contents

Acknowledgements

This book would not have been possible without the material contained within the Archives of Iowa Broadcasting, located at Wartburg College in Waverly. The facility has become the recognized repository for documents and artifacts related to radio and television in the state. A highlight of the collection is a set of videotapes produced by the ongoing Iowa Broadcasting Oral History Project, started by my colleague, Wartburg Professor Emeritus Grant Price, in 1994. Nearly 100 Iowa broadcasters have already shared their memories on videotape for future generations to study. Thanks to the financial support of entities such as the Iowa Broadcasters Association and the continued dedication of Professor Price and Wartburg College, this facility will serve both scholars and the general public for generations, telling the story of Iowa broadcasting.

This book also would not have been possible without the continued interest of various broadcasters and historians in preserving the records of this important medium. Their names are too numerous to mention here, but as the administrator of the Archives collection, my thanks go to every broadcaster, station manager, and citizen who has provided us with documents, photographs, and recordings.

Thanks also go to Duane Wood and his staff at WDG Publishing in Cedar Rapids for learning of the Archives and seeing the value of a book such as this. The editorial help and suggestions provided by Elinor Day were also invaluable in making the book more readable. As evidence of the publisher's commitment to the topic, a portion of the proceeds from sales of this book will go to a fund to support the ongoing collection efforts of the Archives of Iowa Broadcasting.

My greatest thanks go to my wife, Carole Lackey. Without question, she is my strongest supporter and my most accurate critic. She graciously gave up time we could have spent together, so I could write this book. She has indulged my interest in this field, and the career path upon which it has taken us. There is no way for me to properly convey how much I appreciate her continued love and devotion. I owe her more than I can express.

Honor Roll of Sponsors

The following broadcast firms and individuals have supported this project and the Archives of Iowa Broadcasting at Wartburg College with their generous prepublication pledge of commitment.

| KFJB-AM & KXIA-FM | KZIA Z102.9 | KCCI-TV | R. J. McElroy Chair | Des Moines Radio Group |
| Marshalltown | Cedar Rapids | Des Moines | Wartburg College | Des Moines |

"It takes more than tubes, wires, etc., to make a radio station.
It takes emotion, laughter, love, dreams, ideas; it takes people."

R. J. McElroy, during the inaugural broadcast
on KWWL radio on November 4, 1947.

Introduction

Far-off sounds would come into my bedroom at night through a tiny speaker on a clock radio (AM only) I was given for Christmas one year. In those days, before digital tuning, one could move the dial ever so slightly and depending on the weather, sounds from distant places like New York, Minneapolis, Chicago, and Denver could be heard. Whether they were the sounds of a baseball game, an all-night talk show, or a disc jockey with a deep voice "playing the hits," they filled my mind as a boy growing up in Central Iowa in the 1970s. Not unlike those who listened to crystal sets in the 1920s, or those who gaze with wonder upon the television set today, the world of broadcasting captivated me in a way virtually nothing else ever has.

In doing the research for this book, I was glad to know that I was not the only one who as a child would pretend to be on the radio or television; many of today's most famous names in the field fantasized doing play-by-play of sporting events, or impersonated favorite disc jockeys as they played records on their home stereos.

Broadcasting has not even been a part of our lives for a full century, yet today it is impossible to imagine life without it. Our memories are tied to it—happy memories tied to songs we heard on the radio, tragedies remembered by the pictures we have seen on television. Broadcasting has in many ways united us as a people; the commonality of experiences we share instantaneously thanks to radio and television were unheard of only 100 years ago.

Perhaps the unifying force of broadcasting is more prominent in a state like Iowa, with its traditionally rural population. Perhaps that is why the development of radio and television here often was far ahead of that in larger parts of the country—it was just more important to the audience here than in other places. Regardless, the history of broadcasting in Iowa is unique and groundbreaking. The impact of this form of mass communication has altered our lives in virtually every way. And audiences here feel very strongly about the personalities who come into their homes every day.

From the earliest days of experimentation, hundreds of men and women were literally "making waves"—creating an industry that travels through the air on modulated electrical waves, and proving wrong those who swore it could never work.

This book is far from a full history of broadcasting in Iowa; to give due credit to all those who have contributed to the success of radio and television in this state would take many books. Instead, this is a collection of stories about some of the people and places of Iowa broadcasting, designed to show how unique the Iowa experience has been.

Some of the stories were included because the individuals are well-known to a great number of people; other stories were included because they told of unique accomplishments; still others were included simply because I had learned about them, and found them to be representative of the experiences repeated at dozens of similar stations in other parts of the state.

Many wonderful stories about dedicated people are unfortunately not included; I hope they will be properly recognized in another, future book, and that those who read *Making Waves: The People and Places of Iowa Broadcasting* will find it to be a wonderful starting point for the recollection of even more broadcasting memories.

They faced enormous challenges, both technical and financial, in creating an entirely new way for the public to receive information and entertainment. They continue to break new ground today, with ever-changing technology. From the start, they have truly been "Making Waves." I hope you enjoy the memories recalled by these stories of the people and places of Iowa broadcasting.

Jeff Stein
R. J. McElroy Chair in Communication Arts
Wartburg College

Foreword

Electronic communication through radio and television may well turn out to be the defining force which shaped the 20th century. Certainly no other has touched human lives, both as individuals and as a society, more intimately and as pervasively. If proof were needed, it was provided again on September 11, 2001. However, just as Americans were unified by television through that terrible experience at the beginning of the 21st century, as we were through the Kennedy assassination in the middle of the 20th century, there also is a curious irony in the influence media have exercised. That is the socially isolating and fragmenting effect which has been produced by the massive amount of time spent using media, substituting vicarious experience for human contact and resulting in erosion of the role of other institutions in society.

Grant Price (circa 1965)

Some scholars, such as Leonard Steinhorn of American University, argue that in the final decade of the 20th century, media emerged as "The predominating influence in American society—replacing home, church, town hall and work." It all happened over the span of just 80 years.

Even if Steinhorn's premise is only partially valid, it should give us pause to begin reflecting on how this experience, obtained in such a short time, could inform the development of media of the future which is rocketing ahead at an even faster rate in our world of accelerating change. To do that we need to start thinking of it as history. Most of us usually don't regard it that way because radio and television have been so intimately tied into our own life experience. In order to benefit from the lessons which may be drawn from this rapid journey "from the airwaves to the internet" we must collect and preserve this history and make it accessible for study.

If that is regarded as a somewhat esoteric purpose, there is at least one other reason which is just as valid. That simply is to look back and enjoy remembering what we experienced as, first radio and then television, came into our homes and gave us access to a vastly wider range of information and entertainment than otherwise could have been possible. In many ways, the personalities who delivered these electronic messages were as much a part of the family as our relatives and there is value in reminiscing about, as well as learning from, times spent with family.

For anyone who has ever lived in Iowa, as you read this book and examine the pictures which accompany the text, I am certain it will resonate with experiences you have had. Many of them will be associated with the radio and television stations of your area and the personalities who became part of your family through them. A number of those stations set a standard for quality and public service which made them national leaders and models for others to follow.

That is one of great legacies of Iowa broadcasting. It is particularly true in the area of news. Managers at stations such as WHO and WMT invested in the staff and resources required to establish and support departments specifically dedicated to reporting news, weather and sports on radio and television. They were among the first to elevate the status of broadcast news to accepted principles of journalism practice. Others would follow as radio and television rapidly became the primary source of news for Americans, rising to that level by the mid-1960s. Sadly, the fairness and integrity which was the foundation for the trust which undergirded that reliance has been eroded by management practices in the exploding media universe which accompanied passage of the millennium. Perhaps that is one of the issues which needs to be examined under the light of history.

Grant Price
Professor Emeritus of Communication Arts
Wartburg College

Preface

I had the privilege of starting a broadcast news career in 1935, early in the development of electronic news reporting. Thus I had the rare opportunity of watching people who lived on farms and in small towns of the Midwest eagerly grasp their first opportunity to receive news almost instantaneously.

For long years these people had been lucky to see a newspaper once a week. Now the effect of radio news was almost like what happens when rain falls on a parched plant; there was a flowering of awareness, an eager haste to absorb information about what was going on in the world. Quite literally, their lives experienced a major change for the better—and they loved it.

Those of us fortunate enough to be news broadcasters then knew how fortunate we were: Our listeners felt they knew us as

Jack Shelley (circa 1960)

trusted friends who reported accurately and objectively on matters of real importance to them. Before long the shattering trauma of World War II was upon us. My station, WHO in Des Moines, was one of a handful that sent their own staffers overseas to tell the stories of Midwest men and women serving in uniform. I went to Europe with the U.S. Army and to the Pacific with the Navy, and was able to send the voices of these fighters back home. Their families hung on every word, and trust now was joined with gratitude.

The effect of electronic communication on the world has been so gigantic that it is beyond measuring. Iowa broadcasters have played a major role in altering our landscape. It is a story that has needed telling for a long time, and Jeff Stein has risen to the challenge.

Jack Shelley
Professor Emeritus of Journalism
Iowa State University

"A radio station could provide a service to people in the small towns and the farms, in addition to the cities—but particularly for people in the rural areas—that they had never known before. It was just a whole new world opening up for them."

WHO's Jack Shelley, during an interview for the Iowa Broadcasting Oral History Project in 1995.

1 | Sounds Flying Through The Air

As the 20th century began, people in rural areas such as Iowa were quite isolated. Automobiles were still uncommon, and travel from the farm to the nearest town—or even the nearest neighbor—meant hitching a horse to a wagon. In most areas, even electricity was still a far-off notion. The only form of "mass media" that existed was newspapers, and the most common form of entertainment was an evening with friends at home by the light of a kerosene lamp.

The notion of far-off sounds flying through the air and into homes was hard to comprehend. For those of us who treat such occurrences as a necessary part of everyday life, it is hard to imagine a time without radio or television. Once the concept actually began to show signs of becoming reality, citizens in Iowa and across the country were understandably excited.

At the turn of the 20th century, Council Bluffs native Lee DeForest was completing work on his Ph.D. at Yale University. He was trying to find a way to harness electrical current and amplify it; he knew that if the solution could be found, voices could travel between distant points without the need for cables or wires. In fact, he predicted actual radio broadcasting in 1902—but there was still the problem of harnessing the electrical current.

Then in 1906, DeForest invented the three-element vacuum tube, which for the first time allowed electrical currents to be amplified. This was the step that had been missing, and it allowed development of the radio industry to be commercially feasible.

A few years later, AT&T installed DeForest's audion tubes to boost voice signals as they went across the United States over land lines. Soon, the audion tube developed by DeForest was being used in homemade radio transmitters and receiving sets, and the industry was born.

The predecessor to over-the-air sound transmission came from "code stations," where operators sent the dots and dashes of Morse code to nearby receivers without the benefit of wires. Adding the audion tube to such a system could produce low-quality sound transmissions, which quickly became known as "wireless telephony." Now, voices and other sounds could be transmitted from one location to another without wires. This concept quickly revolutionized the way people around the world would get information.

Most early transmitters were homemade by amateurs who were experimenting with the new technology as a hobby. Many entities that started as code stations built by teenagers evolved into the earliest licensed radio stations.

The listening devices were homemade, as well. Many members of "the Greatest Generation" remember hearing their first radio broadcasts on a crystal set, which was quite easy to make; diagrams were included in many magazines of the time. An insulated copper wire would be wrapped around an empty Quaker Oats box. One end of the wire would serve as an antenna, leading out an open window to a tree or post. The other end, called a "cat's whisker," would touch a piece of mineral rock called a crystal that could bring in different signals, depending upon where on the crystal the "cat's whisker" would probe. A battery would be attached for power, and listeners could then pick up the sound of dots and dashes—and later voices—through earphones.

Quickly, however, the novelty of simply hearing an occasional sound from an experimental code station wore off, and the audience was ready for the miracle of broadcasting to become part of their daily lives. A number of early entrepreneurs were ready to provide the service to Iowans.

Col. B. J. Palmer (left) and an unidentified announcer (right) during a broadcast on WOC in Davenport in the early 1920s.

A 1920s-era broadcast in the KWCR studios in Cedar Rapids. The call letters reportedly stood for "Keep Watching Cedar Rapids."

According to records from the Department of Commerce, which oversaw the earliest days of radio broadcasting, in June, 1922, there were 11 Iowa stations licensed to broadcast. One year later, only eight of those original 11 were still in operation; however, another 18 had joined them, bringing the total number of Iowa's licensed stations to 26 out of 592 nationwide. Virtually none of these stations were operated by "professional broadcasters." A look at who was actually operating the radio stations of 80 years ago is somewhat surprising.

Six were operated by schools, colleges or universities, two were operated by banks, two were operated by individuals (the closest thing to "professional broadcasters" existing at the time), another was run by a newspaper, and yet another by a department store. However, most of the 14 radio stations in Iowa in 1923 were owned by electrical or radio companies in towns such as Fort Dodge, Marshalltown, Newton, Gladbrook, Burlington, and Sigourney,

and larger cities such as Waterloo, Davenport, Des Moines, Council Bluffs, and Dubuque. In fact, Fort Dodge, Burlington, and Waterloo each had two licensed radio stations by June of 1923.

The interest of electrical companies in the new field of radio was easy to understand. Since the basis of radio is the process of harnessing signals within an electrical current, it was a natural for those who were installing electrical lines to Iowa's rural areas to be following this use of electricity. And since there were no commercially produced radio transmitters or receiving sets at this time, the business opportunities were also logical.

The story of Marshalltown radio station KFJB is similar to those of many other stations of the time. Employees of the Marshall Electric Company were tinkering with the technology and built a transmitter that could send vocal messages to a properly tuned receiving set. Soon, they began building receivers for their friends, and as word spread, customers began asking for their own sets. In

Shenandoah's Famous Seed Men

It may be hard to believe today, but in the earliest days of broadcasting, two of the country's most famous announcers competed down the street from one another in little Shenandoah, Iowa, then boasting a population of just over 5,000. Both men originally went into radio as a way to sell their seed and nursery products. Before long, however, Henry Field and Earl May were the ringmasters of an exciting radio circus that captivated Shenandoah and much of the country.

"It was like having two P. T. Barnums in the same town at the same time, each trying to outdo the other," Earl May's son Ed once said.

Field and May were competitors in the seed business at the dawn of radio. An Omaha station, WOAW, invited each man to present evening programs, with great listener response. More than 5,000 letters came to the station after a 1923 Field broadcast that featured all his company's employees who could sing or play an instrument. A year later, May's first broadcast offered iris bulbs to the first 10,000 persons who sent cards to the station; 17,800 listeners from as far away as California responded.

Seeing the potential for promotion of his products, Henry Field brought radio station KFNF to the air on February 22, 1924, from makeshift studios on the third-floor of his nursery building. While there was still a ban on direct commercial advertising, Field was able to get around the restriction by offering to answer listener questions about

Henry Field

Earl May

gardening on the air each midday. He would then promptly add the letter writers to the mailing list for his company's catalog.

May continued broadcasting on the Omaha station using a special phone line connected to Shenandoah. By August of 1925, however, his own KMA—"the cornbelt station in the heart of the nation"—was on the air.

Whether it was to "Keep Millions Advised," or suggesting that "Kind Friends Never Fail," the stations battled mightily to outdo each other, well into the Great Depression.

"Everybody wanted to come to Shenandoah. There wasn't much to see or do anywhere else. But in Shenandoah, we had two radio stations and they were very anxious to come here," Mary Field Hamilton, Henry's daughter, said in a 1992 interview.

Field's station included healthy doses of old time fiddling and gospel music, while May's station focused more on information with a broader entertainment format.

The competition between the stations was never greater than during the annual "jubilee" celebrations. When KFNF held its first jubilee to commemorate its second anniversary, the station stayed on the air for 36 straight hours at a time when stations were operating on a limited schedule, only a few hours a day. Not to be outdone, KMA's first jubilee included 72 hours of continuous broadcasting, as well as the promise of free pancakes personally fried by Earl May himself. A total of 53,000 flapjacks were cooked and served during that first KMA jubilee in November of 1925.

Thousands flocked to Shenandoah in the late 1920s for events such as a mass wedding with 14 couples involved, or to watch a

"flagpole sitter" sit atop the KFNF broadcast tower for weeks at a time.

Occasional celebrations were not enough, however, for these two men. In 1927, they competed with one another by building large auditoriums for live broadcasts. Henry Field announced in February of that year that he would build the KFNF Auditorium; a few months later, Earl May announced similar plans for a building he would call Mayfair. While the Field building was built by staff members and local contractors, May's facility was designed by an architect from Omaha to be the largest and biggest radio hall between the Mississippi River and the Rocky Mountains. Field denied spending even as much as $40,000 on his building; May proudly proclaimed that his building cost more than $100,000 to build.

More than 100,000 visitors came to Shenandoah each year in the late 1920s to see acts perform live in the various auditoriums, and therefore on the two radio stations. Field and May each provided free entertainment from morning until night. Soon, the Field and May facilities each added stores and overnight lodging facilities, as well.

But on more than one occasion, the stations and their owners worked together, in an effort to bring greater attention to Shenandoah and to better serve their audiences. Since neither station was licensed to be on the air all afternoon, KMA and KFNF teamed up to broadcast the 1925 World Series. KFNF would broadcast the first innings, then

Shenandoah's Famous Seed Men

listeners would switch to KMA for the completion; Field vice president and announcer Pate Simmons did the broadcasting for both stations, re-creating the play-by-play for the games via teletype wire.

The next year, *Radio Digest* magazine sponsored its annual "World's Most Popular Radio Announcer" contest. Henry Field had placed second in the 1925 contest to network announcer Graham McNamee, but withdrew from the 1926 race and urged his listeners to cast their votes instead for Earl May, to insure that Shenandoah would be recognized across the country. Earl May won the 1926 contest, receiving more than 452,000 votes; however, despite withdrawing from the contest, Field still managed to finish sixth that year with more than 153,000 votes of his own. "The world has beaten a path to Shenandoah," the magazine wrote.

The stations also paid quick dividends for both Field and May. Field's annual seed sales rose from $900,000 in the year before he began radio broadcasts to $2.5 million just three years later. May's company turned its first profit after five years of losses in the same year as his first radio broadcast.

While their intense competition ended in the 1930s, the mark that Henry Field and Earl May left on Iowa broadcasting and their town of Shenandoah is still unparalleled in broadcasting history.

After a visit to Shenandoah during the October 1927 jubilee celebration, Federal Radio Commission member Harry Bellows reported to his fellow commissioners that "the stations at Shenandoah presented an extraordinary example of the place a broadcasting station can hold in the lives of people on the farms and in small towns, not as distinct sources of entertainment, but as a close-at-hand center of actual life."

"The story of a big radio station like ours is fascinating," Earl May wrote in 1945, a few years before his death. "The story isn't too technical when it's told right, either, because the story of radio is necessarily a story of people, and people are always interesting."

Certainly none were more interesting during that time than Henry Field and Earl May.

a manner no different from the largest New York City operators (such as General Electric or Westinghouse), Marshall Electric's owners, Earl Peak and A. J. Clark, decided to produce programs to be broadcast over their homemade transmitter, hoping that the public would buy receiving sets from them. Ultimately, that transmitter would lead to the founding of radio station KFJB, which was licensed by the FCC on June 2, 1923.

The story was no doubt the same in Newton (WIAH-Continental Radio & Manufacturing), Burlington (WIAS-Home Electric and WLAT-Radio and Specialty), Gladbrook (KFIK-Gladbrook Electrical) and Sigourney (WOAD-Friday Battery & Electric), all of which had stations licensed by the FCC in the middle of 1923.

But others saw broadcasting differently—not as a way to make money from selling radio receivers, as the electric companies did, but as a way to deliver a message to a potentially large audience.

The first radio station operated in the state of Iowa that was not begun by a state college or university actually had its start across the Mississippi River in Illinois. In the spring of 1922, Col. Bartlett Joshua Palmer purchased the rights to a Rock Island radio station and moved it across the river to Davenport as part of his Palmer School of Chiropractic.

On February 18, 1922, WOC went on the air, licensed to the Karlowa Radio Company of Rock Island. However, the costs to start the station and continue its operation were great, and owner Robert Karlowa quickly began to look for a buyer. In May of that year, WOC's license was transferred to the Palmer School of Chiropractic, led by B. J. Palmer, and the equipment was moved to the Palmer School property at 1002 Brady Street in Davenport. The station became the first commercial radio station to be licensed in Iowa. The call letters, WOC, reportedly stood for "Wonders of Chiropractic," but in fact were issued sequentially by the FCC. Palmer's purchase began a family connection to some of the best-known stations in Iowa broadcasting—a connection that would last for three-quarters of a century.

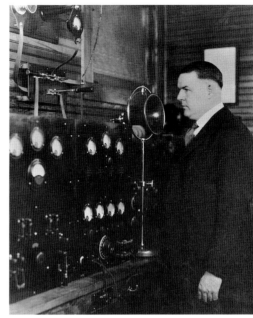

The first radio station in Cedar Rapids went on the air in this building in 1922; WJAM founder "Tex" Perham is seen speaking into the original microphone, at right.

Not long after WOC took to the air, other Iowa stations began a broadcast schedule. On July 30, 1922, an engineer named Douglas "Tex" Perham brought broadcasting to Cedar Rapids when his WJAM began operation in a converted garage on the southwest side of Cedar Rapids. Soon after, studios for the station were moved into three rooms of Perham's home, with the antenna and 115-foot transmitting tower mounted on his roof, creating quite a stir in his neighborhood.

While working as an assistant to Lee DeForest, Tex Perham designed and built the first five "wireless telephone" stations in the United States. Since the word "microphone" had not been invented, announcers spoke into devices called "carbon transmitters." At first, the predecessor to WMT was only on the air for an hour a day, broadcasting each evening from 7 until 8 p.m. In the weeks leading up to the inaugural broadcast, tests were made. Perham offered a five-dollar prize to the listener who reported hearing his experimental broadcasts from the greatest distance. The prize went to a listener 60 miles from Cedar Rapids.

Only ten days later, Cedar Rapids' second radio station took to the air. On August 9, Harry Paar went on the air with a station originally called W9CNF, which soon became WKAA, and in 1928, KWCR. Three years later, brothers John and "Mike" Cowles of the *Des Moines Register & Tribune* bought KWCR from Paar and set up shop with studios on the seventh floor of the Montrose Hotel in downtown Cedar Rapids.

Meanwhile, WJAM left Cedar Rapids for Waterloo in 1928 when the station was sold to Harry Shaw, publisher of the *Waterloo Morning Tribune* newspaper. He changed the station's call letters to match his newspaper, and the now-familiar WMT was born.

Shaw was an active owner during the six years he owned the station. In 1931, he provided the initial funding—a pledge of $52,000, with 10 percent paid up front—for *Broadcasting* magazine (now known as *Broadcasting and Cable,* the nation's premier weekly magazine in the field). Magazine founder Sol Taishoff recalled in 1962 that within a year, Shaw was repaid for his upfront investment of $5,200, as well as another $5,200 a year

Harry Shaw

after that as a bonus, "plus our everlasting gratitude for making possible the founding of the magazine." Shaw was also one of the first presidents of the National Association of Broadcasters, being elected at the group's 1931 convention.

Harry Shaw also understood the importance of a low dial position, because of the way amplitude modulation (AM) waves traveled. He knew that a station at 600 kHz would travel farther than one with more watts of power at, for example, 1600 kHz, so he simply moved WMT to 600 without bothering to tell the Federal Communications Commission.

According to William B. Quarton, whose tenure at WMT spanned most of five decades, Shaw's lawyer told him he had to go back to the 1120 kHz frequency he had been assigned. "He said, 'The hell I am, this is too good,'" Quarton recalled. "They got so tired of seeing him over there (at the FCC) that they said, 'Oh, hell, let those Czech haymakers have it.'"

Shaw sold the station to the Cowles brothers in October, 1934, and by the middle of the next year, they had moved WMT back to Cedar Rapids, combining it with KWCR to create one station. However, WMT maintained studios in both Waterloo and Cedar Rapids until after World War II.

A national company founded in Iowa saw the business possibilities of radio, and on April 11, 1924, the Bankers Life Insurance Company (now known as the Principal Financial Group) first broadcast over radio station WHO. One visitor to the new station's facilities on the top floor of the Liberty Building in downtown Des Moines described the scene vividly; it accurately portrays the layout of many radio station studios during the early days of broadcasting:

The reception room and studio of the new station are luxuriously appointed, the latter room being as near sound-proof as it is possible to make it. The walls are deadened with heavy velour curtains of old rose shade, the entrance being curtained with the same material. Heavily padded carpet eliminates vibration of footsteps. A concert grand piano occupies one end of the studio, and a massive floor lamp stands at the side. In front is a pedestal supporting the microphone, this being on a level with the mouth of the performer. At the opposite end of the room is the announcer's desk, with a switchboard controlling the signals to the radio room. Colored lights flash 'all ready'... 'quiet' and other operating conditions.

Bankers Life president George Kuhns was a strong supporter of the station, and found it to be an easy way to promote his insurance company. Radio stations are required to identify themselves by call letters and city of origin at the top of each hour. WHO would identify itself as "This is WHO—Who?—Bankers Life, Des Moines."

The first decade of American broadcasting was filled with change, as the federal government would frequently change a station's power and dial position in order to eliminate interference. Many stations had to share time with one another. As part of a general reallocation by the FCC on November 11, 1928, WOC and WHO were the two Iowa radio stations selected to share a clear channel. This meant that they would not have interference from out-of-state

The College Component

While many ventured into operating radio stations as a way to promote business, much early experimentation in the field occurred in the physics and engineering departments of the state's major public universities. The State University of Iowa (now the University of Iowa) and Iowa State College (now Iowa State University) had the first licensed radio stations in Iowa. WSUI in Iowa City and WOI in Ames had begun experimental broadcasts and claim their origins pre-date World War I.

In 1911, an Iowa State College physics professor, "Dad" Hoffman, set up an experimental transmission line stretching from the campus water tower to Engineering Hall and asked for money from the college to establish a wireless telegraph station; the first transmission from campus in Morse code occurred a year later.

All amateur radio stations were shut down during World War I, but once the government approved transmissions again in 1919, the experiments quickly resumed.

The first "wireless telegraph" station in Iowa officially licensed by the federal government was owned by what was then known as the State University of Iowa. Given the call letters 9YA, the station was approved in the fall of 1919. The station operated with a voice transmitter built by a student, Carl Menzer. Menzer would manage the station, which would

WSUI founder Carl Menzer

become WSUI, his entire professional career, until his retirement in 1968.

On November 21, 1921, Iowa State College became the first station in America to be licensed by the federal government as an educational radio station, and was given the call letters 9YI. The first non-code broadcast originating from 9YI occurred on that day, when an hour of concert music was presented. Then on April 28, 1922, the FCC granted the station a license with the call letters WOI, and the first regular voice transmission was broadcast.

Soon after, on June 26, 1922, Iowa's first radio station, 9YA, was

granted a license with the new call letters WHAA. The station would assume its familiar call letters of WSUI (for State University of Iowa) in 1925.

WSUI can claim a number of "firsts"—it was the first educational station on the air west of the Mississippi River (although it held a "general" station license), the first radio station to broadcast live from a university classroom, and the first station in the country to offer a radio-only course for university credit. A Burlington man, Clifford Lideen, was bedridden but continued his studies via the radio courses. In

June of 1925, he became the first person to complete his college degree through radio instruction. WSUI's "radio courses" lasted for only three years, due to other commitments by faculty members, but the station continued broadcasting lectures from classrooms on a regular basis.

Even before WSUI's predecessor, 9YA, was on the air, the University of Iowa conducted a course on radio theory and electricity transmitted solely by code sent through the air, which Carl Menzer listened to as a high school student in 1917 from the wireless receiver he built at his home.

The station also presented a series of programs entitled "Radio Aids for High Schools," designed to help secondary schools in their work, as well as the "Iowa School for the Air," a program designed for elementary students which allowed college students the ability to act as part of the programs.

"Radio was such a startling thing at the time. People looked for ways to use it and many people were indifferent to it, including many people in government who never thought it would catch on," said University of Iowa researcher Von Pitman, Jr., who has written about the early days of broadcasting at the university. "But it was the dreamers and visionaries and tinkerers in the best American tradition who made this into something, and colleges provided a home for it."

Many years later, in 1959, the

The College Component

first experiment in stereo broadcasting in the area occurred, using both of the University of Iowa's radio stations. However, in order to get stereo, listeners actually needed two radios—one tuned to WSUI-AM for the "A" channel, the other tuned to KSUI-FM for the "B" channel.

Smaller institutions were also involved with the new technology of broadcasting. The "Wartburg Quarterly" from June 1917 indicated that Wartburg College "Professor C. S. Fritschel, who is an efficient wireless operator, recently dismantled his wireless outfit, for all private radio stations have been closed on account of war. Professor Fritschel's station has been officially sealed up."

Two years later, the same publication reported that "On or about May 15, Professor C. S. Fritschel re-erected his wireless outfit and has been receiving messages. At the outbreak of war he was compelled to dismantle his entire equipment; now, with the first announcement of permission to reinstate the outfit, he set it up in the laboratory."

The college was then located in Clinton, Iowa, and reports indicate that the Wartburg facility was located in the high central tower of the college building, a structure five to six stories tall located on the top of a high hill, which would have provided for excellent transmission and reception.

By 1923, three other institutions of higher learning had broadcast licenses: Graceland College in Lamoni (KFFV), Western Union College in Le Mars (KCRY), and William Penn College in Oskaloosa (KFHL). All continued operation for some time in those early years, which was no easy task given the high mortality rate of radio stations of the time.

According to the annual reports prepared by the Department of Commerce, which regulated broadcasting throughout most of the 1920s, all three stations were still on the air in 1925. However, the Graceland station does not appear on any reports after that year, and the Western Union College and William Penn College stations were both absent from the government's annual report by 1930.

broadcasters, but would have to limit the time each individual station was on the air. The solution: WHO would broadcast during the day and WOC during the evening one week, with WOC then broadcasting during the day and WHO during the evening the next week. While that was a "solution," it was hardly accepted by either party.

Finally, B. J. Palmer decided the real solution was for him to buy WHO, combining the two stations on the single frequency. The Central Broadcasting Company was formed, and on Valentine's Day 1930, the new "WOC-WHO" went on the air, with transmitters and studios located in both Des Moines and Davenport. A construction permit for a new 50,000 watt transmitter—ten times the previous power—was approved, and in 1933, the Davenport facilities were closed and all station activity came from Des Moines. On the fifth anniversary of the "sharing" arrangement, November 11, 1933, the "WOC" part of the station name was dropped; WOC would return to the air as a separate station, on another frequency, exactly one year later.

That "no nonsense" approach was one of B. J. Palmer's trademarks. The most famous alum of the WOC-WHO experience was a young sportscaster named Ronald "Dutch" Reagan, who recalled at WHO radio's 50th anniversary in 1974 the day Palmer decided that the station's "legal ID" was too wordy.

Reagan remembered that Ed Reimers (who would go on to become the voice of the Allstate insurance "you're in good hands" television commercials) was the announcer on duty that day in the mid-1930s. At the top of an hour, Reimers told the audience, "This is radio station WHO, Des Moines, Iowa." Palmer entered the studio and noted that most sponsors use words in their radio ads, and if the rest of the "talking" on the station was too extensive, the value of those words to the advertiser would be less—and that would be bad for business.

Palmer showed Reimers and Reagan how to eliminate unneeded

words in the legal ID. He noted that the words "radio station" were not needed, because if someone was listening, they would already know it was a radio station. "This is" could also be eliminated, Palmer said, because it was too obvious. That left the phrase, "WHO, Des Moines, Iowa."

As Palmer turned to leave, he stopped and then pointed out that "Iowa" was also extraneous, since there was only one "Des Moines" in the world at that time. In B. J. Palmer's mind, even an eight-word phrase was too long if the point could be gotten across in three words—WHO, Des Moines.

"He was the greatest master and teacher of the economy of words I've ever known," Reagan said.

The earliest days of broadcasting did not include what we today would call a "full schedule" of programming. At WSUI in Iowa City in the 1920s, the station would sign on, present a live musical program from the studio, sign off so that the lone station employee, Carl Menzer, could go across campus and set up microphones, sign back on for a professor's lecture on some topic, and so on. One of the first program schedules from WOC in Davenport, during the first week of July, 1922, promises that the station will be on each day at noon for a 15-minute chimes concert, followed by a weather report. Then the station would sign off until late afternoon when an "educational talk" would be delivered. The station would be silent again until the dinner hour, when a chimes concert, baseball final scores and market quotations would be aired, followed at 7 p.m. by an evening musical concert.

Western Iowa was also well represented during the earliest years of broadcasting. The June, 1922, Department of Commerce report indicates two stations licensed in Sioux City. WHAE, licensed to the Automotive Electric Service Company, lasted only a few months. But the station operated by the Davidson Brothers department store, WEAU, signed on in 1922 and provided a continuous broadcasting schedule until 1927.

A broadcast tower used by KFJB, Marshalltown (circa 1940).

As the popularity of radio grew, the morning newspaper in town began to take notice. The owners of the *Sioux City Journal*, the Perkins Brothers, made plans to start a radio station of their own, to be known as KSCJ. At the same time, the Davidson Brothers were advised that they would need to upgrade their operating equipment and transmitter at a cost of $25,000. Legend has it that when the high price tag became known, the Davidsons decided to get out of the radio business; their last broadcast was a few days before KSCJ's first broadcast, on April 4, 1927.

But not all the activity during broadcasting's first decade was in Iowa's largest cities. The hottest action was in Shenandoah in southwest Iowa, where Henry Field and Earl May engaged in a decade-long, ever-accelerating competition to outdo one another with their stations, KFNF and KMA. Using the stations as a way to help promote their respective seed and nursery businesses, Field and May became master showmen, with elaborate festivals and entertainment that drew national attention.

But while many remember those early stations (KFNF was born in 1924, KMA a year later), many are not aware that Shenandoah had a radio station before either of them. In early 1922, W. H. Cass licensed a station called WGAJ in the city; however, government records indicate it was no longer operating a mere year later.

This was not uncommon. In those early days, stations were often licensed on a limited, temporary basis, often for only a few days or months. Some have escaped the review of historians because, although they may have been on the air for months, they might not have appeared in the annual governmental report showing what stations were licensed on a certain report date. In addition, in the beginning, most stations were licensed to operate on the same frequency. They had to battle with nearby operators in transmitting a clear signal to the audience; for the limited and intangible benefits received from what many called a hobby or experiment, a number of operators simply allowed their stations

to "go dark" after the newness had worn off.

But at the same time, it is interesting to note that the first four radio stations licensed by the federal government in Iowa—WOC, WOI, WSUI, and WMT—have broadcast continuously since their licenses were granted more than 80 years ago.

The equipment used by early broadcasters was primitive compared with the technology of today, and often provided unexpected outcomes. The original WSUI transmitter used an old telephone microphone. "It was right in the ground circuit, and it would get so hot that after about five minutes, you couldn't hold it anymore, so we fixed up two of them so you could switch off to the second one while the first one cooled off," station founder Carl Menzer remembered in 1979.

The first generation of true radio microphones were thick, round dinner plate-sized devices, filled with carbon particles. After several hours on the air, the particles would become compacted, so the announcer would have to turn off the power and hit the side of the microphone with a ruler to shake the particles loose so sounds would come from the microphone again.

Power surges caused by the WSUI transmitter led the lights in the campus engineering building to flicker on occasion; some suggested that the blinking lights could be seen further than the signal of the station could be heard.

Things were no different by the early 1940s. The signal coming from radio station KXEL's transmitter near Dysart was so powerful and the radiation was so strong that farmers could not shut off the lights in their henhouses; even with the electrical power in the henhouse turned off, the radiation was enough to make the bulbs glow. Some nearby residents even claimed that music—the sound of the station—came out of their stoves. Des Moines radio personality Steve Gibbons recalls working at KSO in the 1960s; he often amazed visitors to the station by holding a fluorescent light bulb near the door of the transmitter room, then watching as the

The main control room at KCRG-AM in Cedar Rapids (circa 1947).

A Dangerous Business

The business of putting a broadcasting station on the air and maintaining its service is a complicated one. Highly technical machinery powered by electricity can be difficult to maintain, and as the history of Iowa broadcasting shows, at times it has been deadly for those called to service.

The first transmitter used by KFJB in Marshalltown was merely a table-top with two sockets in it to hold the tubes used for sending signals. It was homemade by Marshall Electric engineers Merle Easter and Chauncy Hoover, who made modifications to the transmitter over time.

One day in March 1929, Easter was making an adjustment to the KFJB transmitter with another engineer. He had carefully turned off all power to the unit before beginning work. When he powered up the transmitter again, Easter neglected a wire lying on the floor; he stepped on the wire and was quickly electrocuted. His death—and the large burn mark on the floor of the station—served as a clear reminder of how dangerous engineering for the still-new medium could be.

Iowa's often-unforgiving weather has also affected broadcast stations. Radio station KROS operated from studios in downtown Clinton, with the broadcast tower located on top of the Jacobsen Building, facing Main Street. During a particularly icy and windy day in 1947, the ice which accumulated on the tower became too heavy to withstand the gusts of wind, and the entire structure came crashing to the ground. The tower crumpled on the street near the Walgreen Drug Store. As then-station manager Walt Teich said at the time with obvious relief, "It never touched a soul."

In order to enhance signal range and quality, broadcast towers are as many as 200 stories above the ground and difficult to reach. Often, the only way to get to the top is by scaling the outside of the narrow structure. Usually, construction and maintenance are trouble-free; however, there are often disastrous consequences.

The first of these "tall towers" in eastern Iowa was being built by WMT-TV when it collapsed shortly before completion. The tower was to be 1,600 feet tall, but crumpled in high winds. No one was killed in the collapse, and the tower was quickly rebuilt.

Shortly before noon on October 3, 1973, the 2,000-foot-high KCRG transmission tower located north of Walker in Buchanan County collapsed, killing five persons. Workers had been making modifications on the tower to allow installation of an antenna for the Iowa Educational Broadcasting Network (now known as Iowa Public Television) and public radio station KUNI-FM. IEBN had leased space at the KCRG transmitter site for its own antenna and transmitter.

Channel 9 engineers worked around the clock to put the station back on the air. Some 40 hours after the collapse, KCRG was again broadcasting, with reduced signal coverage, from its old transmitter site near Hiawatha. While the main tower had been destroyed, the transmitting equipment was virtually untouched by the tower collapse.

A newspaper account of the time indicates that area farmers and residents took turns manning sledge hammers to knock the wall out of the transmitter building so that the equipment could be removed and taken to the new, temporary transmitter site. Just under 13 months later, a new 2,000-foot-high tower was erected near Walker, to replace the collapsed one.

KCRG's auxiliary tower near Hiawatha was the scene of another deadly accident only a few years later when a small single engine airplane collided with the tower in poor visibility. Some six feet of one of the plane's wings was embedded in the tower, and three members of one family died when the plane crashed nearby, narrowly missing a mobile home court.

Ten years after the KCRG tall tower collapse, in November of 1983, KWWL's main tower was brought to the ground by heavy ice and strong winds. Channel 7 was off the air until it could resume transmission from a lower, backup tower; as was the case a decade earlier with KCRG, it took KWWL a year before a new, higher tower could be constructed to replace the old one. Unlike the KCRG tower collapse, fortunately the KWWL tower collapse did not result in any injuries.

But another tower collapse a few years later was deadly for three men. On June 2, 1988, a 2,000-foot tower for ABC affiliate KTVO-TV, serving southeast Iowa from studios in Ottumwa, Iowa, and Kirksville, Missouri, collapsed, killing three engineers. Unlike the other stations, however, KTVO decided not to rebuild its tall tower, and instead opted to broadcast permanently from its backup facility, an 1,100-foot tower located near Lancaster, Missouri.

Ronnie Brown (left) and Al Schrock (right) during a KFJB music program in the early 1950s, broadcast live from the Smith Music Store in Marshalltown.

bulb lit up without being attached to electrical current due to the power coming from the station transmitter.

But as proof that "the more things change, the more they stay the same," some Black Hawk County residents complained in 2003 about interference after changes to the transmitter of Cedar Falls station KCNZ, not unlike complaints heard about KXEL 60 years before.

As radio evolved, the public demanded higher quality programming, and expected government regulators to impose certain standards. The Federal Radio Commission, founded as part of the Radio Act of 1927, took steps to do just that. It was already clear that there were more people who wanted to broadcast than there were available frequencies, and those who were abusing the privilege of operating a station needed to be controlled.

One Iowa station owner lost his ability to broadcast in a classic case. In June of 1931, the FRC refused to renew the license of Norman Baker of Muscatine. Baker had operated radio station KTNT since 1926. The government claimed Baker used KTNT—which stood for "Know the Naked Truth"—solely to exploit his medical theories and practices and promote his cancer hospital and merchandise, along with making the occasional "bitter attacks" on persons with whom he disagreed. Baker's case was one of four similar cases decided by the FRC that year, all supporting the congressional mandate that stations should act in the "public interest, convenience, and necessity," rather than solely for personal purposes.

In fact, early governmental rules even prohibited advertising on the air. It was a position that then-Secretary of Commerce Herbert Hoover, who was responsible for regulating broadcasting in the early 1920s, felt strongly about.

KSCJ Chief Engineer Al Smith proudly inspects the Sioux City station's new transmitter in this 1941 photo.

"I believe that the quickest way to kill broadcasting would be to use it for direct advertising. The reader of the newspaper has an option whether he will read an ad or not, but if a speech by the president is to be used as the meat in a sandwich of two patent medicine advertisements, there will be no radio left," Hoover told the Third National Radio Conference held in Washington, D.C. in 1924. "It is inconceivable that we should allow so great a possibility for service to be drowned in advertising chatter."

Even though the official government policy against radio advertising was lifted by the time the FRC was founded in 1927, license application forms still wanted to know how a broadcaster intended to keep the station on the air. One question on the form in the late 1920s asked, "If Applicant does not propose to sell time, how will the station be supported?"

The owners of KSCJ, the *Sioux City Journal*, responded in a document filed February 23, 1928, that "This is primarily a goodwill proposition with the *Journal*, and if we can ever get to a point where we can break even, we'll be happy." In a renewal form dated December 12, 1928, less than a year later, the answer to the question was, "We are amply able to keep KSCJ rolling if we never sell any time. In fact, we are not keen about much advertising, anyway."

Despite that, a station advertising rate card from the year before offered to sell advertising at the rate of $97.50 for a half-hour program, and $185.00 for an hour program.

Broadcasting quickly became a popular career choice for young men in the 1930s. Sometimes, that choice was hard to sell to skeptical parents.

Ben Sanders, who owned and operated KICD radio in Spencer beginning in 1945, recalled telling his father he was interested in working in radio. His father, who owned a Cadillac dealership, told his son he should instead learn how to grease cars.

"I told him that I wanted to go into broadcasting, radio broadcasting. And he told me emphatically that was stupid," Sanders recalled in a 1992 interview. "And I told him, 'Nuts!' I was going to go into broadcasting. He said it'll never last; but he was wrong, it did."

Ben Sanders obviously had different advice for his son, Bill. After working in sales for the WMT stations under Bill Quarton for a number of years, Bill Sanders would go on to succeed his father as owner of the Spencer radio station and become a member of the Iowa Broadcasters Association Hall of Fame in 1990. Both men shared the same sense about how to operate successful broadcasting stations.

"The station is far, far more than a transmitter," Ben Sanders said. Bill Sanders echoed his father's sentiments. "The station is people. Anybody can put up a piece of equipment," Bill Sanders said.

Al Schrock, who spent his entire 45-year radio career at KFJB in Marshalltown, agreed.

"I think the one thing that I enjoyed most as I think about it is the people I worked with," he said. "I was privy to working with a lot of people who were very creative, very energetic, and as I look back, those are the things that I remember most."

The first quarter century of radio—before the advent of television—is remembered by many as the medium's "golden age."

"It seemed that we were experimenting then. We were doing things, taking the chances that we wouldn't today. Radio was more things to more people then," KFJB's Schrock said. "It was more fun to me, and I think, to the others of that time, when we were doing more things and just having more fun. It evolved into more of a hard-core business as the years went by."

That became particularly true when the new kid on the block—television—swept across America in the 1950s. Radio still plays an important role in our lives, but most agree that nothing could match those early pioneer broadcasts.

"Radio was in sheer paranoia when they thought of television."

KRNT radio and television personality Bill Riley, during an interview for the Iowa Broadcasting Oral History Project in 1999.

2 Adding Pictures to Sound

When television first came to Iowa, radio was barely a quarter-century old. The new medium scared even those who were "veterans" of broadcasting. The concept of television as "radio with pictures" was harder to produce than it might have seemed. WMT station manager Bill Quarton summed up the feelings of many television pioneers when, on September 30, 1953, he spoke the first words heard on Cedar Rapids' Channel 2.

"Please do remember that we are not experts. We're trying to do the best we can. We're going to make many mistakes, and you're going to have a lot of fun with it, laughing at our mistakes. But one of these days, we'll end up, I feel confident, with a very good operation. So let me end my little talk with a plea to you to please be patient with us," Quarton told the audience.

And the audience was forgiving. After all, they were eager for television, and any visual image on the screen captivated those who stood in front of store windows, gawking at the miracle before them. Stations, in turn, were eager to get on the air, often before they were truly ready.

Jackie Grant, head of the WMT-TV film department, remembered that the new Broadcast Park facility was not totally completed when the station went on the air. For example, it had no furniture, no water, no food, and no toilets. "When you had to go to the bathroom, you had to get into your car and go to a friend's house or to one in the neighborhood," she said.

WMT-TV rented picnic tables on which to set the original film winders, which were not electrically powered—film had to be spooled onto reels by hand before it could be aired. On the first night the station was on the air, Grant was responsible for preparing the movie "Hopalong Cassidy" for airing on Channel 2.

Her job was to manually splice in the filmed commercials during breaks in the movie. "Hopalong Cassidy" barely got on the air because of the time it took to hand wind the film at the last minute.

While the audience was anxious for television, not everyone thought the new medium was a great idea. Despite the success of the WMT radio operation, Bill Quarton says that when he sought another $300,000 to add to the money they had saved in order to put Channel 2 on the air, local bankers would not give him the money; he had to go to Twin Cities banks for financing.

Iowa's first television station was WOC-TV in Davenport. Only about 400 Quad Cities homes had television sets when the station went on the air on October 31, 1949; within only two months, an estimated 6,000 sets were in use in the area. B. J. Palmer's television station relied on talent from his WOC radio station to staff the new effort.

"None of us got paid. We all went down there because we wanted the experience," longtime station employee Harold Heath said in a 1998 interview. "It was exciting. It was new. We were pioneers. It wasn't until several years later that any of us got paid for working at the television station. It couldn't make any money."

Just a few months after WOC took to the air, on February 21, 1950, WOI-TV began broadcasting from facilities on the Iowa State College campus. The station had no television cameras and simply showed film or slides with announcer narration.

"We really had no models to follow and our equipment was very primitive," former WOI news reporter and Iowa State University journalism professor Jim Schwartz recalled for the station's 25th anniversary in 1975. "We had to put the news together in the station, and then we drove it five miles out in the country to the

A floor crew in action during a live musical broadcast at WHO-TV in Des Moines in the mid-1950s.

transmitter and put it on the air," he said, with only the announcer's voice heard over a basic logo slide. The audience did not actually see the newscaster until months after the station had been on the air, when Iowa State College purchased the station's first studio cameras.

Later in that first year of broadcasting, the station rented a single camera and a remote truck in order to provide live coverage of the college's annual VEISHEA parade as well as a baseball game held later that day. The producer, director, and announcers were seated on the roof of the remote truck, next to the camera.

Those first stations operated without the benefit of a connection with one of the national networks. "We had to originate all of our own shows," Heath said. "It wasn't until several years later that the network came." Since there was no technical way to transmit programs from New York to Iowa live, at first the networks made kinescopes of the shows—films of the actual on-screen image seen in New York. The kinescopes were shipped by mail for replay on a one-week delayed basis, meaning, for example, that Christmas programs aired on New Year's Day, and New Year's programs aired on January 8.

The first interconnection came in the fall of 1950, connecting New York with stations in the Quad Cities, Ames, and Omaha; connections with Cedar Rapids were in place when WMT and KCRG went on the air in 1953, but KWWL in Waterloo had to wait even longer before network programs, such as John Cameron Swayze's "Camel News Caravan," could be seen live. For every television station, one of the first locally produced regular programs was a daily newscast. But those first newscasts hardly resembled the highly packaged programs we are used to seeing today.

"It was rudimentary. Really, what we were doing in the beginning was a radio newscast, and then putting whatever visuals you could find behind it to give it some motion," said Paul Rhoades, who spent 43 years at KRNT radio and television in Des Moines. He anchored the station's 6 p.m. television newscast for 38 years, from the time the station signed on the air in 1954 until his retirement in 1992.

Even with months of planning, starting a local television news operation was not a smooth process. "There's so many doggone things you didn't find out about that someday'll rear up and bite you on the leg," WHO's Jack Shelley said. "We found all kinds of things that we didn't really know about. It was quite a problem in many ways."

The first noon newscast ever broadcast on WHO-TV got off to a rocky start. Len Howe was the anchor for the live 30-minute program. Howe read a story and called for the first piece of film; however, no film appeared on screen. Howe continued and read the next story, calling for the second film segment; what appeared on air was the wrong piece of film. Undaunted, he pressed on, calling for what should have been the third piece of film, but what appeared on the air was yet again the wrong film. "At that point, he stopped, glared at the camera and said, 'There will be no more film on this newscast,'" Shelley recalled.

WMT in Cedar Rapids had an early evening newscast at 6 p.m., anchored by Bill Roberts, from the time it went on the air in 1953. A year later, news director Dick Cheverton assigned staff member Bob Johnson the task of anchoring the first late-night news program, which would air at 10:30 p.m.

Johnson says that Cheverton was convinced the anchor should not sit down while on the air. The backdrop for the news program had maps of each hemisphere with arrows the anchor would point to, to show geography and location of the story. However, such movement was awkward. "That was the problem. We didn't know what to do," Johnson said. Soon after, the WMT-TV anchor simply stood. Later he was seen seated behind a desk, which is the common custom today.

The Fight for Television

Almost immediately after the end of World War II, attention refocused on the promise of television. Radio's success in assisting the war effort and keeping citizens at home informed no doubt enhanced in the minds of many the promise of adding pictures to the sound.

The crush of applications for new television stations quickly outpaced the FCC's ability to respond. After granting only 108 licenses nationwide in the post-war years, in 1948 the FCC imposed a "freeze" on the granting of applications in order to sort out the situation. The freeze was intended to last only a few months, but in fact would last for nearly four years, while an impatient public waited.

Two Iowa-based television stations were approved to go on the air before the freeze. Just as his radio station was the first one licensed to operate as a commercial station in Iowa, B. J. Palmer's WOC-TV in Davenport officially began broadcasting on October 31, 1949, as the first television station in the state. Operating at the time on Channel 5, the station served the approximately 400 homes in the Quad Cities of Iowa and Illinois which had television sets at the time. Soon after, on February 21, 1950, Iowa State College signed on WOI-TV, which then operated on Channel 4. Following the "thawing" of the license freeze, a reallocation of frequencies bumped each station up one number on the VHF dial— to channels 6 and 5, respectively.

But it was not all smooth sailing for many who wanted to run a

R. J. McElroy, flanked by legal counsel Col. William Roberts (left) and Robert Buckmaster (right) on the steps of the federal Court House in Waterloo during the trial which led to the first television station in Waterloo going on the air in 1953.

television station. The FCC could only allow a limited number of stations in each area, and in some markets, the applications for the limited number of television licenses were hotly contested. Station applicants much preferred dial positions 2 through 13 on the VHF, or "very high frequency" band, as opposed to channels 14 through 83 on the UHF, or "ultra high frequency" band.

For example, VHF channels 8, 11, and 13 were allocated in Des Moines, along with UHF channel 17. Channel 11 had been reserved for use as an educational station, later licensed to the Des Moines Public School District. The four major AM radio stations in town fought vigorously for the remaining two Des Moines VHF channels.

KRNT and KSO each applied for Channel 8, while WHO and KIOA sought Channel 13. The fight for Channel 8 was indeed ironic, as both radio stations seeking the license began their lives in Des Moines under the common ownership of the Des Moines Register & Tribune Company, sharing studio space on the 12th and 13th floors of the Register and Tribune Building.

After a fierce fight, KRNT ultimately won the right to broadcast on Channel 8, but only after a unique financial arrangement. In order to avoid a contested hearing, and therefore further delays in getting the station on the air, KRNT and KSO negotiated a settlement, approved by the FCC, for a joint operation owned 60 percent by KRNT and 40

percent by KSO. However, once the FCC granted the license, KRNT immediately bought out KSO's 40 percent share, by prior agreement, and KRNT-TV 8 signed on the air on July 31, 1955.

WHO and KIOA reached their financial settlement more quickly, allowing WHO-TV 13 to beat KRNT on the air by more than a year. Details of the agreement are not clear, but no doubt WHO would have had the upper hand before the FCC in a contested hearing for the license. WHO's owners, the Palmer family, already had a television station on the air with WOC-TV in Davenport, and WHO radio was operating as a "clear channel" station with maximum power and had been on the air for more than a quarter-century. By contrast, KIOA was a relative newcomer, first signing on the air as a "farm and home station" only in 1948. Channel 13 first took to the airwaves on April 26, 1954, as the first VHF station based in Des Moines.

But that was not the first television station to operate in Des Moines. KGTV-TV actually began operations on UHF Channel 17 in 1953. However, by the time WHO-TV took to the air in the spring of 1954, KGTV-TV was already off the air, no doubt due to the financial pressures of starting a new station and the inherent differences between VHF and UHF transmissions. A separate antenna was required to receive UHF signals, they did not travel as far as VHF signals, and many television sets sold at the time were VHF-only.

The Fight for Television

The Channel 17 frequency remained dormant for nearly 30 years, until it was revived in 1983 by what is now known as KDSM-TV.

By comparison, however, the allocation of television frequencies in Cedar Rapids was rather calm. Channels 2 and 9 were assigned to the city, and WMT quickly made application for Channel 2. The radio station was already located to the far left of the AM band, and being assigned Channel 2 would place WMT at the far end of the television band, as well.

The competition was greater for Channel 9, however. The *Cedar Rapids Gazette*, owners of KCRG-AM, applied for the channel, as did a group of local businessmen led by Myron Blank, who operated a number of movie theaters in Iowa. The Gazette Company put KCRG-AM on the air in 1947, and saw how difficult it was to have given its cross-town rival, WMT, a 25-year head start; the company did not want to be behind in television, too.

So a negotiated settlement agreement was filed with the FCC by the Gazette and the Blank group, forming the Cedar Rapids Television Company. The original call letters for Channel 9 were KCRI-TV, and the station went on the air in October, 1953, approximately two weeks behind WMT-TV 2.

The marriage between the Gazette and Blank's group was not a happy one. For example, Blank's group fought for the KCRI call letters, rather than the already-recognizable KCRG, because they felt any mention of "KCRG" would be a free advertisement for the *Cedar Rapids Gazette* newspaper, and that the Gazette Company should pay any time the letters "KCRG" would be used on the new television station. Soon the Gazette Company bought out its partner, becoming the sole owner of the station and reclaiming the call letters KCRG-TV. The station is still owned by the Hladky family's Gazette Company to this day, and is currently the only family-owned VHF television station remaining in Iowa.

The most vigorous competition for a television license in Iowa—and perhaps in the country—occurred in Waterloo between two well-known radio personalities and station owners who were not used to losing.

Joe Dumond started his radio career with WMT in the 1920s. He later moved into ownership of stations in Iowa and other states, capitalizing on the fame he earned by playing the character "Josh Higgins" on network radio on NBC in the 1930s. He founded Waterloo radio station KXEL in 1942, one of the last stations to be licensed and built after the start of World War II. The station's 50,000-watt power insured the station would have a great signal reach.

Across town, R. J. McElroy returned from service in the war to his prior position as a sales person and announcer for WMT, which had maintained local studios in Waterloo even after moving back to Cedar Rapids in 1934. After World War II, however, WMT planned to consolidate its operations, and the enterprising McElroy took advantage of the opportunity to start a station of his own in Waterloo. With the support of a group of prominent businessmen, he founded the Black Hawk Broadcasting Company and put KWWL-AM on the air in 1947.

The FCC had allocated two channels for Waterloo: VHF Channel 7, and the less desirable UHF Channel 16. Both Dumond and McElroy applied for Channel 7, which led to a divisive fight which split much of the local business community.

Despite FCC rules prohibiting construction of facilities before a license was granted, Dumond was so confident he would prevail in winning the license for Channel 7 that he began building a new facility on U.S. Highway 20 near Jesup. A billboard near the site proclaimed it to be the new KXEL Television Center. Dumond assumed that his government contacts in Washington would be of help during the FCC process.

Shortly after the freeze was lifted, Dumond took to the KXEL radio airwaves on June 5, 1952, and proclaimed to his audience that he was ready to begin broadcasting on television, and was being held up only by KWWL. He also spoke to a number of service clubs, frequently saying, "If it weren't for McElroy and KWWL, you would be enjoying television in Waterloo right now."

In order to trap Dumond while he made such statements, KWWL staffers Ed Falk and Warren Mead hid a microphone in the room where the local Exchange Club was to meet, hooked up a tape recorder, and caught Dumond in the act of suggesting that local businesses stage an advertisers' boycott against KWWL—which was a violation of antitrust and trade restraint laws.

Armed with this evidence, KWWL filed a lawsuit against Dumond and his company, as well as a number of local business owners, claiming they engaged in a "conspiracy in restraint of trade." The point was to discredit Dumond and disqualify him as an applicant for the television license.

A trial was held in federal court in Waterloo, and testimony was heard over several days. To this point, Dumond was not aware that there existed any transcript or tape recording of his inflammatory remarks. Shortly after they were introduced into the official court record with a flourish, McElroy and Dumond went for a car ride around Waterloo alone.

After the discussion, McElroy's attorney began drawing up an agreement in which KXEL would withdraw its application for Channel 7, encourage the FCC to award the television license to KWWL, and as if all that weren't enough, to lease the television portions of the KXEL building to McElroy and his new TV station. KWWL-TV 7 went on the air less than three months later, on November 29, 1953.

Dumond never recovered from the embarrassing loss and sold the station not long after, leaving Iowa for Arizona where he engaged in real estate and ran a radio station in Tucson. McElroy operated his company, including the purchase of additional radio and television stations in the Midwest, until his sudden death in 1965. To this day, no station in Waterloo has signed on using the UHF Channel 16 frequency.

Getting pictures on the air for the new medium was not easy. In the days before satellite delivery, film had to be transported via airplane to different locations across the country.

Dwight D. Eisenhower was the first president to allow television cameras at his morning news conferences; but in order for the film to be seen by central Iowa television viewers during that night's 10 p.m. news, Jack Shelley remembers that one of the news film services had to shoot and process the film, make copies and package the film, and rush to Washington's National Airport where the film was flown to Des Moines via Chicago. Shelley said that if the station was lucky, a United Airlines plane would land in Des Moines at 9:30 p.m., a courier from WHO-TV would rush from the airport to the station and put the film on the air during the news without anyone at the station ever having seen it. "We wished by luck and by golly it would all make sense," Shelley said, adding that he would ad-lib narration as he was seeing the film for the first time while it was live on the air.

Sometimes, even landing the plane at the airport was a luxury the station's time limitations would not allow. Early WMT-TV anchor Henry Lippold remembers planes dropping cans of film from the air over the station's Broadcast Park facility, sometimes missing their mark, with the cans landing in fields, roadways—or on one occasion, in a woman's garden while she was weeding it.

Bob Bruner, who spent 29 years at WMT radio and television, once recalled another occasion when an errant film drop could have cost the station an exclusive. At the 1958 national corn picking

contest, held in Marion, WMT cameras recorded a meeting and a handshake between then-Senator John F. Kennedy and President Eisenhower. The station had chartered a plane to drop the film onto a cloth target laid out in an open area near Channel 2's Broadcast Park studios. However, the pilot misjudged the situation, and the film sailed past the target, across C Avenue and into a wooded area by a cemetery. The sight of WMT staffers combing the woods and the cemetery for that can of undeveloped film was no doubt another recordable moment.

Even when stations shot their own film, the procedure for getting it on the air was difficult. For many years, stations like WMT, KWWL and KRNT used Bell and Howell wind-up black-and-white movie cameras, without sound, shooting on 100-foot reels that lasted no more than two minutes.

"We'd go to the darkroom and we'd spool it off into a bucket of developer. And then we'd just reach in with our hands and slosh it around in that bucket for the correct amount of time," Lippold said. "Then we'd wash it and we'd hang it up to dry, sort of like the laundry." That was crude, but it was the only method available at WMT-TV in the late 1950s. The station had built homemade racks on which the freshly developed film was spread out, with fans and a spotlight used for drying the film more quickly. At that point, stations were using what was called "negative film," which would have to be run through equipment that could electronically change the polarity to make it appear normal on the air.

Poster announcing KRNT-TV's inaugural broadcast day—July 31, 1955.

The KWWL tent at the National Dairy Cattle Congress in Waterloo (circa 1955).

For "breaking news," stations would shoot black-and-white photographs using still cameras. The photographs would be mounted on cards placed on a stand. "Believe it or not, I would introduce a picture and the camera would pan over to the picture, and then back to the newscaster," longtime WMT anchor Bob Bruner said in an interview for the station's 40th anniversary in 1993. The studio camera would shoot the photograph on the card, with offstage hands pulling the cards off the easel in sequence. Each member of the WMT news staff was issued a Brownie camera, to make it easier to gather these still photos for use in the newscast. Often, there was barely enough time to develop the film and print a picture to show on the air, so a still-wet photo print would hurriedly be placed in front of a camera, just in time.

Instead of using slides for still images, KWWL in Waterloo used "balops," which were 4-by-5-inch, black-and-white photographic prints, which went into slots on long thin trays. The trays were then pushed through a lantern called a "flying spot scanner." Also in those early days, Channel 7 could not show film directly on the air. Instead, the station used a "shadow box," which was a ground glass screen on which the film was projected much as it would be on a movie screen. A studio camera was focused on the screen and the image of the projected film, as seen through the lens of the camera, was put on the air. The quality was poor, but in those early days, simply seeing an image on a screen was considered miraculous.

KWWL had to show network entertainment programs the same way, by projecting the film onto the shadow box and focusing a camera on the screen. One night, while the station was showing a film of the "Liberace" program, a viewer called to complain that the picture was getting smaller and smaller. And indeed it was—someone in the studio had failed to properly lock the wheels on the camera which was focused on the shadow box screen,

and the camera was slowly rolling away from the screen across the studio.

Later, KRNT began shooting color news film on occasion, but had to outsource processing of the film to a Des Moines business until the station could obtain its own color film processor. Such inconveniences were not uncommon; to save money in its early days, KWWL made a deal with the Waterloo Police Department, which loaned the station an officer who could develop the station's film in the police darkroom. KGLO in Mason City had a longer turnaround time for film—before Channel 3 got its own darkroom facility, the station would send film by bus to KRNT in Des Moines to be developed and sent back.

Live broadcasting often results in the unexpected. Once, while WMT's Bob Bruner was delivering the 6 p.m. "Report to Iowa" newscast, a mail carrier using a shortcut through the station's facility walked in front of his news desk, between him and the camera, in plain sight of the audience watching at home. Across town, a KCRG news anchor sat on a stool to deliver the news. One night, for an unexplained reason, the adjustable seat on the stool began slowly working its way downward to a lower position. The camera slowly followed the "action" as the anchor sank lower and lower.

The presentation of weather information was far different in the early days of television from the computerized, graphic-laden approach of today. When Duane Hunting was the first weathercaster on Waterloo's KWWL-TV, he used what he called a "square barrel" to add a visual component to his five-minute weathercast. The "barrel" was a four-sided box, which could be turned to show the United States weather map, the Iowa weather map, statistics such as high and low temperature and rainfall amounts, and the forecast. In the days before felt-tip marking pens, Hunting had to write on the maps with an empty deodorant bottle filled with shoe polish, meaning everything he wrote was roughly a half inch wide. This

WOI-TV produced live broadcasts of the VEISHEA parade for many years while the station was owned by Iowa State University, as in this 1966 photo.

allowed the characters and numbers he was writing to be seen by the still-primitive cameras and transmitted to the audience.

Hunting's audition for the Channel 7 weather job was not without its problems. When he could not get the makeshift writing instrument to work, the director off-camera suggested he squeeze the bottle. He did—causing it to burst, spilling dark shoe polish all over his clothes.

Things had not improved much when Craig Johnson came to KWWL-TV a quarter-century later, in 1979. Gone were the days of shoe polish—however, a small squeeze bottle filled with tempera paint was used, affording a weathercaster the ability to use multiple colors in map drawing. While today's computer age has drastically changed the way weather information is presented on television, Johnson says he still draws his initial forecast maps by hand.

The audience now has more options than ever, thanks to the Internet. Many stations now make news stories, or even entire newscasts, available via the World Wide Web for viewers to download and watch at their convenience.

Whether on a 4-inch black and white screen in the earliest days, or now through large flat-screen, wall-mounted television sets, for more than a half century, audiences have relied on the visual image brought to them by Iowa's television stations.

From Iowa television's early era: (clockwise from upper left) Henry Lippold of WMT, Cedar Rapids; Dean Osmundson of KTVO, Ottumwa; a floor crew with one of the original studio cameras used at Channel 2 in Cedar Rapids; and the cast and crew of a studio program at KTIV-TV, Sioux City.

Inventions Along the Way

The role Iowans played in the development of broadcasting was not limited to putting stations on the air. Some of the foremost inventors in the field have ties to the state.

Born in Council Bluffs, Lee DeForest has been called by many "the father of radio." He spent his life as an inventor, and by the time he died in 1961 at the age of 89, he held more than 300 patents.

He applied for his last patent on his 84th birthday; the invention was for a television set that was only four inches thick, which could be hung on a wall like a picture. This was the forerunner of the current trend in television sets—flat screen, thin models which can be hung on a wall, avoiding the need for a large cabinet. This was the story of Lee DeForest's life—often being decades ahead of the commercial viability of one of his inventions.

DeForest is best known for inventing the device that made wireless radio broadcasting feasible—the audion amplifier. At the turn of the 20th century, diode vacuum tubes were being used to maintain an electromagnetic current between two electrodes, one positive and one negative. They could repeat signals, but not amplify them. By 1906, DeForest had found a simple but ingenious solution—he added a third electrode between the other two, leading to the new "triode" or "audion" tube, which meant that circuits could be controlled and amplified, and what became known as broadcasting could be commercially feasible.

Lee DeForest

The audion tube became an essential part not only of radio and television, but of devices such as the telephone, radar, and computers, as well. Transistors have long since replaced the audion tubes devised by DeForest, but his invention paved the way for all that would follow.

In fact, it was DeForest who in 1916 invented the first way to record sound onto movies. The film industry, however, was not ready to move to "talkies" yet, and DeForest's method was not universally accepted.

DeForest was unable to enjoy his successes. While he was a genius in the laboratory, his business skills—and often, his choice of business partners—showed a lack of judgment. He spent most of his wealth defending himself in court against other inventors, trying to preserve the patents he had obtained. The experiences left him bitter and critical of what broadcasting had become.

"What have you gentlemen done with my child?" he wrote in an open letter to the National Association of Broadcasters meeting in Chicago in 1946. Instead of providing what he called "high class entertainment," he complained that broadcasters had sent his child off "in rags of ragtime, tatters of jive and boogie woogie, to collect money from all and sundry, for hubba hubba and audio jitterbug." Radio, DeForest wrote, had become "a stench in the nostril of the gods of the ionosphere."

Although the concept of television was not known to most Iowans until the post-World War II era, experimental television broadcasts had been conducted at the University of Iowa throughout the 1930s.

A station known as W9XK was licensed to the university and transmitted a regular schedule of programs from 1933 to 1939, from studios in the electrical engineering department. The television station used the university's radio station, WSUI, to provide audio for the programs. The development of television was so primitive at the time that transmission of audio and video simultaneously was not possible; therefore, those with the appropriate equipment could see the pictures on W9XK and hear the audio by tuning a radio to WSUI.

The Iowa engineers experimented by using a mechanical device that cast light through a rotating, perforated disk to create the image scan. Photo-electric cells made the conversion to electrical energy, which was then transmitted on radio waves to receiving sets. However, the mechanical scan system generated only 45 lines of resolution, rather than the 525-line electrical scan system that was adopted as the industry standard in the early 1940s.

Seeing early on that the mechanical scan system had limited potential, the Iowa scientists in 1936 also obtained an experimental license from the FCC for an electronic television station, which was called W9XUI. "They sent the signals via closed-circuit to other parts of the university, but there's no evidence to suggest that the signal was ever transmitted over the air," according to Cedar Rapids broadcast historian Rick Plummer. The experiments with electronic television continued until 1941, when the American entry into World War II stopped all television experiments at the university; they were not resumed at the conclusion of the war.

The mechanical station continued over-the-air broadcasting until 1939—the same year President Franklin D. Roosevelt spoke for the first time on television from the New York World's Fair during a demonstration of RCA's electronic-scan system.

The mechanical experiments were successful in a number of respects, and were seen beyond the state of Iowa. In late 1935, a viewer sent a letter to project supervisor Dr. E. B. Kurtz confirming receipt of one of the television programs in Somerset, Kentucky, more than 600 miles away.

While the building in which the television experiments were conducted, Old Gold, no longer exists, a plaque outside the present-day physics building still commemorates Iowa's first licensed television station.

Black Hawk Broadcasting chairman Robert Buckmaster reviewing a program in the KWWL control room during the late 1960s.

"Radio is the greatest factor in modern life today."

Earl May, owner of the Earl May Seed & Nursery Company
in Shenandoah, shortly before his KMA radio station
began broadcasting in 1925.

Down on the Farm

The success of Iowa's small towns and large cities alike has forever been tied to agriculture. So it comes as no surprise that early on, Iowa's radio and television stations found an eager audience looking for current farm-related information.

WOI at Iowa State College began to broadcast market reports as early as the spring of 1922. Andy Woolfries, a freshman engineer who helped build the station transmitter a few months earlier, was the person who usually received the reports in code and then repeated them into the WOI microphone. He later was the first farm director at WMT radio, joining their staff in 1942.

The nation's first full-time farm broadcaster also had Iowa ties. Frank Mullen, a graduate of Iowa State College, began at KDKA in Pittsburgh in March of 1923, delivering daily market reports.

The first full-time radio farm department in America, however, was founded at WHO in Des Moines in 1936, when news director H. R. Gross hired a young Davenport newspaper reporter named Herb Plambeck. Gross offered to pay Plambeck $120 a month to start—a pay cut from what he had been making in Davenport. To make matters worse, Gross expected Plambeck to start work the morning after his job interview.

So on August 26, 1936, Herb Plambeck presented his first farm news broadcast on WHO. "It was remarkable that Gross had that kind of confidence, that kind of determination," Plambeck said. "And I always thought if it didn't work out, I could always go back to newspaper work."

But that morning broadcast was just the beginning of Plambeck's first day of work. Shortly afterward, he was informed that he was to do a live program at WHO's Crystal Studio, a 10-by-10-foot square glassed-in studio in the center of the Varied Industries Building at the state fairgrounds. Before a live audience at the 1936 Iowa State Fair that afternoon, Plambeck organized and hosted an impromptu rooster-crowing competition that almost ended his broadcasting career the very day it started.

Plambeck borrowed two prize roosters from the nearby poultry building, ready to entertain the crowd with the contest. But when he picked up the first rooster, a Plymouth Rock, the rooster was silent. He then picked up the second rooster, a Buff Orphington. It was silent, as well. It finally occurred to the new broadcaster that roosters mainly crow at dawn. He quickly spied a role of dark paper near the stage, and hurriedly spread the paper over the cage, darkening it completely. After a brief intermission, the paper was removed and both birds responded with healthy crowing, thereby saving Plambeck from embarrassment and successfully beginning a 65-year broadcasting career.

While it took until the mid-1930s for any Iowa radio station to hire a full-time farm broadcaster, information about markets and other farm news was common from the beginning of broadcasting in Iowa. Sioux City station KSCJ gave listeners the markets three times daily, live from the Sioux City Stock Exchange Building, beginning in June 1927, only two months after the station first came on the air. Joe Hale delivered the live reports for more than 35 years. In all, KSCJ broadcast live market reports from the stock exchange for more than a half-century, until the early 1980s.

The ability to get current information about markets and what today is called agribusiness was nothing to be trifled with. In a 1995 interview, Plambeck (who died in 2002) said, "There is not a day that goes by when I'm with younger people when I don't hear them say, 'Oh, yes, Herb Plambeck. You know, when I was a little

WMT farm reporters Warren Kester (left) and Chuck Worcester (right) sizing up a calf at the National Dairy Cattle Congress in Waterloo (circa 1948).

Herb Plambeck

girl or I was a little boy, whenever you were on, my dad would say, 'Quiet! I want to hear Herb!'"

The information was taken seriously by a trusting audience. Stations quickly learned that announcers without a farm background, who thought "heifers" was pronounced "heefers"or that "ewes" was pronounced "eewees," were not good enough for the sophisticated Iowa farm audience.

Shenandoah's KMA naturally carried farm programming from its earliest days, including regular "farm talks" by Earl May himself and other employees of the May Seed and Nursery Company. In

1937, KMA hired Carl Haden as "farm service announcer and music production manager," but it was not until 1946 that the station's first full-time farm service director was hired. Merrill Langfitt had served as the Page County extension agent and had appeared frequently on station broadcasts. He first hosted the "RFD 960" program, which aired for an hour each morning beginning at 6.

Probably the longest continuously running farm program in Iowa broadcasting history was WHO's "Corn Belt Hour." In the spring of 1937, station officials asked Plambeck to develop a program similar to the popular "Farm and Home Hour" broadcast daily on the NBC Blue network. "The Corn Belt Hour" was aired every Saturday at noon for the next 32½ years—a total of 1,677 shows, with more than 12,500 guests appearing.

The Corn Belt Hour even originated from overseas during World War II. The first Iowa broadcaster to be accredited as a war correspondent was Herb Plambeck, who did the "Corn Belt Hour" live from London during July 1943. It was the first international farm broadcast ever attempted. WHO formed a small network of stations to relay the program from the BBC studios in Britain to Des Moines. Col. B. J. Palmer, the legendary station owner, personally insisted on setting the stage for the WHO audience and lavishly introduced the international broadcast. Plambeck's voice came over the air from more than 4,000 miles away within three seconds after Palmer's introduction—"perfect" timing (especially in light of today's satellite-based delays).

When television entered the picture in the 1950s, farm broadcasting became an important part of its early history, as well. WMT-TV's first farm director was Chuck Worcester, who came to Cedar Rapids and WMT radio in 1946 after hosting a national farm show on the CBS network. He was succeeded by Bob Nance, who hosted the first farm program on Channel 2.

The noontime farm show was a staple on Channel 2 from the

time the station went on the air in 1953, providing the most comprehensive farm news of any station in the United States and setting a record as the longest-running noon farm television show in American television history.

"Nobody really knew how to do agricultural broadcasting at the time, because we were in fact one of the pioneers," Nance said. "We sort of flew by the seat of our pants. We learned by doing."

The WHO farm department expanded its service with a midday half-hour program on central Iowa's Channel 13 called "TV-RFD," which ran for three years in the mid-1950s. While the program served the new television audience, it put great strain on WHO's farm news staff because they were also doing WHO's established midday radio farm programs at the same time. The members of the staff—Plambeck, Keith Kirkpatrick, Lee Cline, Ralph Vogel, and Janet Coppock—often were seen racing from the second floor radio studios down the stairs to the first floor television studios and back to cover the shifts during the busy noon hour.

Making the transition from radio to television gave many farm directors new opportunities to present information. Al Heinz, who spent more than 50 years as farm director of KGLO radio in Mason City, remembers adding television reports on Channel 3 to his existing radio duties. When the first soybean cyst nematodes were identified, he said, "We simply pulled up a plant, washed it off, and showed people what they looked like." It was a

PURINA PRESENTS CHOW-TIME with Bill Hitt KIOA Farm Director — 12 NOON Monday thru Friday — FARM & HOME RADIO KIOA DIAL 940...

method of education that had not existed before.

The first television station on the air in central Iowa, WOI-TV in Ames, was founded by what was then known as Iowa State College, well known for its ties to agriculture. In fact, when the station first went on the air at 6:30 p.m. on Tuesday, February 21, 1950, the first full program shown was called "Farm Facts." It featured a British Information Service film entitled "The Story of DDT." The station's first live studio program aired on March 5, 1950, presenting topics of interest to gardeners.

Channel 5 frequently called upon experts from Iowa State College's Extension Department. Since the station was owned by the college, it was convenient for Extension guests to come to Exhibit Hall, the station's home, for regular broadcasts (which was ironic, since Exhibit Hall's original usage was as a sheep barn).

On Tuesday nights during the 1950s, "Down to Earth" was hosted by WOI farm editor Dale Williams. A station promotional flyer from the time tells us that "economics of daily living, food budgets, landscaping and gardening are typical subjects for the show." The flyer also notes that all of the station's local programs "must be attractively staged as well as expertly performed...Each WOI-TV program has a separate and distinctive set and a complete supply of properties." A photo on the flyer shows Williams and a guest sitting on hay bales—part of the "separate and distinctive set"—discussing soil sample testing.

Sponsors and stations promoted their farm broadcasts, as seen in this 1950s ad for KIOA in Des Moines.

Creighton Knau

The set for WHO's "TV-RFD" featured a gleaming white mailbox, borrowed from Herb Plambeck's farm, with the station name and address painted prominently on it. A painting of a country home among other farmstead buildings served as further backdrop for the program. The rural mailbox was the focal point of the program, allowing announcers to work into the show letters or questions from viewers.

Radio stations with strong farm departments, such as WHO, WMT and KGLO, easily made the transition to providing television viewers with agricultural information. A strong stable of talent,

most of whom stayed with their original stations for many years, contributed to the loyalty audiences felt toward their broadcasters—and vice versa.

The relationship between the farmers and their farm broadcasters has been uniquely close. According to Grant Price, who worked with him in the late 1950s, Chuck Worcester "probably succeeded the best of anyone I've known in getting through that microphone as a personality." The man who hired him, Bill Quarton, agreed. "He had that wonderful quality that few people have," Quarton said. Among the regular features WMT listeners counted on was the weekly "Sunday Visit" from Worcester's own farm home, filled with information about the family's activities.

"I think farmers feel as though they are underappreciated, and so any exposure on radio or television was a way at that time—perhaps still is—a way to tell their story, which they feel oftentimes is either over-romanticized, so that people don't get the idea there is real nitty-gritty work going on, or just plain misunderstood," said Ron Michaelson, who served as WMT-TV farm director from 1972 to 1974.

"I guess it's the friendly type of thing. If somebody's lost a steer that's jumped over the feedlot fence, we'll help them find it," longtime KMA farm broadcaster Creighton Knau once said. "We are next-door people, and we try to get out and shake hands with as many people as we possibly can and if we have some neighbors who have some problems, we're going to be there if we can help."

WHO's Plambeck served as farm director for nearly 34 years, before leaving to become an assistant secretary of agriculture in Washington during the Nixon Administration. Two of his employees—Kirkpatrick and Cline—each spent more than 40 years with WHO, and can still be heard on the station today. WMT's early farm director, Chuck Worcester, was legendary, even though his career was tragically cut short at its peak when he was killed in a 1961 automobile accident. His successor, Bob Nance, held the position for two decades before entering private business, only to be called back to the WMT airwaves in the early 1990s. Farm broadcasters such as Jack Gowing, Tom Beavers, Warren Nielson, Jim Ross Lightfoot and Creighton Knau enjoyed long tenures behind the KMA microphones from the 1950s to the 1990s.

One of the most popular programs on KMA radio was Frank Field's 7:15 a.m. weather forecast, which aired on the station from 1940 to 1974. Prior to that, Frank was a regular on his father Henry's radio station, KFNF, but left for KMA after family control of KFNF ended. The weather forecasts included a healthy dose of practical information for those in gardening and agriculture. In addition, Frank Field's "Over The Garden Fence" program aired on KMTV-TV from the time the May Broadcasting station went on the air in Omaha in 1959 until the program ended ten years later.

Simply passing along current information was the minimum service many stations provided to their listeners and viewers. From the plowing matches and corn picking contests of the 1940s and 1950s, to the "Favorite Farmers Daughter" contests of the 1960s and 1970s, to the tractorcades of today, Iowa broadcasters have been closely involved with their audiences.

In the late 1930s, the advent of mechanical picking meant that traditional corn husking contests were quickly becoming a thing of the past. WHO's Herb Plambeck was lamenting the change while playing golf with a college classmate; the two came up with an idea for a contest that would be based on the land, since the land would always be there, and would also further the cause of conservation.

The first statewide WHO plowing match was held in Mitchellville in 1939, and drew 8,000 people. Eventually, the event became a national phenomenon, with presidents and other national figures attending. More than a half-century later, a quarter of a million

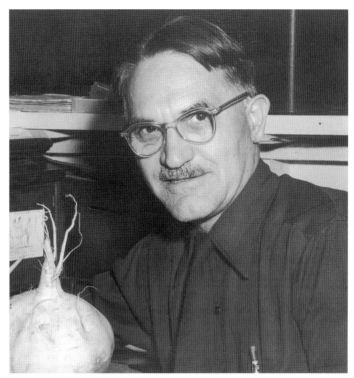

Frank Field

people attended the plowing match held in Colfax, Iowa, which had grown to a three-day affair.

"We just felt these people out here who produce this food, the farm family, are so vital to the nation's economy, to the state's economy, to our well-being, that anything we could do to make them feel they were important was worth doing," Plambeck said in an interview at the time of the 40th anniversary plowing matches, held in Marshalltown in 1979.

On the other side of the state, WMT was making a name for itself by hosting annual corn picking contests. Even though the picking was done by machinery, the spirit of the original picking contests carried on, with judging criteria including how much corn could be picked and how well tuned the machinery was for safety concerns. This event also grew quickly in popularity, becoming a national event spanning two days and attracting hundreds of thousands of people.

One of the most famous WMT National Corn Picking Contests occurred in 1958 on a farm east of Marion. Senator John F. Kennedy of Massachusetts crossed paths in a field with President Dwight D. Eisenhower. The film of their now-famous handshake was a harbinger of things to come, as Kennedy would succeed Eisenhower in the White House a few years later.

In 1949, KMA's Ed May, who assumed responsibility for the station after his father's death, budgeted $65,000 for what was called the "Six Year Farm Program." The KMA farm department would focus its attention each year for six years on a single special problem confronting farmers—weed and insect control, livestock improvement, land use, mechanized farming, farm life improvement, and human and animal nutrition. The focus included many special programs dealing with that year's topic, as well as four Farm Field Days annually, where farmers would come to Shenandoah to hear experts and see demonstrations of new techniques.

Many stations also were visible presences at various county fairs. KFJB in Marshalltown was a regular participant in broadcasts from fairs in counties around the station's home in Marshall County; fairgoers in Hardin, Grundy and Tama counties frequently saw the KFJB microphones at their events, interviewing participants and reporting fair results. Annual broadcasts from the Gladbrook Corn Carnival were also a staple of KFJB's summertime programming. Later, many broadcasters followed the lead of KIWA's Frank Luepke, who frequently took the station's live mobile unit from its base in Sheldon to fairs, farm meetings, field days, and other

Chuck Worcester

agricultural events in northwest Iowa.

Many of Iowa's farm broadcasters were quite versatile. KGLO's Al Heinz was not only a farm broadcaster, but also hosted a daily children's television show—the "Triangle 3 Ranch"— as well as a weekly televised Monday night barn dance program. WMT's Bob Nance sang in a barbershop quartet, "the Vigortones," for nearly 50 years, and was named to the national Barbershop Hall of Fame in 1996. Chuck Worcester was the announcer for the weekly television programs featuring bandleader Leo Greco and his Pioneers, which were syndicated to stations in Iowa and Illinois.

Both radio and television broadcasters had high credibility with their audiences, and their sponsors—producers of agricultural products—often maintained long-term relationships with them. Occasionally, however, advertisers put them to the test—and they delivered.

In the early 1940s, John Wisdom, owner of the Wisdom Hereford Ranch near Bloomfield and the Wisdom Livestock Company in Des Moines, became the 6:30 a.m. Farm News sponsor on WHO radio. On Christmas Eve 1943, rather than having an announcer read the normal message, Wisdom appeared on Plambeck's show in person and did a surprise commercial. He offered 12-by-10-inch illustrated 1944 calendars to anyone who wrote WHO asking for one—free. Calendars were hard to find during the war, but Wisdom had been able to secure 5,000 of them. The only announcement of the calendar giveaway was that single commercial during the early morning farm broadcast.

Herb Plambeck was nervous. Not only was this a clear test of the effectiveness of his broadcast, but there would be no mail delivery for three days, so he had no immediate way to know if he would pass Wisdom's test. It quickly became clear that the only person who needed to be nervous was Wisdom.

On the first day of mail delivery, Monday, December 27, a total of 4,255 calendar requests arrived. A whopping 15,000 requests had arrived within a week. The final mid-January total: 16,518 letters, coming from 43 of the 48 states, five Canadian provinces, Mexico, England, and from many servicemen. Wisdom ordered another 10,000 calendars—still not enough to meet the demand, but he never again questioned the effectiveness of radio advertising.

The growth of Kent Feeds from a company with a small plant in Muscatine, Iowa, to one with plants in a dozen states is directly tied to the company's association with the Leo Greco band on radio and television.

"The feed without a filler" began sponsoring Greco's band in 1951. The relationship continued for 18 years, as the band appeared regularly on up to two dozen radio stations and a half dozen television stations, as well as in ballrooms throughout the Midwest. "Leo and his Pioneers" was named the number-one-drawing ballroom band in America for four straight years in the late 1950s, until the magazine that sponsored the contest discontinued its annual poll of ballroom operators.

"You'd go into a ballroom and pack them in like sardines, and you knew radio was doing it because that was the only vehicle you had...It was terrific," Greco said.

In the early 1950s, Kent Feeds had tried a giveaway of their pig nuggets product via print advertising, with almost no response. After Chuck Worcester mentioned the pig nuggets giveaway just once during Greco's 5:45 a.m. music program on WMT radio, more than 200 inquiries came within a single week. On another occasion, a single announcement by Worcester on Greco's evening television program—of a chick giveaway at Kent's Bellevue facility—led to all the chicks being gone by 8 a.m. the next day.

Greco claims Worcester ad-libbed all his live commercials during those days, reviewing a sponsor's script once and then tossing it aside. Yet all the important product information, along with a genuine feel, came through.

But not everything went as planned, especially during the early days of television. One year, WMT wanted to boost interest in its Saturday farm program, so it partnered with the local Wilson & Company to host a weekly swine judging competition in the station's studios. A dozen hogs in three classes were presented over a month-long period, with viewers voting on their favorite to win the "Bronze Pork Chop Award."

To make the setting more realistic, the station had corralled the hogs with wooden fencing, with sawdust on the studio floor.

Extension in the Field

As a land grant institution, Iowa State University has established a proud tradition of service to Iowans, especially in providing extension and outreach services. From the earliest days of broadcasting, Iowa State Extension and its broadcasting service have worked to provide information of great interest to Iowa's agricultural community.

As a boy growing up in Waterloo, like many who had an interest in the new world of radio, Andy Woolfries had built his own amateur station. He enrolled at Iowa State College in 1921 to study electrical engineering and quickly became one of a three-man team helping to build a radio-phone station at the Ames school. On November 21, 1921, at the age of 17, he pushed the button that put station 9YI on the air; the station was licensed as WOI in April of the next year.

At the suggestion of ISC Extension director R. K. Bliss, Woolfries and others at the station began to copy the opening and closing prices on the Chicago hog market, which were broadcast in code by the Great Lakes Naval station, and rebroadcast those reports in voice over WOI radio. Daily reports on butter and egg prices provided by the Stevens Point, Wisconsin, USDA office came soon after.

By the fall of 1922, Bliss began to assign Extension specialists to broadcast over WOI radio in their free time. As Woolfries later wrote, by the next year, the USDA considered broadcasting to be useful employment for the staff, who no longer had to broadcast in their "free time."

By 1928, after the FCC ordered all stations to broadcast with a regular, "continuous" schedule, Extension Service programs were regularly scheduled in an early morning half-hour. Extension Editor Blair Converse scheduled the speakers, and Woolfries acted as host for the various programs. During the 1930s, Samuel Reck moved from South Dakota to become an Extension editor in Iowa and became a regular participant in the WOI program, "Farm Facts."

As recounted by farm broadcaster John Baker in his book, *Farm Broadcasting: The First Sixty Years*, the ability of radio to reach wide audiences was quickly proven when a February 1936 blizzard wiped out a series of nearly 100 county 4-H Club meetings. The 4-H leaders arranged a series of broadcasts to be aired over WOI, with two 4-H programs aired each week for several weeks covering the topics that would have been talked about during the county meetings.

Later, during the early 1940s, Reck acquired disc recording equipment and started sending a series of recorded programs to stations throughout Iowa under the title "Keep 'Em Eating."

There were major changes at the college in 1942. Reck moved to New Jersey as an extension editor and Woolfries moved to WMT in Cedar Rapids as that station's first full-time farm director.

Iowa State alum C. R. "Dutch" Elder became Extension Editor and continued to take part in WOI's several daily farm programs. WOI hired Iowa State alum Dick Hull to replace Woolfries; Hull had been an extension editor in Minnesota. A year later, Hull was named WOI station manager, and the farm broadcasts were taken over by Dale Williams, who had been a county agent in Minnesota. Williams conducted early morning and noon programs for nearly four decades, until the early morning program was discontinued in 1970.

When WOI-TV came on the air in 1950, Williams teamed with assistant editor Dick Cech to start a daily television farm program. In addition, by the 1970s, Williams taped eight four-minute-long radio programs each week and distributed them to 50 other stations, as well as a series of four-minute-long

videotaped features sent to four other television stations in Iowa. Before his retirement in 1980, he also provided two more programs each week via telephone recording to those radio stations calling in for them.

The ability of farmers and merchants to have real-time market information was of great benefit, and led to much of the early popularity of radio in the Midwest. In 1933, the heart of the Great Depression, Congress threatened to cut the USDA appropriation for market news. Within only 48 hours, some 35,000 Iowa farmers had signed petitions to keep the market reports coming; as a result, Congress did not cut the appropriation.

The WOI market programs were taken over in 1943 by Ronald "Cap" Bentley, an Extension marketing specialist, who shifted the focus to include more reporting on commodities, market interpretation, and indicators of future price trends.

From the post-World War II period until the 1960s, the number of minutes of market reports on WOI radio tripled. When Bentley retired in 1965, one of his longtime assistants, Dallas McGinnis, became market director. McGinnis was a familiar figure on WOI radio and television until his retirement some 25 years later.

One week, a hog jumped the wooden gate and ran under the tripod of one of the studio cameras. As the hog continued to make his escape, a camera operator had to "ride" the camera—and the hog—around the studio during the live broadcast.

Many Iowa radio stations continue to provide farm and agribusiness information. The same cannot be said for television, however. The last two full-time TV farm reporters in Iowa—Wade Wagner of KGAN-TV and Dale Hansen of KWWL-TV—each saw his job phased out by corporate owners during 2000. Television farm reporters in central Iowa disappeared long before that time.

The one exception is Iowa Public Television's famous farm program, "Market to Market," which began life as "Farm Digest" in 1974. Noted farm broadcaster Chet Randolph hosted the program from its beginning until 1991; Mark Pearson has been the host since that time. While based in Iowa, the program is aired on public television stations in other states, as well.

Even radio farm broadcasting is very different today than it was in the 1950s and 1960s. Originally, farm news consisted solely of crop and livestock commodity reporting; today, reporting includes the total lifestyle of farmers.

"The atmosphere out in rural America is much different and our needs are much different, and so consequently, the communications needs of the farmer and other agribusinesses are much different than when I got started in the business," the late Creighton Knau, who began his broadcasting career as a student at Iowa State College in 1948, said in a 1985 interview.

"When I started, we were telling people how to do it—how to get those 100 bushels of corn per acre" at a time when the average yield in Iowa was only 60 bushels per acre, Knau said. "We did a series of programs on television from Iowa State University

Chet Randolph

on how to produce 100 bushels of corn, and we were kind of laughed at. We were talking about how to do it, how to get the fertilizer there, what kind of seed to plant, how deep to plant it— the very basics. Today, the farmer is way ahead of us on that. Now he wants to know what his politicians are doing, what the international market is doing, because when, for example, the European Economic Community sneezes these days, we catch a cold over here. So it's a whole different ballgame."

"Take it easy, play it safe, and be careful."

The traditional closing words of "Dr. Max" Hahn, who hosted a children's program on WMT-TV in Cedar Rapids from 1961 to 1981.

4 For The Children

They were clowns, cowboys, and space travelers, steamboat captains, doctors, and puppets. They showed cartoons, interviewed guests, and took pratfalls, all to keep generations of Iowa's young people entertained—and along the way, to teach them valuable lessons, as well. They were the hosts of children's programs on radio and television.

Mention names like Dr. Max or Floppy, or places like the house with the Magic Window or Romper Room, and Iowa's baby boomers will still get a far-off look in their eyes, and smile as they remember the time they spent with these daily broadcast visitors to their homes.

In the early days of television, every station had a local children's program in the late afternoon. But long before, many radio stations also sought to entertain the youngest members of the audience.

Cedar Rapids radio station KWCR, owned by the Cowles family of the *Des Moines Register & Tribune*, featured the husband-and-wife duo of Doug and Jackie Grant reading the "funny papers" on Sunday mornings—long before Mayor Fiorello LaGuardia read the comics to children during a newspaper strike in New York City. When KWCR moved to Des Moines, the concept moved too, with the "Sunday Funnies" becoming a regular feature on the *Register's* KRNT radio in the 1940s. Various staff members contributed each week. When the show became a daily feature, the afternoon comics were acted out live on the air by a young announcer named Bill Riley and a Roosevelt High School student named Cloris Leachman.

In the fall of 1946, thousands of Iowa children began yelling out "Hey, Bob!" It was the start of a five-year run that proved the power of radio.

The previous year, the head of the Des Moines safety council approached KRNT management with an idea for a children's program called "Hey, Bob," with "Bob" standing for "be on the beam" or "be on the ball." Riley was asked to host the show.

"If we could teach children safety the fun way, and have them enjoy yelling 'Hey, Bob' when someone is jaywalking or something," Riley said, the message had a better chance of getting through. A rather grotesque-looking dummy was the physical presence of "Bob"—to this day, Riley still has "Bob" in his Clear Lake home.

The first show was aired in the fall of 1946 at the KRNT studio, with seating for 50 children. The program was designed to be fun; children threw pies, blew up balloons, competed in bubblegum blowing contests, and the like. The show was such a success that by the next week, the elevators and studios in the building were jammed. By the third week, the program was moved to the Paramount Theatre, and soon the 1,300-seat theater was regularly filled to capacity.

"One year, I remember driving to the Paramount Theatre, and it was 11 below zero and the line of children waiting to get into the theater went clear around the corner and a block up the street," Riley said. For the presentation of big shows, such as the Ice Follies, the program would occasionally be moved to the larger KRNT Theatre, which seated 4,200 people, but even that was not large enough at times.

For a dairy month promotion in June of 1949, the local dairy sponsor reported giving away 10,000 cups of ice cream—more than 4,000 to those in the theater, and another 6,000 to those who were waiting in line but had to be turned away at the door.

Duane Ellett and Floppy of WHO-TV delighted central Iowa children for parts of four decades.

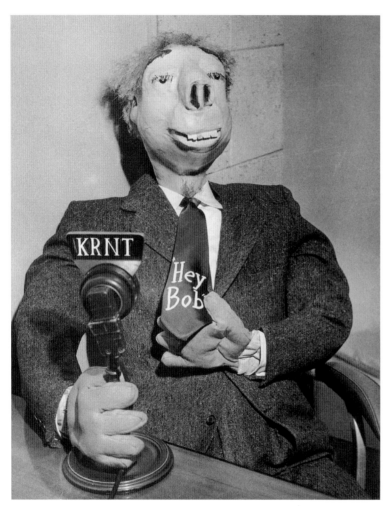

The notorious star of the "Hey, Bob!" radio show of the late 1940s.

But while the power of the "Hey, Bob Safety Legion" was strong, and the program received many national awards, it proved to be no match for television. By the fall of 1952, the show had left the KRNT radio airwaves.

By that time, central Iowa children had been exposed to the house with the "Magic Window," the longest continuously running children's show in American television history. First taking to the air in 1951, the program was seen on WOI-TV in Ames for 43 years. The producer and host of the program for all but the first three years was Betty Lou Varnum, the versatile WOI staffer who at various times also hosted a teen dance program and public affairs shows, and coordinated the station's election coverage.

The program occupied some of early television's prime real estate. For example, in 1953, the program aired at 5 in the afternoon, just after Gabby Hayes and Howdy Doody, and just before the Lone Ranger. The show included syndicated programs such as "Tales of the Riverbank," featuring the adventures of Hammy Hamster, and cartoons such as Felix the Cat. But it was the projects and crafts made with snubby-nosed scissors (as opposed to pointed ones which could hurt young children), along with the interaction between Varnum and her puppet friends, that made the program unique.

Gregory Lion, Dusty the Unicorn, and Catrina Crocodile lived in the Magic Forest, and interacted with Varnum to help introduce the animated features. They would help draw open the curtain, with Varnum calling out to "turn on the motor, turn on the lights" of an unseen projector so the feature could be shown.

Thousands of Central Iowa children learned how to use construction paper and glue, thanks to the Magic Window. But showing a young audience how to make things was not easy. "One of the things I found difficult in the beginning was working upside down and backwards, and now it's gotten to the point that I have to read maps that way," Varnum said.

From the day Channel 9 signed on in Sioux City, in March of 1953, the Canyon Kid was there. For 32 years, Jim Henry presided over the Canyon Kid's Kartoon Karnival.

"I guess the purpose of the show was to entertain children. Along the way, I wanted them to get some sense of how to live right, like be kind to your friends, obey your mother and father, those kinds of things," Henry said.

A native of Brooklyn, N.Y., Henry was stationed in Sioux City during World War II and decided to make the area his permanent home. When Channel 9, then known as KVTV, went on the air, the station was looking for a children's host. He had been active in community theater and thought, "This is all brand-new. They don't know any more about it than I do."

He decided the best format for the program would be to emulate a kids' club in an average backyard. He'd be the "president" of the club, with 15-20 children live on set each day. The easiest costume to come up with was a simple Western shirt and jeans, and he called himself the Canyon Kid. The station liked the audition, but thought they could come up with a better name for the show. In 32 years, no one did.

For the first month of the show, Henry sported a cowboy hat and a string tie, but those parts of the costume did not last. One thing that did last was his rather heavy Brooklyn accent. How did he account for a cowboy having a Brooklyn accent? He freely admitted to the children that the accent did not come from the canyons out west, but rather from the canyons created by the tall buildings in New York City.

An estimated 75,000 children appeared on the program over its three-decade run. Henry says he is amazed that people will still recall verbatim what they said on the show decades before, and remember what happened to them the day they appeared on the Canyon Kid program.

While the Magic Window and Canyon Kid were pioneers in

Iowa children's programming, programs designed for children were a part of early television in eastern Iowa, as well. Just three months after the station went on the air, WMT-TV premiered Miss Ruth Anne's School in January of 1954. The program lasted only two months, making way for cowboy Marshal J, who, along with his horse Nugget and dog Rascal, kept children entertained for nearly six years. When the Marshal rode off to continue his television career in California, Channel 2 officials were looking for a replacement. They asked a longtime community theater performer named Max Hahn if he wanted the job.

Hahn was no stranger to broadcasting, having performed in radio theater in the mid-1930s on both KWCR and WMT radio in Cedar Rapids. He was working on the night shift as a printer at a local firm at the time, and agreed to take on the TV duties in addition to his regular job.

"They didn't know what to call me. They didn't want a ship's captain or cowboy," Hahn recalled in a 1981 interview. Then someone at the station decided he should be called "Dr. Max." "Gee, that sounded awful. Dr. Max? I thought it was a terrible name for a show," he said. Regardless, on January 23, 1961, complete with safari jacket, Dr. Max the world traveler debuted on Channel 2. It was the beginning of a 20-year run.

Other stations in the Cedar Rapids/Waterloo market tried children's programming of their own. Sheriff Steve hosted a show on KCRG, and KWWL had Captain Jet, but they were no match for the good doctor. In 1963 and 1964, for example, the Dr. Max Show exceeded the ratings of the other two combined. One promotion, a Mickey Mouse coloring contest, netted 25,000 entries from four states.

For a time, Dr. Max was on for 60 minutes in the morning with a program designed for young children, and for another 90 minutes in the late afternoon with a program designed for older, school-age children. Foghorn Leghorn, Deputy Dawg,

Eastern Iowa children spent mornings and afternoons with Dr. Max and Mombo on WMT.

Huckleberry Hound, and other "colortoons" appeared on the "magic board" for children to see.

Early in the show's run, an off-stage noise accidentally carried over the microphone. To cover for the noise, Max blamed it on an unseen character, "Mombo." For a while, anytime something would go wrong on the live show, Max would simply blame Mombo.

After a while, children started writing in, asking to see Mombo. Hahn called upon a community theater friend, Fred Petrick, to appear a few times on the program as Mombo. Petrick devised a clown character, who was simply supposed to sit at Dr. Max's feet to satisfy the children's curiosity about "Mombo." But the children were still not satisfied. They began writing, asking for Mombo to talk. Soon, the two or three guest appearances became a run that lasted the length of the show. Mombo began doing magic tricks, and the duo made thousands of personal appearances across the state, at community events, store openings, parades, and the like.

A unique concept in local children's programming was Romper Room. The program, which appeared in a number of markets across the country in the late 1960s, was the brainchild of a Baltimore couple who devised a basic outline for what local Romper Room programs around the country should do each day, but provided no full script. The concept allowed national marketing, including the sale of merchandise such as "romper stompers" and "posture baskets." In eastern Iowa, "Miss Bonnie" was in charge of the classroom on KWWL-TV 7, while central Iowa children watched "Miss Nancy" on WHO-TV 13. Each day, the Romper Room teacher would hold up a "magic mirror" which could "see" the children watching at home. She would then call out various children's names; such as, "I see Bobby, and Sally, and there's Jim."

While the specific name and character played by the children's program host may have been different, the premise was the same at stations throughout the state. Quad Cities children grew up with the Cartoon Showboat, which aired on WOC-TV from 1964

"Miss Bonnie" Noonan and the KWWL Romper Room classroom in Waterloo in the mid-1960s.

to 1974. Four different captains piloted the Showboat during its decade on the air, including "Cap'n Ernie" Mims, who was the last. For a time, WHO-TV in Des Moines aired "The Lucky 13 Ranch" program, playing off the interest in "cowboy movies," which were popular at the time.

In Mason City, Bart Curran presided over "Bart's Clubhouse" from 1958 to 1976 on KGLO-TV. According to Curran, the set and premise was simple. "It was like an old-fashioned clubhouse kids would build in the backyard," he said in a 1994 interview.

When KTIV-TV went on the air in Sioux City in 1954, "Commander Four" was there to contact Buck Rodgers or Flash Gordon and bring their adventures to the northwest Iowa audience. Hosted by Red Quilleash as the commander, the station brought the old movie serials back to life for a new audience. The station's "Space Legion Headquarters" would send cards to children to decode with "secret decoding devices." The messages would provide guidance such as "ride your bike carefully" or "drink your milk."

Bill Riley made the switch from radio to television on KRNT with, among other things, the Breakfast Club, which aired for a half-hour at 7:30 a.m. weekdays. The club claimed 40,000 children as card-carrying members. Riley also hosted an hour-long Variety Theater program in the afternoons, featuring standards such as The Little Rascals.

Puppets were popular, particularly in central Iowa. Captain Redbeard and his sailor sidekick, Seasick, hosted Kadipus Land on KDPS-TV (later KDIN-TV) in Des Moines in the 1970s. But without question, for more than 30 years, the most popular puppet on Iowa television was Floppy.

Created by WHO announcer Duane Ellett, Floppy made his debut in the mid-1950s on a program called Pet Corner, which was designed to help find homes for shelter pets. By 1957, Floppy had his own show, with Duane providing the "personality" behind a wall. The on-air foils for Floppy's jokes were a series of young female co-hosts. Before long, however, Duane and Floppy were back on camera together and became one of Iowa's great two-man stand-up acts, with very little change in format over the decades.

"I gave it about two years when we started," Ellett remembered in a 1985 interview. "But it has picked up momentum and kept growing. We found out along the way we didn't have to get new cartoons—we had new kids being born all the time, so that was kind of a cheap way to manage that."

In between various cartoons, children who were given cardboard question marks would get to ask Floppy a riddle. No matter how many times Floppy was asked, "What is the biggest pencil in the world?" or "Why did the man put his car in the oven?", he always acted surprised when the laughing youngster would say, "Pennsylvania," or "Because he wanted a hot rod."

Tickets to be a part of the in-studio audience for The Floppy Show were hard to get, with reservations required one year in advance. Fan clubs sprang up on Iowa college campuses, where wearing a Floppy T-shirt was considered the height of fashion in some circles.

"I wish the ratings surveys took into account the college and university groups, because they are the fanatics," Ellett said.

As was the case with all late-afternoon, locally produced children's programming, however, the weekday "Floppy Show" was pushed aside in 1984 to make room for syndicated programming designed for adults. Floppy still appeared on a weekly program along with other puppets, called The Floppytown Gazette, until Duane Ellett's sudden death in 1987. After his death, Ellett's family donated Floppy to the State Historical Society of Iowa, where he is always on display—trademark red sweater and all.

Without exception, the programs were low budget and were broadcast live, usually without any rehearsal. Special effects were limited. The programs relied on the imagination of the children who were watching.

Fred Petrick, who played Mombo the Clown for 20 years, recalled in a 1993 interview that they seldom resorted to trick photography—except on one memorable occasion involving a lawnmower.

Petrick said he and host Max Hahn saw a lawnmower in the station before their show one day, and decided it would make a good prop for a skit. The set had a carpet which was actually laid in two pieces. Mombo started up the lawnmower, with Dr. Max encouraging him to be careful. The camera shot the upper half of Mombo's body while he pushed the mower across the set, allowing unseen stagehands to pull the carpet pieces apart. When the shot widened to show the entire set, it appeared as if he had mowed a clean strip across the carpet, much to Dr. Max's dismay.

Most local hosts originally did live commercials during their programs, until the Federal Communications Commission changed the rules and banned the practice. Some of their experiences made many local hosts happy to stop doing commercials.

During one program, Channel 3's Bart Curran was to do a live commercial promoting McDonald's milkshakes. As a prank, one of the crew members had spiked the milkshake with a shot of

KRNT personality Bill Riley welcomes a troupe of Bluebirds to his "Variety Theater" program in Des Moines.

Jim Henry as
Sioux City's
"Canyon Kid."

for as much as six months at a time. One of his sponsors was Peter Pan bread, and Hahn said after more than 100 daily commercials for the product, "you got the idea of making sandwiches."

"When I started out in children's television, I really had no lofty ideas about educating children," Ellett said. "I just really wanted to make something entertaining for them. But then when I got older, I started thinking more about the educational aspect of it."

While their primary purpose was to entertain children, these programs also helped develop a sense of community involvement and personal responsibility in the young audience. Over an 18-month period, with the help of Des Moines children, KRNT's Bill Riley was responsible for raising $156,000 to aid in the construction of the Des Moines Children's Zoo.

For eight years, the Dr. Max Show sponsored "My Important Book," a pocket-sized booklet where children could make lists of their "important" things. The books, which sold for 50 cents including postage and handling, were mailed from the station. They also included "Dr. Max's Rules for the Day," such as obeying your parents, saying your prayers, and brushing your teeth. Regular guests on the Dr. Max Show included a police officer, an individual from the local humane society, and a representative from the local nature center, among others. Max Hahn himself was a regular reader at the Saturday morning story hour at the Cedar Rapids Public Library.

alcohol. After one drink, the unsuspecting Curran was unable to speak. To make matters worse, a regional manager from McDonald's was in the studio that day to see how well their advertising dollars were being spent .

Channel 2's Dr. Max once noted the difficulty of ad-libbing a 60-second commercial for the same sponsor five days a week, often

The young audience was impressionable, and parents were concerned about the programming. For many years, the Dr. Max

Betty Lou Varnum hosted WOI-TV's "The Magic Window," the longest-running local children's program in American TV history.

Show aired films of The Three Stooges. However, by the mid-1970s, the station pulled the Stooges due to concern from viewers about the violence depicted in the programs. Other stations had to defend violence in cartoons such as Tom & Jerry, and the Road Runner and Wile E. Coyote. (It is more than a bit ironic that the daytime talk shows that replaced children's programming in the late afternoon hours, when children are still in the viewing audience, regularly depict a great deal more "violence.")

One bit of children's show violence was not actually seen by the Sioux City television audience, according to Jim Henry. Each week on the Canyon Kid program, one day was designated as "Pet Day," when the children in the audience would bring their pets to the studio. On one show, when Henry himself was on vacation and the station's sports announcer was substituting, one child showed his turtle to another child, who had a pet raccoon. Unfortunately, nature took its course, with unfavorable results for the turtle.

"You become a celebrity when you have cows and dogs and llamas named Max," WMT's Dr. Max said in a 1981 interview commemorating the 20th anniversary of the program. A young fan once showed Hahn his two pet frogs—one named Max and one named Mombo. "So you see, you are famous when kids start naming animals after you."

Sometimes, the "naming" is more serious. Sioux City's "Canyon Kid" recalls once meeting a young woman who said that when she was a child, Henry had a girl named Rochelle on the show. The young woman said she thought that was a pretty

name, and decided then and there that if she ever had a daughter, she would name her Rochelle. The woman then introduced Henry to a young girl—her daughter, Rochelle.

"All I knew was that we were doing a show for children, with children, and that I needed to be as interested and take them as seriously as I would an adult, and so that when we talked, I always thought of dealing with children on that basis, that what they've got to say is very important, and it just worked," Henry said.

"It's a feeling of satisfaction that the kiddies out there and the people liked us, and when you please people, it gives you a good feeling," Fred Petrick, Channel 2's "Mombo," once said.

Some thought that doing a daily program in front of a live audience would get old after a while. In a 1980s interview, Duane Ellett disagreed. "With each group of young people that enters the studio down there, I see a lot of new faces and new little individuals, and it's something that I look forward to," he said.

"Is there anything nicer than being known to and loved by children? And that has been one of the most warm and wonderful parts of doing Magic Window all these years," Varnum said in a 1994 interview.

Long before books such as "All I Needed to Know, I Learned in Kindergarten" became popular, eastern Iowa children learned all they needed to know through Dr. Max's daily sign off—"Take it easy, play it safe, and be careful."

In different words and different ways, that message was delivered by all of the dozens of children's shows originated at Iowa radio and television stations.

A Word From Our Sponsors

It is hard today to think of any alternative to the current system of commercial broadcasting which dominates our country. In our free enterprise system, tangible goods are bought and sold; broadcasters have nothing tangible to sell, simply the air through which the signals travel. So despite past government efforts to prohibit commercial advertisements from the broadcast airwaves, the way that the great majority of stations stay in business is to sell pieces of the broadcast day to those who wish to advertise their goods and services.

A 1934 "rate card" for KWCR in Cedar Rapids indicated that during the evening hours, a person could buy sponsorship for a half-hour radio program for $45; if the sponsor were willing to purchase that half-hour of time once a week for a year, the rate dropped to $27 per week. Conversely, a half-minute commercial cost $7; if that commercial were run once a week for a whole year, the per-commercial rate dropped to $5 each. The evening hours were the most costly time in which to purchase advertising, as it was considered "prime time;" today, those evening hours are television's prime time, while the most expensive time to buy in radio are the early mornings, "drive time."

By the end of the 1930s, one of the ways the Cowles stations tried to compete with WHO's broad signal was to form the Iowa Network, occasionally sharing programming between Cowles-owned stations and offering advertisers combination

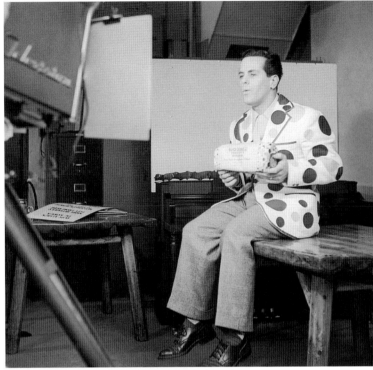

Bill Riley delivering a commercial for Wonder bread.

packages. As the station with the largest signal, WMT was the heart of the network, but as advertisements in national publications in the 1930s pointed out, "WMT can be bought in combination with WNAX and KSO or KRNT at an exceptionally low rate." Advertisers, therefore, received a discount if they advertised on multiple Cowles properties.

Broadcasters could not be shy about recruiting advertiser dollars. WHO, for its part, also advertised in *Broadcasting* magazine, soliciting national advertisers. WHO pointed out its large 50,000 watt coverage in

a 1952 ad, but also indicated that due to the station's "tremendous goodwill by helping various community organizations throughout Iowa...literally tens of thousands of families have become our personal friends," which meant "responsive listeners for WHO advertisers."

When R. J. McElroy was known as the "most curious man in the world" as part of WMT's Voice of Iowa broadcasts, he would ask trivia questions of passersby. The program sponsor was Kleen-Maid bread, and everyone got a miniature loaf of the bread for appearing on the Voice of

Iowa program. When people got a question right, McElroy's tagline was "Right as Kleen-Maid!" to give the sponsor extra promotion.

When McElroy went into the Army in 1942, he was replaced on the Voice of Iowa program by Howdy Roberts and Red Rowe. McElroy reported on how he was doing during his first months in the service with the following message sent back to the audience: "I hope you all keep buying Kleen-Maid and listening to Howdy and Red so that the program will still be on the air when the war is over and I can come back and spend happy hours with you again," McElroy said.

During the early television years, sponsorship of programs included signage on the set; even newscasts were sponsored, with company logos prominently displayed on the anchor's news desk. In Des Moines, for example, Jack Shelley would do the WHO-TV news with a Standard Oil sign on his desk, Bill Milldyke would anchor WOI-TV's news with an IMT Insurance logo in the background, and in the most famous example, the Anderson-Erickson dairy sponsored Russ Van Dyke's late news, which traditionally ended with Van Dyke taking a long drink of milk from a glass.

But those who ran the Iowa State University-owned television station, WOI-TV, were not as free to solicit advertising as their competitors. The State Board of Regents originally set a policy limiting advertising on WOI to national accounts, including advertisements during network

A Word From Our Sponsors

programs. This policy was approved on January 17, 1950, less than five weeks before the station went on the air.

Local advertisers were effectively shut out of television advertising in central Iowa for a number of years because of the policy, since WOI was the only station on in central Iowa until 1954, and many were not happy about the advertising ban.

Less than a year after the station went on the air, in May, 1951, the policy regarding "the assignment of broadcasting time" was reviewed and again approved by the Regents in its original form. Yet that was not the end of the discussion.

In November, 1951, the Central National Bank in Des Moines asked for a change in policy to allow local advertising on WOI-TV. Again, the Regents agreed that the policy governing advertising should not be changed. A representative from a Des Moines advertising agency met with the Board in January, 1952 to further lobby for a policy change, but he was again unsuccessful.

Later, however, Tone Brothers, an Iowa-based business which operated nationally, filed a formal complaint with the Regents, since the station was carrying commercials for Folgers coffee—a Tone's competitor—but would not sell time to Tone Brothers. The policy was eventually modified so that the station would accept in-state commercials, but would not actively solicit advertising from Iowa businesses. However, once the policy was changed in any way, the overall interpretation of the policy became

more liberal, and under pressure from the television networks which aired programs on WOI-TV, even beer and cigarette advertising was eventually accepted by the station.

But once Channel 8 and Channel 13 went on the air, the increased competition along with the lackluster advertising solicitation policy adversely affected WOI-TV's bottom line. The drop in profit was so significant that discussions regarding selling the station began as early as 1958, when college President James Hilton was directed to confer with a broker regarding the value of WOI-TV on the open market. (While nothing came of that effort, the discussion of selling the station would arise on more than one occasion in the mid-1970s, and again in the early 1990s before the station was finally sold on March 1, 1994.)

In the early days of television, commercials were done live, sometimes with interesting consequences. More than once, KRNT's Russ Van Dyke took a long drink of Anderson-Erickson milk at the end of his newscast, only to find that it had been spiked with a shot of alcohol, or that someone had switched the regular milk with buttermilk. Regardless, Van Dyke had no choice but to smile and act as if the milk he had just drunk was the best he had ever tasted.

The late Harold Heath recalled in a 1998 interview a number of unexpected occurrences during live commercials. The rules in the late 1950s prohibited beer companies from actually showing a person drinking

the product on air; a bottle could be brought up to a person's mouth, but they could not take a drink. On one occasion, an announcer told the audience of the virtues of Black Hawk Beer and brought the bottle to his lips; at that point, the director was to switch to another camera shot, but he was late in making the switch and the audience saw the announcer dump the beer and scowl as if the mere scent of the beer made him ill. Needless to say, the Black Hawk Beer company was not pleased.

Station marketing and promotion takes on a variety of forms, all designed to increase the audience—which allows stations to charge more for the commercials they sell, and in turn, to make more money.

One of the more ingenious advertising promotions was begun by rock station KRNA in Iowa City in the late 1970s. The station was one of the few commercial radio stations in Iowa City which did not broadcast University of Iowa basketball games, but the station did want to establish a tie to the successful program coached by Lute Olson.

The partners running KRNA, Eliot Keller and Rob Norton, came up with the idea of working with the Iowa basketball department to create a poster. Many teams had team photos and schedules printed on posters which were popular with fans; Norton's idea was to take the concept to a higher level.

Using commercial photography and an elaborate setting, the first KRNA basketball poster was printed, titled "A Class Act." The players, in

full uniform, were seated around a formal dinner table at a local restaurant. Waiters in formal attire were shown serving them a multi-course meal. The uniqueness of the setting was an immediate hit with fans. The posters were originally a station promotion, handed out by KRNA during remote broadcasts at area businesses. Later posters in the series included the team in a county courtroom, with different players assuming the roles of judge, attorneys, and jurors, in a takeoff on the basketball "court" theme.

However, a change in NCAA rules limited the free distribution of the posters, which are still printed annually under the sponsorship of the radio station Keller and Norton currently run, KZIA in Cedar Rapids; posters are now available for sale by the Iowa athletic department. They remain popular with collectors today.

The old FCC rules regarding the number of minutes per hour a station could air advertisements, however, are no longer in effect, and have given way to program-length commercials known as "infomercials." Some longtime broadcasters are not sure that deregulation like this was a good idea.

"The free enterprise system in the final analysis is the best, and so we have to put up with some of these things like over-commercialization," former WMT station manager Bill Quarton said nearly a decade ago. "I think they're killing the goose that laid the golden egg by over-commercializing."

Early WMT-TV children's host "Marshal J" and his dog "Rascal."

"I felt I got the greatest satisfaction out of the news part of it.
I had the most fun doing the sports."

Ken Kew, whose 32-year career at KGLO radio and television in
Mason City included both anchoring newscasts and doing play-by-play
of University of Iowa athletics.

5 Good Sports

In the spring of 1922, some Marshalltown sports enthusiasts strung a cable from the KFJB radio studio to Franklin Field, three blocks away, and broadcast a track and field meet—the first live remote broadcast of a sporting event in Iowa. But even these young pioneers could never have imagined that 60 years later, an Iowa television station would be the first local station in America to originate an NCAA football broadcast and send it back to the station via satellite. It seems that Iowa broadcasters have always satisfied sports fans' desires with groundbreaking programming.

While Marshalltown's KFJB was not officially licensed until June 2, 1923, the station was broadcasting regularly more than a year before that. Earl Peak and his partner in the Marshall Electric Company, A. J. Curtis, encouraged the efforts of two of their employees in developing an audio receiving station. Merle Easter and Chauncy Hoover had been experimenting with a code signal station in the back of the Marshall Electric building. It was taking too long to encode and decode messages, so Easter added a tube to allow audio transmission to take place so he could more quickly communicate with a fellow enthusiast in Ames. The homemade effort soon became one of the first radio stations in Iowa.

Earl Peak had experience working for various rural telephone companies, and had founded Marshall Electric in 1914. In May 1922, the skill of these young men led them to try something new. It seemed like a natural progression to them, but no one had ever tried it before.

Earl's son Eugene, who still lives in Marshalltown, was 10 years old at the time, but had already spent much time hanging around his father's business. He recalls personally being one of those who helped string an audio line from the business, down West Main

Street for three blocks to the new athletic facilities. This track meet is the earliest recorded notation of a live remote broadcast of a sporting event in Iowa, and perhaps the first of a track meet anywhere in the country.

"We put the line in," Eugene Peak remembers, "and in the fall of 1922, we did high school football from Franklin Field." In U.S. radio history, there is no documentation of any other high school football game being broadcast live from the field earlier than this, making KFJB's high school football broadcasts the first of their kind in America.

Soon after, the station began broadcasting high school football and basketball games throughout the region, using telephone lines to send the signal back to the station—a practice still in common use today. In the days before press boxes, KFJB sports announcers would carry their own "portable press box" to games— sheets of plywood that could be quickly assembled to create a "booth" in the stands to limit the amount of crowd noise that came over the air and provide some shelter for the announcer.

Live coverage of sporting events quickly became a favorite source of programming, not only to members of the audience but for broadcasters, as well. The audience could experience the athletic event without having to travel to see it in person, while the broadcaster had a ready source of inexpensive programming to fill air time.

On February 21, 1924, the first play-by-play of University of Iowa basketball was aired on WSUI radio in a game between Iowa and Illinois. A direct phone line was strung from the Armory where the game was being played to the WSUI control room in the engineering building. Reports from the game site were fed to

"Tait" Cummins was a fixture behind the WMT sports microphone throughout the 1950s and 1960s.

KFJB in Marshalltown was one of the stations that brought its own press box to the games. Often the workings of the broadcast was more fascinating to children in the stands than the game.

stringing an audio line with which to do the games, and wanted the athletic department to provide $100 worth of plywood for the booth. The athletic director responded that while it was nice the radio station was broadcasting the games, it was not worth $100 to the basketball team to build the booth.

One of the first statewide radio networks to cover a major sporting event was formed in 1939 for the Iowa high school basketball championship tournament. The Iowa Dairy Commission was in charge of arranging the broadcasts, and selected three stations that it felt had sufficiently strong signals to serve the entire state. Commercial station KMA in Shenandoah and non-commercial stations WSUI in Iowa City and WOI in Ames carried the coverage live.

Carl Menzer in the studio, who would repeat what he heard on the telephone through the microphone on the air. A newspaper article promoting the broadcast promised that within two minutes of a basket being scored, the information would be relayed to listeners.

Once actual play-by-play was possible from the game site, WSUI's Menzer wanted a small booth built in the Armory to improve the quality of the broadcasts. The college dean wrote a letter to the athletic director noting that WSUI had spent a lot of money

It was not uncommon for university-owned stations like WSUI and WOI to broadcast their institution's athletic contests; WOI had broadcast an Iowa State football game in the fall of 1922, the station's first year of existence. The stations continued these broadcasts even into the 1960s. However, the ability for universities to earn millions of dollars from selling broadcast rights to commercial stations has changed that.

One thing that has not changed, however, has been intensive coverage of state basketball tournaments by Iowa's radio stations. Press row at Veterans Memorial Auditorium in Des Moines is typically jammed each March with local broadcasters, bringing the tournament stories home to their listeners. The colorful banners, denoting station call letters and location, ring the upper level of the Auditorium in what is known as "Radio Row."

Fans have appreciated the dedication their sportscasters have shown in following the hometown teams. In Clinton, the high school press box is named for Hank Dihlman, who called more than 5,000 games over a 40-year career on KROS radio there. In 1959, KFJB sports director Dale Smith was honored for his years of service at a special halftime show during an October football game. The Marshalltown High School Bobcat marching band created a number of formations in tribute: spelling out the KFJB call letters and the word "DALE" on the field, and forming a microphone and a turntable complete with moving record. Smith was sports director for the Marshalltown station from 1949 to 1970.

Then as now, it was costly for stations to travel with their favorite teams and produce broadcasts of road games. One solution that was prevalent in the 1930s and 1940s was for a local announcer to "re-create" ballgames based upon information sent by a teletype. Famed WHO and WOC sports announcer Ronald Reagan was well-known for his coverage of Chicago Cubs baseball games, despite the fact that he never left the studio in Des Moines.

Throughout his political career, Reagan delighted in telling stories of how the teletype wire would feed information about each pitch of a game, which Reagan would then relay to the audience as if he were in the ballpark, complete with sound effects, all sponsored by Wheaties. On one notable occasion, Reagan was delivering his re-created play-by-play when the wire suddenly went dead. Reagan stalled for time by having the batter foul off pitch after pitch, after pitch. He had the batter foul off a near-record

Dale Smith

number of pitches in a row before the teletype signal was restored and his accurate re-creation could continue.

More than one Iowa sportscaster grew up listening to Reagan's broadcasts, and turned to a career in broadcasting as a result. Sports broadcasting legend Jim Zabel recalls listening to Reagan broadcast University of Iowa football games while growing up in Davenport. Zabel began his career at WHO in 1944, not long after Reagan's departure for Hollywood, and has spent his entire on-air career there. He has interviewed Reagan some two dozen times—to help promote a new Reagan movie when it premiered in Des Moines; during his television career; and later while he was governor of California and then president of the United States.

Mason City broadcaster Ken Kew, who also did play-by-play of Hawkeye athletics during his 32 years of broadcasting on KGLO radio and television, knew from the time he was a sophomore

LONDON   NEW YORK   DES MOINES   DENVER   LOS ANGELES

You Expect more from STANDARD and Get it!

Sports director Jim Zabel at the WHO-TV anchor desk (circa 1960).

STANDARD

JIM ZABEL

in high school, when he heard Reagan re-create a game, that he wanted to cover sports for his career. One of Kew's first sports memories was listening to the famous Jack Dempsey-Gene Tunney prize fight on a crystal set.

Some may be surprised to learn that re-creation of sporting events by teletype carried on long after Reagan's time. In the mid-1950s, Waterloo radio station KWWL broadcast the games of the minor league Waterloo White Hawks baseball team. Sports director Claire Rampton and Frosty Mitchell handled the broadcast duties, live from the stadium while the team was at home, and in the studios with the help of the Western Union telegraph when the team was on the road, to save the cost of traveling around the Midwest. Down the road, Bob Brooks was the voice of the minor league baseball teams in Cedar Rapids from 1949 to 1962, traveling with the team for the first decade and re-enacting road games in the studio from ticker tape feeds from 1959 to 1962.

Viewers in eastern Iowa were eager for the first day of broadcasting by WMT-TV on September 30, 1953. They certainly were looking forward to news and musical entertainment programs—but perhaps more importantly at the time, Channel 2 was scheduled to air the World Series, which was in fact the first program aired on the station after introductory comments by manager William B. Quarton.

WMT was a CBS affiliate, and the World Series was to be aired on NBC. However, since there was no NBC affiliate in eastern Iowa at the time, WMT sales manager Lew Van Nostrand traveled to New York and made a special deal with NBC to allow the baseball games to be aired on Channel 2. As Quarton remembers, NBC agreed that WMT could air the games, but at a cost of $5,000. However, NBC never billed the station—and Quarton didn't remind them.

Probably the first sports announcer to gain popularity as a broadcast personality was originally known to eastern Iowans as an award-winning sports writer and editor for the Cedar Rapids Gazette, authoring the popular "Red Peppers" column. Lawson "Tait" Cummins began his 37-year career at WMT radio in 1947. The first live program on WMT-TV was an interview between Cummins and Hawkeye football coach Forest Evashevski in 1953; the first local program aired regularly on Channel 2 was "Sports with Tait."

One of those coach's shows with Evashevski drew the attention of the Big 10 conference. During the show following the 1953 Iowa-Michigan game, discussion focused on a controversial call where an Iowa player was called for holding. Coach Evashevski thought the play cost his team the 14-13 game. "Evy made sure we had that play on film. On the show we ran it over and over and stopped the film at the play," Cummins once recalled. The conference commissioner then imposed a new rule regulating television shows featuring conference games, forbidding the shows to stop the film while showing plays.

At first glance, Cummins did not fit the mold for broadcasting. His voice was gravelly, he got excited during games, and he did not possess the "look" of many in television. But he was a solid journalist, and had a huge following.

"He didn't have a phony bone in his body, and I think that that came through," his wife and professional partner Dotty said in a 1993 interview. "I wish I had a nickel for everyone who ever said to me, 'I don't care about sports, I just like to watch your husband on television.'"

Tait Cummins was the sports face of Channel 2 for its first 11 years, before leaving television in 1964 to work exclusively in radio. The change was Tait's idea.

"I'm ugly as hell and I knew the station's management was about at the end of its rope with my appearance. So I went to see the boss and told him if I ever had to make the decision of doing either TV or radio rather than both, I'd take radio. I was off

Dutch and the Cubs

Governor Ronald Reagan of California was the keynote speaker at WHO radio's 50th anniversary luncheon in 1974. Reagan delighted the audience with stories from his time as a broadcaster in Iowa from 1933 to 1937. None of the stories was more famous than his tale of re-creating a Cubs-Cardinals baseball game in the mid-1930s, when the two teams were contending for the pennant.

Ronald Reagan

Reagan explained that information about the game came by teletype in the form of Morse code, which would have to be interpreted and passed on to him. On this particular day, Curly Waddell was at the teletype key, deciphering the information for Reagan. It was the bottom of the ninth inning, and the Cardinals' famous pitcher, Dizzy Dean, was on the mound.

"I said, 'Diz comes out of the wind up, and here comes the pitch.' Curly was shaking his head 'No,' but I thought he just didn't like something. And I took the paper and it said, 'The wire's gone dead.' I had a pitch on the way to the plate!

"There was only one thing you could do that doesn't get into the scorebook—I had him foul it off. I looked at Curly, and Curly looked at me, and I just couldn't say to that audience in the ninth inning,

'We've lost our service. We're going to give you a brief interlude of transcribed music.'

"So I talked about Dizzy Dean. I slowed him down a little, I had him use the resin bag a lot, I had him shake off signs, then a lengthy wind up, and Diz finally let go with another pitch, and the batter fouled that one off to the right. Then he fouled one off back to the stands. And then he fouled one off back of third base, and I described the fight between the two kids trying to get the ball.

"Then he fouled one off that just missed a home run by a foot. Now I'm beginning to sweat because I'm beginning to set a world record for a man staying at-bat, and that is going to get in the news.

"Until finally, in the nick of time, Curly sat up and started typing. And I started another ball on the way to the plate, grabbed the wire, and it said, 'Batter popped out on the first ball pitched.'"

television that night," Cummins said in a 1979 interview with the *Des Moines Register.*

He broadcast Hawkeye sporting events for WMT radio for 24 years before retiring in 1971; however, he produced daily shows and covered stories for the station until his death in 1984 at the age of 78. His ties to the Hawkeyes were so strong that he became the first non-athlete ever to be presented with a letterman's award by the university. As was the case with many Iowa broadcasters, Cummins was an active participant in supporting a number of charitable causes, most notably Camp Courageous near Monticello.

A one-time rock and roll disc jockey who became a station owner also broadcast Iowa athletics for 35 years. Frosty Mitchell bought radio station KGRN in Grinnell in 1960 for $65,000, founding what became known as Mitchell Broadcasting, which owned stations in cities such as Knoxville and Mount Pleasant.

A young Des Moines lawyer helped Mitchell with the legal work for the company, and agreed to help the fledgling business by taking stock in the corporation in exchange for the value of his legal services. An avid sports fan, the young lawyer served as color commentator when Mitchell began broadcasts of Hawkeye football that fall. He and his wife themselves later bought a radio station in Estherville. The young lawyer might still be involved in sports broadcasting today, but instead chose to pursue a career in politics.

So when Robert Ray decided to run for governor in 1968, Frosty Mitchell had to find a new sportscast partner, due to equal-time rules for candidates. But the partnership continued off-the-air; Mitchell served as Ray's campaign manager in 1968.

Named Iowa Sportscaster of the Year three times, Mitchell created a network of as many as 30 radio stations, primarily in smaller markets, which carried his Hawkeye football broadcasts. He also served for nearly 20 years as color commentator for the statewide televised broadcasts of Iowa's boys and girls high school basketball tournaments.

Iowa broadcasters bringing the word of the coaches to sports fans: (clockwise) Ron Gonder with Drake University football coach Jack Wallace; Tait Cummins with Iowa basketball coach Eddie Anderson; Pete Taylor with Iowa State football coach Johnny Majors; and Iowa basketball coach Lute Olson with Frosty Mitchell, Sharm Scheuerman, and Bob Hogue.

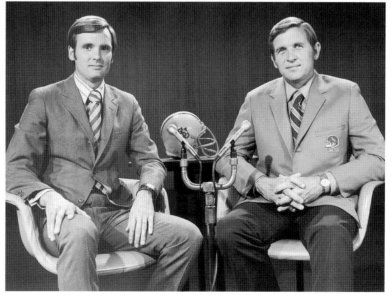

Bob Brooks

Ron Gonder

A number of others were also well known for their longtime association with Hawkeye sports broadcasts, including Gene Claussen of KXIC in Iowa City, Kent Braverman of KCJJ in Iowa City, and Blean Calkins of KWPC in Muscatine.

But today's audience probably best remembers a trio of broadcasters, all of whom were still doing play-by-play of Iowa football and basketball when the University of Iowa granted broadcast exclusivity to a single network in 1997.

At the time, each was heard on dozens of radio stations around Iowa, serving as the lead voice for his own respective network. When their amazing strings were ended by the new agreement, they had amassed a total of 132 combined years of broadcasting Hawkeye sports. Each had also anchored television sportscasts during earlier days when his respective radio station also owned a television station. And each had a devoted following—fans who could not imagine listening to anyone else.

Bob Brooks' association with what was then known as the State University of Iowa began while he was a high school student, volunteering at radio station WSUI. He has continued a regular association with Hawkeye press boxes since 1944. At the time of WSUI's 60th anniversary in 1979, Brooks remembered those early days, and said just getting to the games was an adventure.

"We traveled in those days by train, usually without the benefit of any sleeping car or anything. If you could find a seat, fine. But the trains were so crowded that you usually had to sit in the men's room, on the floor, in the aisle or some place. The hotels quite a few times couldn't even accommodate the team. They could give you only a few rooms, so people would have to sleep in the bathtub," Brooks recalled. "If you played Ohio State in Columbus, for instance, you had to leave on Thursday night and you didn't get back until Sunday night because of the route of the train. And sometimes the train was so slow that you could get on the back of the observation car and throw some cinders at the telegraph poles as they went by—that's how slow the thing was moving."

A mainstay of Cedar Rapids sports broadcasting, Brooks spent 28 years on KCRG radio and television, and 21 more years on KHAK radio. To this day, he still makes regular appearances on KMRY radio and KCRG radio and television broadcasts, covering coaches' press conferences and commenting on current sports issues. In addition, Bob Brooks was named the recipient of the 2002 Chris Schenkel Award by the National Football Foundation and the College Football Hall of Fame, only the seventh person to ever receive the honor. He was also named Sportscaster of the Year six times.

Frosty Mitchell

Jim Zabel

Ron Gonder's Iowa broadcasting career began at KRNT radio and television in Des Moines in the mid-1960s. Though Gonder is most closely associated with University of Iowa athletics, among his early duties during his time at Channel 8 was hosting the Iowa State University football show featuring Coach Clay Stapleton. KRNT-TV advertised in 1965 that Des Moines viewers could watch football game films with Iowa coach Jerry Burns on Sunday afternoons and Iowa State coach Clay Stapleton on Monday evenings.

Gonder moved to WMT-TV in Cedar Rapids as sports director in 1969. He picked up Hawkeye radio play-by-play duties in 1971, succeeding Tait Cummins. After WMT-TV was sold in 1981, Gonder moved exclusively to WMT radio, were he continued broadcasting Hawkeye football and basketball games and doing morning sportscasts. He was the sideline reporter for the first three years of the consolidated Hawkeye football network broadcasts, and retired from WMT in 2000.

Jim Zabel began work at WHO radio shortly after graduating from the University of Iowa in 1944. He still delivers regular afternoon sportscasts for the station. His 52 consecutive years of calling play-by-play for University of Iowa athletics is a record that undoubtedly will stand forever.

Zabel was a workhorse for WHO, hosting two of the longest-running local television sports programs in American broadcasting history. "Beat the Bear" aired after the late local news on Sunday nights, and featured the head coaches from Iowa, Iowa State and Drake, discussing sports and offering predictions about the outcomes of the next week's games. The program aired during the 1960s and 1970s, and was revived with a different format in the 1990s.

"Let's Go Bowling" was a mainstay of Sunday morning television on Channel 13 for nearly a quarter-century. The one-hour program featured bowlers from around the state, known as the "Out of Towners," taking on a team from various local Des Moines bowling alleys. The versatile Zabel would do "play-by-play" of the action, with a commentator adding "color."

During the 1970s, it was not uncommon for Zabel to anchor the television sports at 6 and 10 each weeknight, after having hosted a two-hour radio talk show on general topics in the afternoon; taping that week's "Let's Go Bowling" and "Beat the Bear" programs at other times; and at night and on weekends, doing play-by-play for as many as 126 high school games a year, plus the full schedule of University of Iowa (and also at times, Iowa State and Drake) games.

Gene Claussen

Pete Taylor

Zabel was also the television play-by-play voice of the Iowa girls state basketball tournament for nearly two decades, and in more recent years, spent his summers broadcasting on radio the exploits of Kurt Warner and the Iowa Barnstormers of the Arena Football League.

Brooks, Gonder, Zabel, and Mitchell—and even Robert Ray and Forest Evashevski—are members of the Iowa Broadcasters Association Hall of Fame.

Iowa State fans who followed the Cyclones on the radio were no less devoted to their announcers, but the number of stations carrying Iowa State games was far more limited. For many years, a number of stations—such as KRNT and WHO in Des Moines— originated broadcasts of Iowa State games, but only as a backup to Hawkeye games or on a tape-delayed basis. KRNT radio advertised in 1957 that roughly half of the Iowa State games would be broadcast, often as the second, tape-delayed half of the football doubleheader. Sports director Al Couppee, along with Ron Shoop and Win Douglass, provided the game commentary that year. Announcers Bud Sobel and Ron Gonder were pictured in a KRNT advertisement that ran in the football game programs at both Iowa and Iowa State in 1965.

Later, KRNT originated all the Cyclone games, featuring the

station's radio and television sports director, Pete Taylor. Iowa State has had an exclusive broadcast arrangement for much longer than Iowa, centralizing its broadcasts within a single network in 1989. In 1990, Taylor left Channel 8 after 22 years as the station's sports director to work full-time for Iowa State University as associate athletic director for external relations, a role which included providing the play-by-play for the broadcast network authorized by the university. Taylor was the play-by-play voice of the Cyclones from 1969 until his sudden death in March 2003. He has been succeeded by John Walters, who had been the Cyclones' television play-by-play announcer.

A number of broadcasters with Iowa ties went on to national prominence. The late Texas Rangers broadcaster Mark Holtz got his start while a student at Wartburg College in Waverly, doing ballgames for radio station KWAR-FM. In addition, two broadcast members of the major league baseball Hall of Fame credit their start to WSUI in Iowa City.

Milo Hamilton worked at the University of Iowa-owned radio station while a student there in the late 1940s, and went on to become a broadcaster for seven major league baseball teams, including the Pittsburgh Pirates, Chicago Cubs and Houston Astros. The Fairfield native was inducted into the baseball hall of fame in 1992. Harry Kalas, the longtime Philadelphia Phillies announcer, was inducted into the Hall of Fame as the Ford Frick Award recipient in 2002; he graduated from the University in 1959, and also broadcast Houston Astros games in the 1960s.

WMT listeners heard Bert Puckett broadcast Cedar Rapids Raiders baseball games throughout the 1930s. Because the team was afraid live broadcasts would cut down on ballpark attendance, Puckett was not allowed inside the park and was forced to do his play-by-play while sitting on a nearby housetop overlooking the field. Finally, in 1941, his final year with WMT, he was allowed to do broadcasts from inside Hill Park. In 1942, Puckett left the station to become the voice of the Chicago Cubs, where he was better known as Bert Wilson. In fact, Wilson and Milo Hamilton worked together as the broadcast team for the Cubs for two years during the late 1950s.

Radio station KSTT in Davenport also originated broadcasts of University of Iowa sporting events, and many of their play-by-play announcers went on to national prominence. Among the stable of KSTT announcers were Fred Manfra and John Cloughessy, who went on to broadcast sports for the ABC Radio Network, and Wayne Larrivee, who has been the play-by-play announcer for no fewer than three NFL teams in the past quarter-century: the Kansas City Chiefs, the Chicago Bears, and the Green Bay Packers, whose games he has broadcast since 1999. A two-time Emmy award winner, Larrivee is also well known for television play-by-play work on college football and basketball games.

The mid-1970s saw a unique undertaking in Iowa broadcasting— the formation of a statewide television network to broadcast University of Iowa basketball games.

Today, it is hard to remember a time when virtually every game of every major college team was not seen somewhere on television. But 25 years ago, a college game broadcast on television was a special occasion.

Prior to the 1978 season, KWWL station manager Bill Bolster had an idea. All the games were already broadcast by radio stations, with announcers the audience had grown to know. What if the games were broadcast on television the same way? Bolster envisioned originating the games and sending them to other stations around the state on a mini-network.

Two home game broadcasts were proposed for the first year, but Iowa athletic director Bump Elliot was afraid that if the games were live on television, attendance would suffer. In order to calm Elliot's fears, in addition to a substantial rights fee, Bolster offered to pay for every empty seat in the Iowa Field House if the first year's broadcasts led to a lack of attendance the next season. Bolster made the promise without checking with station officials first. "I have no idea what financial risk I ran in saying that," he once recalled.

However, attendance did not suffer, Lute Olson's teams continued to play well (including an appearance in the Final Four in 1980), and the broadcasts were a huge success with the television audience. At its peak, ratings showed that Iowa basketball was being watched by two out of every three eastern Iowans.

The Iowa Television Network operated for nearly a decade, and was so popular that rival ad-hoc networks of stations sprang up to carry the games that ITN did not broadcast. By 1980, virtually every Iowa basketball game was on television, long before the establishment of all-sports cable networks.

Not to be outdone by its in-state rival, Iowa State University and its WOI-TV founded the Cyclone Television Network, turning a vision of then-new basketball coach Johnny Orr into reality. Former WOI station manager Bob Helmers was in charge of the network, and remembers that setting up for each broadcast was the most daunting task, since the facilities were all different, and were not as well equipped for television broadcasting as they are today.

Despite that, in the nearly 20 years of the network, the only

Televised Hoopla

University of Iowa basketball had fallen on hard times in the 1970s, when a young coach from California named Lute Olson came to Iowa City and started to turn the fortunes of Hawkeye basketball around.

At the same time, an avid sports fan named Bill Bolster was running KWWL-TV, the NBC affiliate in his hometown of Waterloo. He thought it would be a good idea to give the Hawkeyes more visibility on television.

The result was a groundbreaking marriage that took the popularity of college basketball in Iowa to an all-time high, and smashed television ratings records across the state.

Before the 1978-1979 season, Bolster proposed an experiment— televising three basketball games on an ad-hoc network of stations around the state. If the project was a success, then his network would broadcast all of Iowa's home games the next season. Despite some apprehension by Iowa athletic director Bump Elliott about the telecasts hurting attendance, the deal was made.

Ron Steele of KWWL-TV and Tony Powers of WHO-TV made up the broadcast team for the three experimental games. The next season, the Iowa Television Network carried all of Iowa's home games that were not carried by one of the national networks, with Bob Hogue,

Bob Schultz and Frosty Mitchell on the call.

Bolster recalls that if any seats in the Iowa Fieldhouse were unsold as a result of the games being televised, he agreed to pay the university for the cost of the tickets. "And I paid them $225,000 for the rights for three years for all Iowa home games, but I got a rebate of $75,000 each time they appeared on national television on NBC," Bolster said in a 2002 interview. "At the end of the contract, they owed us money because they had been on NBC so many times that year," however Bolster did not ask the university to pay the difference.

The network was set up with one station in each of Iowa's television markets so that the entire state of Iowa—and fans in six adjoining states—could follow the Hawkeyes from the comfort of their living rooms. As the team's fortunes soared, so did the ratings. At its peak, the Iowa Television Network broadcasts were seen in 80 percent of the Iowa homes watching television when the games were on.

The size of all of Iowa's television markets combined totals approximately the population of St. Louis, Missouri; so to help him determine the appropriate amount to charge advertisers, Bolster contacted friends in St. Louis to see how much they would charge for a program that got a 70 rating and an 80 percent

share in prime time, like the Iowa basketball telecasts did.

"It would have been millions of dollars," he said, "and we were running this literally out of a Winnebago with some tape machines in Waterloo, Iowa."

The popularity of Hawkeye basketball spawned rival networks of stations that sought to carry whatever games Bolster's Iowa Television Network did not hold the rights to carry. Fans would gather in homes, bars, and church halls all over Iowa to watch the Hawks play. Bill Bolster and Lute Olson were even invited to be the "best men" at a wedding at a Storm Lake retirement home; the bride and groom met while watching the basketball games on the television set in the home's lobby.

Four of the five stations on the network were NBC affiliates, and at first, the network was not happy about having some of its popular programming, such as "Hill Street Blues," pre-empted on a regular basis. Bolster got the network to go along by agreeing to heavily promote NBC shows during the ball games, including when the pre-empted shows would be aired. As a result, Iowa outpaced the rest of the country by about 20 percent in the ratings for those shows, thanks to the promotion during the games.

Even presidential candidates who were stumping the state looking

for votes before Iowa's presidential precinct caucuses would arrange to attend University of Iowa basketball games, because they knew they would get free statewide television exposure during the halftime interviews.

Iowa's Final Four appearance in 1980 coincided with the development of all-sports cable television networks, and as game broadcasts became a more specialized field, groups like the Iowa Television Network found it harder to compete for broadcast rights.

Finally, after a nine-year run, the Iowa Television Network signed off; ESPN now holds the rights to most college basketball games in America, including those of the University of Iowa.

Lute Olson moved on to coach at the University of Arizona, where he won a national championship. In 1983, Bolster became the general manager of KSD-TV in St. Louis, and later, WNBC-TV in New York, before becoming the chief executive officer of the international CNBC business news empire.

But the network that Bill Bolster created stands alone as a unique collection of forces that have rightly earned their place in American sports broadcasting history.

"It was huge. It was amazing," he said, nearly 25 years later. "And God, it was fun, to run that out of Waterloo. God, it was fun."

The Iowa Television Network, the first-of-its-kind in the country, broadcast Iowa basketball games from a converted Winnebago operated by Carnaby Square Teleproductions, a division of Black Hawk Broadcasting. William Ronat tests one of the field cameras (above); the network was the brainchild of Bill Bolster, pictured in the Winnebago's control room (right).

time a broadcast ever had to be canceled was when the Cyclones were playing in a holiday tournament in Springfield, Massachusetts. It was discovered a mere two hours before game time that a key part of the satellite truck, which had been parked outside the auditorium to transmit the game broadcast back to Iowa, had been stolen. A replacement could not be obtained in time for that day's broadcast, but a new part was installed in time for a game the next day.

By that time, the station's use of satellite technology was commonplace. Back in 1981, WOI-TV became the first local station in America to originate a live NCAA football game broadcast via satellite, when it transmitted the San Diego State-Iowa State game back to Ames from California. While the Cyclones lost to San Diego State 52-31, it continued WOI-TV's history of being first with new technology. That was a far cry from the 1950s, when WOI sports reporter Dale Williams broadcast games using the latest technology available at the time—a series of microwave relays sending the signal from the game site back to the station.

"Radio, next to family, was the most important thing in their lives."

Billie Oakley, longtime Shenandoah radio homemaker, during a 1992 interview about the early days of radio.

"The Man on the Street" and More

One thing has been true since the beginning of broadcasting—when an announcer appears with a microphone or a camera, a crowd will soon gather. Despite the prevalence of home video recorders, the mystery and magic of broadcasting continues to fascinate people, even in the 21st century.

Early broadcasters took advantage of the public's curiosity by creating programming designed to encourage audience participation. These programs, generally called "man on the street" programs, typically aired during the midday hour and featured an announcer with a live microphone at a public gathering place—a department or discount store, a hotel lobby, or a busy sidewalk. The announcer would encourage those passing by to stop and chat before live microphones, often offering prizes as incentives.

Most analysts credit the invention of such programs, at least in Iowa, to Art Shepard. Shepard began his "man on the street" broadcasts at Ottumwa radio station WIAS in the late 1920s, and is believed to be the second person in America to host such a program on a regular basis. These were the days before live, remote broadcasts could be transmitted easily via telephone lines, so the station strung a microphone cable from the studio, through a window, over the top of the building, and down to the street below in front of the Hotel Ottumwa. The broadcaster could roam from the station as far as a microphone cable would stretch.

During the early broadcasts, Shepard had to carry a large microphone, known as a double-button carbon microphone. In addition to its dinner-plate size, it weighed about four pounds, making it awkward to use during a live broadcast. Shepard lobbied station engineers to secure a more portable microphone. Finally, he was outfitted with a much smaller microphone which could be worn on his lapel, yet still pick up the voices of passersby to whom he was speaking.

On the first day with the new microphone, Shepard was standing as he normally did, on the sidewalk in front of the Hotel Ottumwa. He reached out and grabbed a passerby by the arm and asked, "Hello, sir, where are you going?" The man, who did not see Shepard's new microphone pinned to his coat, promptly answered, "None of your goddamn business!"

It was the first—and last—time Shepard used the smaller microphone.

Shepard moved his "man on the street" program to KWCR in Cedar Rapids when the Cowles brothers, members of the *Des Moines Register & Tribune* family, purchased the station in 1931. The station was later merged into WMT and the show continued, renamed at various times "Question Man" and finally "The Voice of Iowa." Art Shepard's "man on the street" program was the nation's first commercially sponsored program of its kind airing weekdays.

Shepard's show was broadcast in front of The Little Flower Shop in downtown Cedar Rapids, near the F. W. Woolworth store. The Woolworth store manager, Ralph McElroy, struck up a friendship with Shepard. Whenever Shepard could not find a person to question during his program, McElroy would come out and impersonate a passing salesman, or play some other role. Shepard recommended McElroy for a sales position in WMT's Waterloo office, which he took in 1935. That led to McElroy hosting his own "man on the street" program there soon after.

The concept of the noontime interview program was so popular that beginning in late 1935, the station actually aired two versions

KFJB's Bill White interviews a central Iowa resident during the "Man on the Street" program from the S. S. Kresge store in Marshalltown in the 1940s.

of it daily—one with Shepard from Cedar Rapids, and one with McElroy in Waterloo. Others who later became well-known for hosting sidewalk interview programs on WMT included Benne Alter and Dean Landfear.

"Michael" McElroy, as he was known on WMT, was billed by the station as "the most curious man in the world." McElroy prided himself on digging up interesting facts and asking passersby to guess the answers to these "trivia questions." Whether or not the contestant gave the correct answer, a prize was always awarded. For many years, the program's sponsor was Kleen-Maid bread, and program guests always walked away with a miniature loaf of bread. If they had answered McElroy's question correctly, he would proclaim, "Right as Kleen-Maid!" In March of 1940, WMT offered a free loaf of the souvenir bread, as well as 100 questions compiled by "the most curious man in the world," to anyone who sent a request to the station; more than 14,000 loaves were mailed out to McElroy's fans, a record for any WMT promotion to that date.

The business card that McElroy handed out to promote the program, aired daily from in front of the downtown Black's department store in Waterloo, bore his picture and signature, as well as the WMT call letters, and his trademark saying:

Some facts you have to know
To make your daily grind.
But there are facts you want to know
To broaden out your mind.

McElroy compiled a scrapbook, found in his office at the time of his death in 1965, that displays a number of postcards sent by listeners just after his program's 1935 debut. It appears that McElroy sponsored a "funniest postcard of the week" contest to encourage support for his show; one week, a ticket to the Iowa-

Minnesota football game was the prize.

The scrapbook is full of hand-written postcards from all over the state, encouraging WMT to continue the new McElroy program. The cards include comments such as "We like 'the most curious man in the world' fine...More time should be allowed him, however," and "I surely will be very much disappointed if this program is taken off the air as I think it helps us all in brushing up our wits a bit." Some individuals sent letters bearing the signatures of up to 25 people, in mini-petition format. A favorite, from Cedar Falls, reads:

We, the undersigned, wish to show our utmost appreciation
of your program at dinnertime. It helps to digest the food
much more rapidly. After a morning of hard labor, and we
are all poohed out, we feel all refreshed and ready for the
afternoon's job. We hope that you'll continue with this program.

With support like that, the program continued for many years, until WMT closed its Waterloo studios in 1947, and McElroy founded his own Waterloo-based station, KWWL. He continued his daily program on KWWL, renaming it the "Voice of Northeast Iowa," to avoid confusion with WMT's program. McElroy's program aired on radio, and later on both radio and television, until 1959. In fact, the microphone and power outlets are still in place on the front of the old Black's building on Fourth Street in Waterloo.

Iowa's capital city was not without its version of a radio "man on the street" program. KRNT radio (and later, television) aired "What Do You Say?" weekdays at 12:15 for some 20 years, beginning in the 1940s. Each day, a current topic from the news would be chosen, and host Russ Van Dyke would get opinions on the topic from passersby. Over the course of its run, Van Dyke and the staff chose more than 5,000 topics, taking the program from its normal home in downtown Des Moines to the Iowa State Fair

Dean Landfear hosted WMT's "Voice of Iowa" program during the 1950s and 1960s. Landfear is seen here (clockwise, from upper left) interviewing children while large crowds watch (upper left and upper right); sharing a laugh with baseball Hall of Famer and Iowa native Bob Feller; and receiving an honorary title as "Chief Blabbermouth."

and other remote locations. The program focused on local, rather than national, issues, enhancing the station's goal of serving the metropolitan Des Moines area.

The "man on the street" program was not limited to large cities, however, and in fact, was repeated in cities and towns, large and small, across the state.

One of the longest continuously running "man on the street" programs was aired on KFJB in Marshalltown. The program started in the 1930s, and began with live broadcasts from Bliss Anderson's pool hall and soda fountain on Main Street in downtown Marshalltown. The program aired six days a week at noon, except during World War II when the federal government asked radio stations to stop airing such programs for fear that sensitive information might inadvertently be revealed by citizens.

During most of its more than 40-year run, KFJB's "man on the street" show originated from the S. S. Kresge store at the corner of Center and Main streets. While a number of personalities took their turns at the "man on the street" microphone—including originating host Chuck Cook, longtime station manager Bill White, Al Schrock, Jim Hyatt, Marv Baker and others—hosting the show was the primary daily responsibility of sports director Dale Smith for more than 20 years, primarily during the 1950s and 1960s.

One of the program's longtime sponsors was the local Strand Baking Company, which provided KFJB with miniature loaves of Strand's bread to hand out to program participants, similar to the prize handed out by R. J. McElroy during his programs. The souvenir loaves were a great audience attraction—not that one was really needed. The program itself always drew a crowd.

"It started out pretty much as a discussion program with given topics. In later years it developed into sort of a community billboard type of thing," Schrock said. "It was not uncommon to have 8 or 10 or 15 people lined up, literally queued up, taking turns to plug

various events that were coming up, church functions or high school events, things of that nature."

The program was popular not only with listeners at home, but with the live audience, as well. "I do remember we had some regular customers there," Schrock said, "some individuals that we knew by face that were there just to be on the radio. They really delighted in being on the radio, and I presume going home and talking about it to their friends." Seldom was there a lack of persons to talk to on the air; "if the day was rainy, it might be more difficult," he said, but KFJB's "man on the street" host never had to worry about filling the 15 minutes of air time.

As citizens flocked to shopping malls instead of downtown areas, "man on the street" programs slowly died out. KFJB's midday program ended in 1980. But the concept may be making a comeback. In the summer of 2002, as part of a switch to an all news-talk format, KFJB resurrected "man on the street" as a weekly Friday morning feature, at a local coffee shop just a half block from where thousands of early "man on the street" broadcasts were conducted.

Ken Kew of KGLO, who hosted countless live interview programs in downtown Mason City during his long career, enjoyed the duty.

"I was always convinced that you could bring any person in off the street, do a 10-minute interview with them, and it could be interesting because I have never known a person yet who didn't have something interesting that they could talk about," Kew once said.

The concept of "man on the street" programs took on a new form in the 1960s, as telephone call-in shows became popular. While the new format did not have the feel of a live broadcast in front of an audience, it avoided the need for the technical considerations associated with originating broadcasts from outside the studio. In addition, with the advent of television, the public was no longer drawn to a radio personality standing outside with

A rare photo of the first "man on the street" in Iowa, Art Shepard (left), interviewing the manager of the Cedar Rapids F. W. Woolworth store, R. J. McElroy (right), during the WMT "Voice of Iowa" days of the early 1930s. It was not long before Shepard suggested that McElroy go into broadcasting, and soon "Michael" McElroy also had his own "man on the street" show on WMT, based in Waterloo.

Central Iowans weighed in on important issues through Russ Van Dyke's daily midday "What Do You Say?" program. Here, Van Dyke took the show to the Iowa State Fair in the 1950s, where an eager crowd waited to talk to the television audience.

a microphone. Radio was not as "magical" as the new medium of television.

Two of Des Moines' best known broadcast personalities hosted radio talk shows opposite one another in the 1960s. At KRNT radio, Bill Riley hosted an afternoon talk show, "Party Line," that aired from 1:30 until 3:30 weekdays. The program was a challenge for Riley; when the show ended, he had to race to another area of the building to host a television program for children which began at 3:30. "Party Line" aired from 1960 to 1971. Riley told callers that "you can say just about anything you want if you keep it to one minute." He said he never tried to be confrontational, but merely let the callers talk and give their opinions on whatever topic they wished.

The program was canceled in 1971—not because of low ratings, since the program was rated No. 1 in its time slot—but rather because the sales staff thought the program attracted an older audience, which was not as appealing to advertisers.

Across town, sports broadcaster Jim Zabel also hosted a two-hour weekday call-in show, appropriately named "Call Jim Zabel," which aired from 1 until 3 on WHO radio. The program played off of Zabel's gregarious nature, and featured interviews, the trading of recipes, and general conversation. A series of cookbooks was printed, made up of recipes submitted by callers to the show.

WHO featured numerous hosts operating under the "Phone Forum" program title during the 1960s and 1970s. Today, the station produces a weekday call-in program from 9 until 11:30 a.m.

hosted by Jan Mickelson. Since 2001, much of the program has been simulcast on sister station WMT in Cedar Rapids, making the show a true "conversation spot" for people in all 99 Iowa counties.

Many stations serving an area smaller than that served by WHO or WMT still use a daily call-in program as a way for citizens to voice their opinions on local issues of importance to them.

For example, Randy Rasmussen is at the microphone for the 8 a.m. weekday "Open Line" broadcast on KSCJ in Sioux City. KGLO's Tim Renshaw hosts "The Friday Show," a weekly mid-morning talk program in Mason City, while KBUR features "Burlington's Talk Show" weekday afternoons at 1.

For nearly 50 years, Iowa City residents have learned about their community through a daily visit with Dottie Ray. Her program has aired on KXIC radio weekday mornings since 1957 and features live interviews conducted from her home, promoting upcoming civic and community events.

One of the more popular types of audience participation radio programs has been the "buy/sell/trade" shows, where listeners call in and offer various items for sale—in essence, a "garage sale of the air."

The first such show in Iowa is believed to have been started at KFJB in Marshalltown, called "Help Your Neighbor." The program originated in the early 1950s when Al Schrock heard a similar program while on a driving vacation in Wisconsin. He brought the idea back to central Iowa, and it became a fixture on the station for 45 years, ultimately airing each morning at 9:30.

"That was new at the time, involving listeners in the actual on the air dialogue. I thought, 'Boy, that's neat,' and we came back and we tried it," he said. "At first it was more of a tip sharing type of thing; we didn't get into the buy and sell until a little bit later, but it was immensely popular."

The "buy/sell/trade" element was only a part of KFJB's show. Schrock said that for much of the program's run, one day a week was devoted to the exchange of recipes, and another was devoted to open discussion of community issues; he recalls that one topic which dominated the Friday discussions for many weeks was fluoridation of the local water supply.

The station would keep a log of each caller to the show, what the person had offered for sale or trade, and their contact phone number; this was important, because KFJB would typically receive many calls during the rest of the day from listeners who wanted information about something offered for sale on "Help Your Neighbor."

The program aired without the seven-second delay typically used by stations today, allowing them to bleep out objectionable material before it goes over the air. "That's one issue that I've thought about many times. We were taking a terrible chance, I think, in doing it the way we did. But I don't recall once that we had a call that was out of line," Schrock said. "That's amazing."

Today, many radio stations still carry on the tradition of "buy/sell/trade" programs, including KMA's daily "The Elephant Shop" show, the "Wheel and Deal" program on KROS in Clinton, KSCJ's weekend "Swap Shop" program, and KBUR's "Trading Post," which airs on Saturday mornings.

From their earliest days as a curiosity—a way to fill time, promote the station, and give citizens a chance to watch radio in action—to today's chance for listeners to call and offer opinions or ask questions of expert guests, these programs help the station fulfill the congressional mandate of all stations: "to serve the public interest, convenience and necessity." Whether by the old "man on the street" programs, or telephone call-in shows, the unique interaction between broadcasters and their audience remains alive and well, nearly three-quarters of a century after Art Shepard took a microphone to the sidewalks of Ottumwa.

Guests on the "Voice of Iowa" took on all forms. Here "Michael" McElroy talks agriculture with an unidentified cow at the National Dairy Cattle Congress in the pre-World War II era.

Where Stations Get Their Call Letters

Radio and television stations are identified not only by the channel or frequency on which they broadcast, but also by a collection of letters, commonly known as call signs or call letters.

In the earliest days, call letters were in groups of three, and began with either the letter "K" or the letter "W." As more and more stations took to the air, the federal government decided to further regulate the process, and increased the number of letters for each set of call letters to four. In addition, stations that operated east of the Mississippi River would begin with the letter W, while those that operated west of the Mississippi River would begin with the letter K. Stations already in existence at the time of the change were allowed to keep their old call letters, so as not to confuse listeners.

Previously, stations were simply assigned call letters by the Federal Communications Commission. Now, stations have the right to request specific call letters from the FCC, and if they are not currently being used, are commonly assigned. Many times, stations will select a set of call letters to identify their ownership, location, or to serve as the acronym for a phrase.

Some of the more unique combinations include the following:

Newspapers

WMT	Waterloo Morning Tribune
KGLO	Globe-Gazette (Mason City)
KCRG	Cedar Rapids Gazette
KRNT	Register and Tribune (The "R"n"T," Des Moines)
KDTH	Dubuque Telegraph Herald
KSCJ	Sioux City Journal

Owners, Generally

KASI	Ames Stationers, Inc.
KCCI	Cowles Communication, Inc.
KGAN	Guy Gannett Co.

"Iowa"

KIOA	Des Moines
KIOW	Forest City
KIWA	Sheldon
WOI	Ames (Iowa backwards)
KXIA	Marshalltown
KZIA	Cedar Rapids
KIAQ	Fort Dodge
KKIA	Storm Lake
KIAI	Mason City

Seed Companies (All Originally Started by Seed Companies)

KSO	Clarinda—A. A. Berry Seed Co. "Keep Serving Others"
KFNF	Shenandoah—Henry Field Seed & Nursery "Kind Friends Never Fail"
KMA	Shenandoah—Earl May Seed & Nursery "Keep Millions Advised"

Universities/Colleges/Schools

WSUI	(State) University of Iowa
KSUI	(State) University of Iowa
KWAR	Wartburg College
KUNI	University of Northern Iowa
KCUI	Central University of Iowa
KBVU	Buena Vista University
KRUI	University of Iowa ("Kampus" Radio)
KCCK	Kirkwood Community College
KDPS	Des Moines Public Schools
KWDM	West Des Moines Valley HS
KDCR	Dordt College (Dordt College Radio)
KWIT	Western Iowa Tech CC
KIWR	Iowa Western CC (Iowa Western Radio)
KRNL	Cornell College ("Kornell")
KMSC	Morningside College ("Morningside College")
KICB	Iowa Central Community College (Iowa Central Broadcasting)

TV Network Affiliations

KFXA	Cedar Rapids (FOX)
KFXB	Dubuque (FOX)
KPWB	Des Moines (WB)
KPXR	Cedar Rapids (PAX)
KFPX	Des Moines (PAX)

Rare "3" Call Letter Stations (Grandfathered "W" Stations)

WOI	Ames
WOC	Davenport
WHO	Des Moines
WMT	Cedar Rapids

Cities

KGRN	Grinnell
KWLO	Waterloo
WDBQ	Dubuque
KLGA	Algona
KXIC	Iowa City
KDSM	Des Moines
KLBA	Albia
KBUR	Burlington
KCHA	Charles City
KCHE	Cherokee
KCLN	Clinton
KDEC	Decorah
KDSN	Denison
KKDM	Des Moines
KADR	Elkader
KVFD	Fort Dodge
KHBT	Humboldt
KNIA	Knoxville (Knoxville, Iowa)
KOEL	Oelwein
KTVO	Ottumwa (TV for Ottumwa)
KOAK	Red Oak
KSOU	Sioux Center
KQWC	Webster City
KLEM	Le Mars
KMCH	Manchester
KMAQ	Maquoketa
KSUX	Sioux City (airport code is SUX)
KIFG	Iowa Falls

Other

WOC	Wonders of Chiropractic
KHKE	for Herb Hake
KCOB	in the heart of corn country

In the Home and in the Kitchen

In a time before it was customary for Iowa women to work outside the home, they spent many long days working—alone—in rural Iowa farmhouses. Especially in the early days of broadcasting, the opportunities for conversation between farm women were infrequent.

The homemaker programs allowed women on the farm to come together in ways that were not otherwise possible. While the very first programs in the mid-1920s shared recipes, the women hosting them also shared their lives, discussing their husbands, their children, and their various activities. Many broadcast from microphones in their own homes, sitting at their kitchen tables, speaking as if the audience members were there on the farm with them.

"Neighboring is what the homemakers did in the early days of radio," Shenandoah radio homemaker and author Evelyn Birkby once said.

While most stations had a resident "homemaker" on staff, perhaps no one embraced the concept as aggressively as did the two famous stations in Shenandoah.

Henry Field had five sisters, four of whom became actively involved with his KFNF radio station. Jesse Field Shambaugh, the founder of local 4-H clubs and the county superintendent of schools, took to the airwaves to discuss raising children. The youngest sister, Susan Field Conrad, was a potter and on-air promoter of arts and crafts. Helen Field Fisher often discussed flowers during her radio talks, in keeping with the gardening and seed theme of the Field company. In 1926, Leanna Field Driftmier, herself the mother of seven children, took over a program started by Helen called "The Mother's Hour." It later would become the famous

"Kitchen Klatter" program, which became the longest running show in radio history—60 years.

Across town, at KMA radio, Jessie Young became the first full-time homemaker at Earl May's station. She took to the air with her husband Floyd in a music act in 1926, and later that year began the "Stitch and Chat Club" program. Her radio shows spawned a series of popular cookbook pamphlets in the 1930s and 1940s, with collections of recipes for foods ranging from candy to salads to sandwiches.

Another longtime personality was Bernice Currier, who became one of KMA's most beloved homemakers during her career at the station. She first took to the KMA microphone in 1928, and after a stint on radio stations in South Dakota and Texas, returned to the Shenandoah station in 1948 for 15 more years before retiring at the age of 73.

Audiences quickly came to depend on their new radio friends. When an automobile accident in 1930 left "Aunt Leanna" Driftmier seriously injured, her brother Henry Field installed a broadcast line so she could continue talking with the radio audience from her bedside; later, the microphone was moved to her kitchen permanently for the Kitchen Klatter program. By 1932, KMA's top homemaker, Jessie Young, followed the lead and put a microphone in her own kitchen, adding to the authentic, natural feel of the programs.

While Shenandoah was a small town, and competition between the two stations was vigorous, the radio homemakers frequently jumped back and forth between the stations, with the audience gladly moving back and forth, as well. For example, in 1939, when her brother no longer controlled KFNF, "Aunt Leanna"

Shenandoah's "The Farmer's Wife," Florence Falk, doing her daily radio broadcast from the family farmstead in the early 1960s.

KFNF founder Henry Field posing in the 1920s with his five sisters: Helen Field Fisher, Martha Field Eaton, Jesse Field Shambaugh, Leanna Field Driftmier, and Susan Field Conrad.

moved Kitchen Klatter to KMA. At one time, KMA had as many as five homemakers on staff, broadcasting live each day.

Meanwhile, eastern Iowa women were not left out; the familiar voice of Libbie Vaughan greeted them from the earliest days of radio.

Her real name was Faye Vaughan Magee, but she was known to thousands of WMT listeners as Libbie. The program was called "The Magic Kitchen," co-hosted by L. Von Linder, better known on air as "Lindy."

Libbie joined the staff of WMT in Waterloo in 1927 and immediately became identified with the original "Josh Higgins of Finchford" program, created by Joe Dumond. The Magic Kitchen premiered on WMT in 1933, and two years later, also aired on The Iowa Network over sister station KSO in Des Moines. Libbie Vaughn was WMT's first "women's editor," and The Magic Kitchen spawned a monthly newsletter featuring recipes and poems, as well as hand-drawn ads for such program sponsors as Scott Towels and Town Crier flour. The program lasted until 1944;

Libbie Vaughan also broadcast occasionally on KWWL radio after that station went on the air in 1947.

In addition, for 15 years during the 1930s and 1940s, WMT radio presented the "Listen, Ladies" program. For the first eight years, the program was hosted by Wilma "Kay" Adams; Marjorie Norrgard hosted the program later.

All of the women became well-known to their audiences, and were trusted parts of the listeners' days. The natural background noise of typical household sounds from the kitchens added to the comfortable nature of the programs. While many programs were live from kitchens in a town or city, KMA became the first to offer a daily program live from a farm when Florence Falk took over for longtime favorite Adella Shoemaker, who left KMA in September 1952 to host a syndicated program.

For 11 years on KMA, and then for another 12 years on KFNF and KOAK, Falk talked to listeners directly from her rural home. She told of daily life on the farm, including the adventures of

The Role of Women in Broadcasting

Women in broadcasting have often been limited to such stereotypical roles as hosting homemaker programs. The history of Iowa broadcasting, however, is full of examples of women who have played a significant role in station ownership and management.

According to broadcast historians, the first radio station in America to be licensed to a woman was in Vinton, Iowa, in 1922.

Robert (Zim) Zimmerman was a mechanic and electrician in Vinton, and known around town as an avid radio fan. He even had a makeshift car radio in operation in early 1922. Robert and his wife, Marie, a native of Jesup, Iowa, had hoped to start their own station in Vinton, and had saved $150 toward the purchase of transmitting equipment. In an interview with the local newspaper, Zim asked interested radio fans to donate money to help the couple purchase the rest of the necessary equipment; he estimated he needed another hundred dollars.

Apparently, this tactic worked, because soon Marie and Robert were filling out the required paperwork with the Department of Commerce so they could get a broadcast station license.

Using his knowledge as an electrician, Robert built the station, but it was Marie to whom the license was issued, and it was she who became the station manager and chief announcer. Her limited commercial license was issued on July 21,

1922, with the call letters WIAE, and the station went on the air soon after.

A program log printed in Radio Digest magazine in August 1922 indicated that the station usually broadcast for an hour at a time three or four nights a week, plus a Sunday afternoon concert. A local politician, the Republican candidate for county auditor, even made a pitch over the station's airwaves.

Unfortunately for the Zimmermans, WJAM in Cedar Rapids went on the air at the same time. It was bigger and better equipped, and as 1922 went on, the Zimmermans' studio in their house was evidently no match for WJAM. Ultimately, the money ran out, and Marie Zimmerman did not renew the station's license in April 1923 (station licenses were renewed every three months at that time). The department officially deleted the license in late June, less than one year after WIAE went on the air.

By the early 1940s, broadcasting had become more established and more women were making broadcasting their careers.

When Edna Herbst decided to attend college during World War II, she went to the University of Iowa not because it had a strong broadcasting curriculum, but because it had radio station WSUI. She was on the student staff of the university station all four years of college. The war gave many women a chance to appear on the air in new capacities, since the men who had traditionally

filled those roles were in military service. Herbst was one of the first women ever to work in the WSUI news room.

After graduation, she took a job with the Iowa Tallcorn Network in Des Moines, but soon moved to Cedar Rapids, where the Gazette Company was putting two new radio stations on the air in 1947. Herbst spent nearly 40 years at KCRG radio, and later, television, working in public affairs for the stations, engaging in community outreach. During the 1970s and 1980s, she was a key writer and presenter of the station's editorials, and she served as general manager for the stations and was a member of the company's Board of Directors.

Another woman who was asserting herself at the University of Iowa during World War II was Dottie Klein, who would become known to Iowa City radio audiences as Dottie Ray. She was the editor of the *Daily Iowan* newspaper in 1944, and did some broadcasting on WSUI while a student.

In 1957, KXIC owner Gene Claussen asked her to host a daily interview program. Now, 47 years later, she still broadcasts live from her Iowa City home for 15 minutes each weekday. The program broke ground because it did not fit the traditional "women's role" of homemakers programs.

"I wouldn't have dared do that," she said in a 1997 interview. "Everyone knew I was a terrible

cook, and couldn't sew." Instead, the program focused on local events, and ways that listeners could be involved in the Iowa City community.

"I've always loved the show because I like people," Ray said. She has never missed a broadcast; even when she accompanied her husband, the late university dean Robert F. Ray, on a trip to England, Dottie Ray tape-recorded programs from overseas and mailed them back to KXIC to be aired each morning.

Since the program originated from her home, listeners were able to share a bit of the Ray family home life, from children to pets. In fact, the family dog Bozo even received Christmas cards from listeners. "Bozo got more Christmas cards than I did," Ray claimed.

The program has been a familiar part of the Iowa City community for generations, airing just before noon weekdays. Ray said a listener once told her that when her son heard the theme music for Ray's show, he immediately pulled out the peanut butter and bread, knowing it must be time for lunch.

For many years, Ray was also the commentator for live University of Iowa commencement broadcasts on WSUI radio.

As the broadcast industry matured, more women began to take on management roles. Alvina Britz began her broadcasting career in 1947 in Wisconsin, and moved to Ottumwa and radio station KBIZ in

The Role of Women in Broadcasting

1954. Soon after, KBIZ owner James Conroy put KTVO-TV on the air, licensed to Kirksville, Missouri, but operating out of Ottumwa, Iowa. Ultimately, Britz found herself managing the television station. Splitting loyalties between two cities in two different states was not easy, especially when it came to news coverage.

"The problem is not so much doing it, it's how to do it and how to satisfy those people," Britz said in a 1985 interview, "because the Iowans always thought we had too much Missouri news and Missourians, of course, thought we had too much Iowa news." In fact, Britz said that the station's news director actually timed the news coverage to make sure the distribution between the two state audiences was equal.

Britz also played a role in broadcast associations at both the state and national level. She was a national board member of the American Women in Radio and Television, and in 1979, became the first female president of the Iowa Broadcasters Association.

"That was an interesting experience because we have some excellent, great broadcasters in the state of Iowa," she said. "People who are involved and concerned about our industry and concerned about the responsibility that we hold as a licensee to serve the public interest and necessity. They are probably the most outstanding group of broadcasters in any state in the union."

Britz began a long-planned retirement in 1984. But after 30 years at Channel 3, she quickly missed broadcasting and resurfaced as the manager of a Kirksville, Missouri, radio station group after only a month and a half.

"Someone asked if I ever had any goals in life, and I said my goal was to do the job that was asked of me to the best of my ability," she said.

Before long, other women who had worked their way up to broadcast ownership positions, such as Betty Baudler of KASI/KCCQ in Ames and Mary Quass of KHAK-FM in Cedar Rapids, would take their turns as president of the IBA. And since 1991, the organization's executive director has been Sue Toma, the former WMT-TV and WHO-TV personality.

Tippy the dog (there were ultimately five family border collies named "Tippy" during the life of the show) and her husband (usually referred to as "The Farmer"). Often, Falk would speak directly to the audience on personal business, with comments like, "If anybody sees The Farmer in town, would you remind him to bring home a loaf of bread?"

Just as homemaking tips and recipes were handed down from generation to generation, so were the radio homemaker programs. When Leanna Driftmier retired in 1959 after 33 years on the air, her daughters continued the program for another 27 years.

The programs were not limited to commercial stations, however. Even the first educational station on the air in Iowa, WSUI in Iowa City, presented a homemaker program in the 1950s. "The Women's Hour" included recipes, household hints, interviews, and readings from popular books.

As television came to Iowa, so did many homemaker programs. The longest-running and best-known homemaker television program was aired on WMT-TV in Cedar Rapids. Beginning on September 28, 1954, and lasting for nearly 20 years, eastern Iowans settled down after lunch for 30 minutes of "Home Fare." The program was broadcast live each day from a kitchen and living room set at the station's Broadcast Park studios.

The first host was home economist Marguerite Ashlock, who presided over the show for ten years. In 1964, Jackie Grant, Mary Walker and Georgia Frederick began co-hosting the program for the rest of its run.

"It gave me an opportunity to sell my idea of better nutrition, better health through eating food, and better health through preparation of food," Ashlock said in a 1993 interview. "One of the reasons Home Fare lasted so long was that we tried to give them something more than just an ordinary recipe."

But before a recipe could be shared on the air, it had to be tested. Jackie Grant said she would try recipes at home, producing a finished product which she would then bring in to the studio, where she

Jackie Grant hosted WMT-TV's "Home Fare" program for the last half of its 20-year run.

would repeat the procedure step-by-step on the air. "It was fun to teach people how to do it," Grant remembered.

Not all of the audience was made up of women; Grant says mail sent to the program indicated that many men home on their lunch hours stayed until Home Fare was over.

Even though television was gaining in popularity, radio "homemaker" programs were still popular for those who had a domestic tip to share. In 1963, WMT began the "Open Line" program, which aired six mornings a week for 37 years; in the year 2000, the program was reduced to a weekly one-hour offering on Saturdays but has continued the basic recipe-sharing format founded by Jim Loyd more than 40 years ago.

Radio station KDTH in Dubuque featured the morning "Kracker Barrel," hosted for 32 years by Betty Thomas, who succeeded her husband Bill as host of the popular program upon his death in 1966. During her years on the air, Thomas' listeners contributed

thousands of recipes and household hints which were compiled into five books. Her monthly newsletter featuring selected recipes from the show was sent to subscribers in all 50 states.

For many years, KROS in Clinton aired the hour-long "Homespun Lane" program, founded by Margaret Gideonsen. "We did an awful lot of recipes and household hints and how to cure this, that, and the other thing," Gideonsen said. "It was great fun."

Famous guests often stopped by radio and television homemaker programs. "Kukla, Fran and Ollie" star and Iowa native Fran Allison came back to Cedar Rapids for WMT-AM's 45th anniversary in 1967. She offered to make tomato pudding on Home Fare, but did not want to wear her glasses on camera. She could not see well without them, however, and inadvertently turned the skillet on high rather than low. The smoke from the melting butter quickly filled the studio, and the skillet caught on fire—all on live television.

Mary Brubaker was a familiar sight on Des Moines' Channel 8 for many years. At left, she is seen in 1975 with presidential candidate Jimmy Carter; at right, an earlier photo during a cooking segment.

On her morning program on Channel 8 in Des Moines, Mary Brubaker once hosted a former Georgia governor who was running for president. Jimmy Carter even rolled up his sleeves and assisted in the making of a meatloaf prior to his breakthrough in the 1976 Iowa caucuses.

Local celebrities often got into the act, as well. Jackie Grant recalls doing a knitting segment, with the camera focusing only on her hands. She would do a stitch, then undo it and repeat the move slowly so that viewers could follow along. WMT meteorologist Conrad Johnson boasted that he learned how to knit with an old shoestring instead of yarn by watching Grant demonstrate the technique on the program.

Homemaker programs always generated a great deal of mail from the audience. Soon, stations determined that the best way to quickly respond to frequently asked questions was through regular newsletters. At one point, the *Kitchen Klatter* magazine claimed 100,000 persons on its monthly mailing list. WMT radio's Open Line program led to the creation of many supporting

enterprises, including a monthly bulletin which reached a circulation of more than 9,000 in the early 1970s, as well as multiple cookbooks. WMT-TV's Home Fare program also generated a popular monthly newsletter. The homemaker newsletters were filled with references to sponsors, without whom the programs would not exist.

Product endorsements were a significant part of the early homemaker programs. Recipes were not made simply with flour, but with Town Crier flour; spills were cleaned up not with paper towels, but with Scott Towels. In fact, the Kitchen Klatter program was so successful, it even spawned its own line of "Kitchen Klatter-brand" products, including laundry detergent, bleach, household flavorings, cookbooks, and party books.

Listeners took seriously every word the radio homemaker said. They were the example many listeners followed as a confidence builder; if the radio homemaker could do it, so could the woman listening at home. On one occasion, the Earl May company purchased a train carload of prunes at a discount. The task of

The daily "women's" program on Des Moines' Channel 8 was hosted for many years by Mary Jane Chinn Odell, who left Iowa for a career in Chicago broadcasting, only to return and become Iowa's Secretary of State during the 1980s. Notables who visited her program over the years included (clockwise, from upper left) Art Linkletter, Eleanor Roosevelt, Garry Moore and Durwood Kirby, and "Miss America" host Bert Parks.

Bernice Currier

Evelyn Birkby

Billie Oakley

generating a market for these less-than-desirable products fell to Bernice Currier. She was so successful in devising recipes using prunes, and convincing the audience to try the recipes, that the original carload was sold out and May had to order even more prunes to meet the demand.

That loyalty led to a strong following beyond the walls of the studio. The homemakers were also an important part of many community events, including demonstrations at countless county fairs. KMA in Shenandoah continued the station tradition with large, live-audience demonstrations in the Mayfair Auditorium. The annual "KMA Christmas Cookie Teas" originated in 1954. By 1958, two separate programs were needed in order to accommodate

all who wanted to attend; more than 35,000 cookies and recipes were shared that year. In the mid-1960s, the "KMA Meat-A-Rama" meat cutting and cooking demonstration "proved to be one of the most interesting demonstrations for many years," according to the monthly "KMA Guide" for September 1965.

The skill of the Shenandoah radio homemakers became well-known beyond their local area, as sponsors often syndicated their programs to other stations around the country. Edith Hansen's KMA program was syndicated at one time to more than 90 stations.

"It was something that was unique and I have a feeling that the intensity of that, and the way in which it expanded into the lives of so many people in such an important way, was unique

Libbie Vaughn

the first Marconi award, presented in 1989 by the National Association of Broadcasters, for excellence in radio. "It's A Woman's World" first aired in 1949, and signed off for the last time in 1987 as "The Billie Oakley Show."

In later years, the daytime television programs originally designed for women expanded beyond recipes and broadened their scope to include discussion of current topics of interest. "Modern Woman" was a 30-minute program on WMT-TV during the 1960s and 1970s. The program was renamed "Weekday Live" in the 1970s, and was hosted by Sue Toma.

KRNT-TV (later KCCI-TV) in Des Moines also featured a daily interview program, first hosted by Mary Jane Chinn (later known as Mary Jane Odell) and then by Mary Brubaker. "The TV-9 Morning Show" aired on KCRG in Cedar Rapids for many years, first hosted by George Patrick and later Denny Frary.

to this area, these two radio stations and the people who were here," said Evelyn Birkby, whose quarter-century on the air as a Shenandoah radio homemaker began at KMA in 1950 with the "Down A Country Lane" program. In 1991, Birkby collected her memories of the era—as well as favorite recipes—in a book called *Neighboring on the Air: Cooking with the KMA Radio Homemakers.*

By the early 1990s, though, only Billie McNeilly Oakley remained on the air in Shenandoah as a true radio homemaker. Her first radio experience was at age 15, when she won Henry Field's 1931 KFNF amateur singing contest. Decades later, she could lay claim to a syndicated radio program that aired at one time on as many as 40 stations, and to being the recipient of

WHO-TV in Des Moines featured host Pat Valentine in a variety of formats; KWWL-TV in Waterloo included a "women's segment" that followed the midday news and was called "Today with Joan" (later "Today with Beth," as the program hosts changed).

The migration of those interview and cooking shows to the early morning and midday local news programs reflected the changing role of women in society and the changing needs of the audience.

But there are still ample opportunities for listeners to call their favorite local radio station to ask for the pumpkin bar recipe they heard on the air last week, continuing a broadcasting tradition that now dates back nine decades.

> "This was a time, of course, when people didn't have as much money to go out and do other kinds of things, and so radio provided very cheap entertainment, stimulation, education, and news for families. Otherwise, many would not have had it, and so it was a terribly important medium that way."

University of Iowa Communication Studies Professor Samuel L. Becker in a 1994 interview for WSUI radio's 75th anniversary.

8 Entertainers on Stage

One of the earliest challenges faced by broadcasters was filling all the air time available to them. In the days before tape recordings and network broadcasts, all the programming was live. Local amateur entertainers were often used to fill the many hours of the broadcast schedule, performing live music on the air.

The story of Dorothy Ehr Chamberlain of Jesup was not uncommon. As an 18-year-old, she and her friend Florence Brown auditioned to appear on WMT in Waterloo. A station official heard the duo sing a few songs, and gave them the standard "don't call us, we'll call you" response. The teenagers were happy just to have auditioned.

The surprise came when they were called back to sing the following Saturday night. The audience response was favorable, so they were invited back every Saturday night for the next year as part of a one-hour program that included Joe Dumond playing the accordion. The girls performed as the "Air Harmony Twins," a name given them by Dumond.

They were even invited to take their act to Chicago and appear on WGN, but the girls' parents thought they were too young and would not let them go. Their performing careers ended not long afterward. The girls were never paid for their radio singing, but they were given tickets to the top caliber theater shows playing in the Waterloo area, and were asked to sing at functions in their hometown.

Many times, the musical performances were associated with commercial products. Brothers Vern and Wilbur Schield of Waverly appeared on WMT as "The Limestone Boys," a singing partnership that promoted the quarry where the boys worked, without violating the rules then in existence for direct radio advertising.

"We couldn't advertise, otherwise we would have had to pay. We didn't have any money to pay for anything, but they called us 'The Limestone Boys' and we got a little advertising," Wilbur Schield remembered. The Limestone Boys appeared on WMT for about two years in the 1930s.

At Iowa City's WSUI radio, most of the musical entertainment was live, but when there were no live performers available, station manager Carl Menzer would use his own windup phonograph for musical assistance, despite the fact that during much of the 1920s, the station's music library consisted of only seven records. By necessity, those same seven records were played frequently. The repetition bothered one listener, who sent Menzer ten of his own records to help supplement the station's supply.

Rules in effect at the time required stations to make it clear when the music the audience was hearing was not live, or later, that programs were pre-recorded. Today, the situation is completely reversed—programs featuring live entertainment are so rare that stations heavily promote the "live" element.

It certainly helped to know what the audience wanted. In the mid-1920s, KFJB in Marshalltown aired three hours of live music by various "Bohemian bands" on Sunday afternoons. Three staffers were kept busy handling requests by telephone, with calls often coming in at the rate of one per minute.

From one end of the state to the other, listeners were treated to local favorites during radio's first quarter century. Sioux Citians enjoyed the music and antics of the "Timberoojans" on KSCJ radio in the 1940s. Mason City radio station KGLO featured the "Kornbelt Kernals," who would perform six mornings a week at 6:15. KGLO also attracted talent from its surrounding area, including

The venerable Shrine Auditorium in Des Moines, later known as the KRNT Radio Theater, was home to many live radio broadcasts, including the adventures of the citizens of Sunset Corners each week on WHO's Iowa Barn Dance Frolic.

The Air Harmony Twins: Dorothy Ehr and Florence Brown

company secretary to sing along, and the head of the farm seed department to serve as announcer for the program.

Field's station aired a two-hour "barn dance" Mondays through Saturdays, consisting of mostly amateur fiddlers and musicians. Later, the program would be held in the station auditorium, and admission was always free.

The concept of the "barn dance" sprang up at a number of spots around the country, notably at WLS radio in Chicago in the mid-1920s. But it didn't take long for Iowa to have a famous "barn dance" of its own.

Beginning in 1931, a half-hour program originated on WOC radio in Davenport that would become one of the best-known live entertainment programs in Iowa radio history. A year later, the "Iowa Barn Dance Frolic" moved to Des Moines along with the rest of the WOC staff, and found a new home on Palmer-owned WHO radio, where it would become an institution for nearly 30 years.

The program was expanded to three hours each Saturday night, presented before a live audience at the President Theater. In 1935, the program moved to the Shrine Auditorium in Des Moines, where the Iowa Barn Dance Frolic aired for most of its run—two hours each week beginning at 8 o'clock. (Later, when the auditorium was sold to WHO's broadcasting rival and became known as the KRNT Theater, the barn dance identified its home simply as the "Radio Theater.")

A 1936 Barn Dance Frolic "souvenir program" identifies the cast of the show, including Peter MacArthur, who was termed the "director in chief" of the broadcast. The versatile MacArthur had spent 20 years on the musical comedy stage before beginning his radio career in 1921, and followed the Barn Dance Frolic from WOC to WHO.

By 1938, after only a few years on the air, the show was synonymous with WHO. A station promotional booklet, the "WHO

"Merle and the Rhythm Boys" from Grafton, and "Happy Jack and His Group" from Rudd. Decades earlier, Henry Field had the "Cornfield Canaries" and "Seedhouse Girls" singing on KFNF.

During KMA's first official week of programming in September 1925, no fewer than 175 performers took to the Shenandoah station's microphones. Across town, at KFNF, employees of Henry Field's seed company regularly entertained on the air. It was not uncommon for the building custodian to be the fiddler, the

"Howdy" Roberts and Fran Allison perform before an audience at the National Dairy Cattle Congress in Waterloo in the 1930s.

Picture Book," refers to the show as the "Sunset Corners Frolic" after the fictional town around which the program was loosely based; the "barn dance" name was too well established, however, and the apparent attempt to change the focus of the show to something less rural was quickly abandoned.

By the late 1940s, WHO estimated that a half-million people had traveled to Des Moines to witness the live broadcasts of the Iowa Barn Dance Frolic. The program often went on the road, too, broadcasting from a number of communities in conjunction with special occasions. The attraction between the performers from the fictional town of "Sunset Corners" and their audience was significant.

"When they listened to a radio station, they listened to a person whom they liked, and they decided this was part of their family. It was incredible," barn dance announcer Jack Kerrigan recalled. People would come from all over Iowa to fill the 4,500-seat auditorium each week, with some attending performances two or three times each month. Yet they never appeared to tire of the Barn Dance Frolic.

"They would hear Lem Turner tell the same jokes week after week, and they'd still laugh uproariously," Kerrigan said.

The number of letters and postcards the show and its performers received was astounding. In 1935, nearly 300,000 pieces of mail were received from listeners in the state of Iowa alone; in fact, in that year, mail was received from each of the then-48 United States, plus 13 countries. A number of such well-known performers as Louisiana Blue, Yodeling Cowboy Jerry Smith, Mountain Pete and His Mountaineers, and Lem and Martha were regular favorites.

Kerrigan remembers the four Williams Brothers from Wall Lake performing on the barn dance. Kerrigan was the announcer for that segment of the program. "I used to lift Andy up on a box so he could be tall enough to sing over the microphone," Kerrigan said. Andy Williams went on to a successful recording and television

career, and still performs today, a long way from the Barn Dance Frolic days when he joined brothers Ben, Don, and Dick on the Shrine Auditorium stage.

A 1952 WHO program schedule shows that Barn Dance performers were frequently heard during the rest of the week, as well. Lem Turner, whose real name was Tom Lewis, had a one-hour program beginning at 4 a.m. six days a week; "Lem Turner's Coffee Shop" was followed by a half-hour program featuring the "Crack-O-Dawners." Later in the morning, "The Buckaroos" made two separate appearances, and a male quartet known as "The Songfellows" followed Jack Shelley's 12:30 newscast three days a week. When television came to Des Moines in 1954, the barn dance was broadcast on both WHO radio and television from Channel 13's new studios.

The "barn dance" concept quickly caught on in a variety of formats around the state. When TV came to Mason City in the 1950s, KGLO produced the John Deere Barn Dance every Monday night. Farm director Al Heinz was the one-hour program's master of ceremonies. The popular program had two squares of dancers going concurrently; dancers were booked a year in advance to appear.

The KFJB County Marshals were a favorite of that station's weekly barn dance programs, which were held at the Coliseum in downtown Marshalltown for three years just after World War II. The County Marshals band was made up primarily of radio station staffers, who often had their own musical shows on KFJB during the week. In addition to performing at the weekly barn dance, the KFJB County Marshals were in demand around the listening area, playing at dances and other events.

The adults who paid 50 cents each for a ticket found themselves treated to a full evening of entertainment. In addition to the one hour live broadcast, which featured an amateur contest, the County Marshals would provide another two hours of music off the air for dancing. But there was a catch—those in the audience had to help clear the chairs from the main floor after the broadcast before the dance would start. "This was standard procedure. Everyone pitched in," Schrock said. "The sooner they cleared the floor, the sooner the dance started."

The weekly KFJB barn dances typically drew as many as 2,000 people to downtown Marshalltown on Saturday nights. "I would say that of all the promotions the station has ever carried, it was the most dramatic and the most effective," Schrock said. "This was an event that helped promote the radio station, it helped us mature and I think was largely instrumental in positioning the radio station in the community."

As the WHO Iowa Barn Dance Frolic was in its heyday, across the state another well-known station was providing its audience with a great deal of live music, as well.

A square dance caller and star of the original WLS Barn Dance in Chicago, Tom Owens moved to Cedar Rapids in 1937 and brought his band, "Tom Owens' Cowboys," to WMT radio. They were a fixture on the station for decades, even after the death of Tom Owens in 1956.

For parts of four decades, the Cowboys used WMT as their home base, traveling to perform in a five-state area. Nationally known for their recordings on the Mercury label, the band performed on the air for a quarter century, with more than 6,000 live shows on WMT radio and television. After Owens' death, longtime band member Johnny Ketelsen took over, later fronting his own popular band.

In December 1945, Owens needed an accordion player, and a young man named Leo Greco signed on. A few years later, Greco left to start his own band, "Leo Greco and his Pioneers." By the early 1950s, WMT radio had three well-known bands frequenting the airwaves: Owens', Greco's, and a band founded by morning announcer Ralph "Howdy" Roberts.

Those Who Started in Iowa

Iowa has proved to be a successful training ground for a number of persons who became known nationally for their work, both in broadcasting and entertainment. Among those who passed through Iowa on their way to national prominence include:

Richard Threlkeld

Broadcast Journalists

Harry Reasoner
Humboldt native
(later, CBS and ABC)

Tom Brokaw
KTIV-TV and WSUI
(later, NBC)

Tom Pettit
KCRG-TV
(later, NBC)

Richard Threlkeld
WMT Radio/TV
(later, CBS and ABC)

Jack Cafferty
WHO-TV (later WNBC and CNN)

Steve Bell
WOI-TV (later, ABC)

Brian Ross
KWWL-TV
(later, NBC and ABC)

Jerry Bowen
ISU (later, CBS)

Carole Simpson
WSUI (later, NBC and ABC)

Peter Hackes
WSUI (later, NBC
and then an actor)

John Cochran
WSUI (later, NBC and ABC)

Joseph Benti
WSUI (later, CBS)

Don Kladstrup
WSUI (later, CBS)

Performers

Fran Allison
WMT Radio
(later, "Kukla, Fran and Ollie")

Everly Brothers
KMA/KFNF
(later, recording artists)

Andy Williams
WHO Barn Dance
(later, TV and recording artist)

Ronald Reagan
WOC/WHO radio sports
(later, actor and politician)

Simon Estes
KRNT radio, "Talent Sprouts"
(later, world-renowned opera)

Steve Allen
Drake University (later, first "Tonight Show" host)

Cloris Leachman
KRNT radio, reading comics
(later, actress)

Roger Williams
WHO radio
(later, recording artist)

Managers

Dennis Swanson
WMT-TV (later, ABC Sports, WNBC, founded "Oprah")

Bill Bolster
KWWL (later, WNBC, CNBC)

Live music was a staple of early radio and television. The KFJB County Marshals played for appreciative audiences in central Iowa in the 1950s (upper left) while audiences filled auditoriums in Des Moines for WHO's Iowa Barn Dance Frolic for nearly 30 years (upper right). Tom Owens' Cowboys were well-known for appearances on WMT radio and later television (lower right). And even though it was radio, some acts found it helpful to dress the part, right down to the cornstalks in the studio (lower left).

The life of a band leader was difficult. The Greco band would appear on WMT radio in the early morning (originally at 5:45, and later at 6:30) three days a week, yet would perform live shows six to seven nights a week at ballrooms in eastern Iowa—and in later years, in 10 states around Iowa. "Howdy Roberts and the WMT Rangers" toured for 21 years, performing three to four nights a week. "Any place that had asked us, we were there," Roberts once said.

The tradition continued in the television age. In fact, the first original entertainment on Channel 2 in September 1953 was a presentation by Tom Owens' Cowboys and Leo Greco and his Pioneers.

In the pre-television days, the "WMT Family Party" was broadcast before a live audience on Saturdays at noon for many years. Like WHO's barn dance, it was set in a fictional small town, the home of "Neighbor Bob," played by well-known WMT personality Bob Leefers. Crowds of up to 2,000 came weekly to the Paramount Theatre in Cedar Rapids for the Family Party broadcasts, which ran on WMT radio for nearly 20 years.

Another popular program, "Quaker Party Time," featured the largest cast of any regularly scheduled program in WMT radio history. That program originated from Quaker Oats' Stuart Hall before an audience of employees.

The last of WMT's big live broadcasts was "Noontime RFD," heard daily from Studio E at Broadcast Park. The program often featured all three bands—those led by Greco, Owens, and Roberts—in a single show.

Live music from hotel ballrooms and dance halls around the state was common on Iowa's radio stations in the 1930s and 1940s. Sometimes the programming needed to start at a certain time, causing problems for those who were operating stations.

On one occasion, WHO board operator Ronald Reagan told news director H. R. Gross that his newscast had to end by a certain time so the scheduled dance band music could begin. Gross ignored Reagan's signals, and kept reading news. When Gross ended one story and took a breath, Reagan cut him off and went live to the hotel for the scheduled musical program.

Unfortunately, Reagan had forgotten to turn off Gross' microphone, and Gross' expletives could be heard in the background behind the music. The Des Moines police department called the station, threatening to shut down the dance band performance because "you've got some drunk in there" at the hotel—not knowing that it was really an angry news director back at the station with a live microphone.

The original musical entertainment on radio was provided by amateurs, but as noted, that soon gave way to professional musicians on the staff of each station. During the 1940s, KMA had

Leo Greco

Bill Riley interviews a Talent Search contestant at the Iowa State Fair

KMA Country School No. 9, circa late 1940s. Standing left to right: Jerry Fronek, Zeke Williams, Ike Everly, Marge Parker, Bob Stotts (behind black-board), Joan Williams, Elmer Axelbender, and Merl Douglas. Seated, left to right: Steve Wooden, Eddie Comer (with glasses), Mack Sanders, Glenn Harris (teacher), Jeanie Sanders, Harpo Richardson and Wayne Van Horn.

as many as 50 musicians on staff; KFNF had 20 more on the payroll. At one time, WHO had 75 persons on their talent staff, who were paid per program; this allowed them to work at other jobs, as well. Entertainers would play on many shows in a single day, using different instruments and different names to make the audience believe the staff was larger than it really was.

During the 1950s, however, many of the live music, comedy, and drama shows left the air as television became popular. Soon, "live radio"—as it had been known for parts of four decades—was merely a memory. But many performers had used Iowa radio as a stepping stone to greater fame. In addition to those already mentioned, two well-known acts can credit their beginnings to radio in Shenandoah.

The Blackwood Brothers gospel group made KMA radio their home starting in 1940, and moved to Nashville and great fame ten years later. The group did not receive any pay while working at KMA, but earned a great deal of income from selling songbooks on the air and promoting upcoming concerts.

Ike and Margaret Everly moved to Shenandoah from Muhlenberg County, Kentucky. Ike became a studio musician at KMA, while Margaret learned to sing and play to supplement the family's income. When their two sons, Donald and Philip, were old enough, they also learned to play and sing. Ultimately, the family moved to KFNF from KMA, where the one-hour "Everly Family Program" aired at 6 a.m. six days a week. Starting in radio when they were just 10 and 12, respectively, Don and Phil Everly later went on to great success as popular music recording artists in the 1950s and 1960s.

Although the trend was toward professional radio entertainers, amateurs still had a role to play in entertaining audiences—and some of the amateur talent was quite young. One of the all-time favorites was the "Rath's Kiddies Review" amateur show on WMT radio, hosted for more than a decade by Howdy Roberts on

Shenandoah radio entertainers the Everly Family—father Ike flanked by sons Donald (left) and Philip (right), with mother Margaret (seated). Don and Phil Everly went on to fame as 1950s-era rock and roll stars.

Saturday mornings from Waterloo's Paramount Theater. When the station closed its Waterloo studios after World War II, the program was moved to the WMT Radio Theater at the YMCA in Cedar Rapids. Its name was changed to "Hiltbrunner's Talent Time" to reflect the music store that became the program sponsor.

"They would come from miles around to be on this thing," Roberts said. "The kids would line up for two blocks square to get in."

But without question, the most lasting legacy of the "talent show" era was that left by the State Fair Talent Search radio and television programs founded by KRNT's Bill Riley.

In the mid-1940s, Riley began hosting the "Rath Talent Review" amateur hour on the Des Moines station. The program was so popular that a spin-off called "Teen Time" was started on Sunday afternoons. The program was designed for 13- to 21-year-olds to demonstrate their talent.

Soon, yet another program was developed for even younger performers, who were called the "Talent Sprouts." It was there that a 12-year-old Centerville boy sang the song "Little Jesus Boy," gaining his first real exposure as performer. He went on to become a world-renowned opera singer—and Simon Estes never forgot the man who gave him his start, returning to Iowa in 1993 to sing at the State Fair in honor of Riley's retirement.

The talent program gained statewide attention when Riley convinced organizers to make the competition part of the Iowa State Fair. Since 1959, the State Fair Talent Search has been a popular annual feature of the fair, and the main performance stage at the fairgrounds has been known as the "Bill Riley Stage" since 1993.

When KRNT-TV went on the air in 1955, the program moved to television, airing weekly for 20 years. Riley toured the state, hosting tryouts in towns and cities across Iowa. The more talented performers would be brought to Des Moines to appear on the broadcasts. With the exposure on television and the performances at the state fair, the show's popularity spread quickly.

More than 100,000 Iowa children have appeared in the talent search shows around the state over the years. Nearly 100 shows are still held annually in towns large and small, with the winners coming to the state fair for the final competition. The State Fair Talent Search finals are still broadcast live from the fair each year on Iowa Public Television, with hosts Bill Riley, Jr. and Terry Rich now presiding over the competition. Bill Riley, Sr., who started the talent search as a radio show nearly 60 years ago, still attends the fair—in fact, he has attended every single day of every Iowa State Fair since 1946.

Early radio entertainment also branched into sketch comedy programs. "Punkin Valley," one of the first ongoing series on radio anywhere, aired on KFNF in Shenandoah from 8 to 8:15 each night for many years, telling of a local fictional family and their trials and tribulations.

Not to be outdone, the "KMA Country School District No. 9" program aired nightly for 18 years beginning in 1924. The vaudeville program was mostly ad-libbed, often with Earl May himself as the schoolteacher. The program was curtailed during the gas rationing of World War II after more than 4,000 performances, but was revived for another run in the late 1940s.

Perhaps the best-known comedic performers on WMT were "Toby and Susie," in real life Neal and Caroline Schaffner. They were veterans of programs such as NBC's National Barn Dance, and their

Fran Allison as "Aunt Fanny"

first sponsored daily program originated from WMT.

It was a 15-minute program that aired on a number of stations for four years in the late 1930s and early 1940s. The Schaffners were experienced performers on the traveling tent show circuit, and like many entertainers, found the stability of radio a refreshing break from the grind of traveling. "Toby and Susie" began their career in the tent show business in 1922, and were still touring into the 1960s.

Other longtime WMT personalities, such as Benne Alter and Douglas Grant, participated in the daily programs. Toby Tolliver and Susie Sharp's "Corntussle News," a publication of humorous stories and anecdotes, was mailed to an eager audience on a regular basis, similar to the newsletters produced by radio homemakers of the time.

Thousands of people started their day listening to WMT radio for The Singing Cowboy. Noontime programming included "The Iowa Cornhuskers Show," featuring the Les Hartman German Band and Joe Doakes (real name Lyle Harvey) and his accordion. Fran Allison, who grew up in LaPorte City, developed a popular character called "Aunt Fanny," a country girl who looked at the world in an amusing, common-sense way. Her sponsor was the Galloway Company manure spreader, and her promotional line—reportedly originally ad-libbed by Allison—was, "We stand behind our product!"

Howdy Roberts remembers that a man associated with Chicago radio heard Fran Allison as "Aunt Fanny" while traveling through the area, and suggested that WBBM audition Allison. From there, it was on to the ABC radio network and years of performing the Aunt Fanny character on "Don McNeal's Breakfast Club." She later teamed up with Burr Tillstrom to create "Kukla, Fran and Ollie," which became an early hit on the NBC television network.

Despite her fame, Allison never forgot her Iowa roots. "She was one you don't find too often," Roberts said, noting that Allison would always come back to WMT for anniversary events, long

Lyle Harvey as "Joe Doakes"

after her national television popularity soared.

Jack Kerrigan, who later was program director for WHO radio and television, sang, announced and wrote 1,300 episodes of a 1940s comedy program called "Melody Madhouse." The program, which aired six days a week at 7:45 a.m., took a great deal of time and effort, but as Kerrigan recalls, "That's the most fun I ever had in my life, writing that comedy show." The program was even brought back in 1950 for a short time as a half-hour weekly program.

Benne Alter

A popular feature of the "Musical Clock" program, which Howdy Roberts hosted on WMT radio for 31 years, was a skit in which Roberts and an engineer created "interviews" with stars, using quotes from network shows interspersed with unrelated questions from Roberts. The wisdom of "Uncle Zeb" and reminders for listeners to renew their driver's licenses were also staples of the program. At the time of the first radio ratings in the early 1940s, data showed that 90 percent of all radios turned on at the time were tuned to WMT's "Musical Clock" program. (The "Musical Clock" program originated with Benne Alter on the Cedar Rapids station; after Roberts retired, Jerry Carr hosted the program as part of his morning show for a number of years.)

At times, however, the entertainment on early radio stations was rather sophisticated. "KSO Poets," a book published in 1935, was a collection of poems which had been broadcast over the station.

The book's introduction says that "KSO, the *Register & Tribune* station, Des Moines, was the first broadcasting system in the country to set aside definite time for the regular broadcasting of poets native to any particular state." The program started in 1933, and titles of poems in the book ranged from farm themes ("Ode to Iowa Corn," "Lure of Corn," "A Load of Hay") to more general titles ("Madonna of the Knitting Needles," "The Little White Church On the Hill," "Fireside Song of an Old Hunter," and "Concerning a Percheron Stallion").

In the preface to the book, Isabel M. Hoffman, chairman of fine arts for the Iowa Federation of Women's Clubs, wrote, "The spirit of man finds release through various media. To those who find that escape through the writing and reading of verse, the Iowa Poets' Corner of KSO has been a window which has opened each week to singing souls and sent their songs through the ether to responsive hearts. The creative instinct is a shy, elusive thing and

Joe Dumond created a character called "Josh Higgins of Finchford" while he was a staffer at WMT in Waterloo in the late 1920s and early 1930s. He parlayed the character, who was based on Dumond's experiences growing up in rural Iowa, into prominence on the NBC radio network. In the late 1930s, he returned to Iowa, purchasing a controlling interest in radio station KBUR in Burlington, and later founding KXEL in Waterloo in 1942.

the encouragement given it through this means has resulted in a definite contribution to Iowa's literary output."

Beginning in the 1930s, a fixture on WOI radio was "The Book Club," where works of literature great and small would be brought to life. Doug Brown was the host of the Book Club for nearly 40 years, starting in the early 1960s. He did the voices of all the characters, from old women to young boys; some have written that it seemed like there were 30 people in the studio instead of just one. It might take weeks to get through a single book, but loyal audiences were there to hear the half-hour installments each weekday.

Brown's talents were many and varied. For many years, he also hosted the classical music show "The Music Shop" on WOI (another long-running program, founded by Andy Woolfries in 1925), and was the play-by-play voice of college wrestling for Iowa Public Television for 27 years.

In addition to the comedy programs produced by many local stations, radio dramas were also written and performed. At the University of Iowa, radio station WSUI was the site of a number of original productions of student-written works, including a play written by a young Tennessee Williams, who was a student at the Iowa Writer's Workshop at the time. Over a period of two decades, speech and communication professor H. Clay Harshbarger supervised the groups of students who created the productions. In the 1930s, the professor and his students annually produced live radio dramas from the WSUI studios for national audiences on the NBC radio network.

Renowned communication studies professor Samuel Becker recalled the programs with fondness for WSUI's 75th anniversary in 1994, and noted that they were not easy to produce.

"This was a fine art—the creation of sounds that would help people create all of the scenery, all of the background, and all of

Doug Brown

the action in their minds," Becker said. On one occasion, student Herb Kanzell wrote a western. "Clay Harshbarger made the mistake of also casting Herb, and so he was in the studio when we were doing the show. We had a blank pistol that was supposed to go off at some point but it failed, it didn't go off. There was this deadly pause, and Herb ran to the microphone and said, 'Bang!' We all fell on the floor. It was just wonderful."

A wide variety of musical tastes was also served by radio stations. Douglas Grant's varied career in radio began at WIAS in Ottumwa in the late 1920s. He moved to the Cowles-owned Cedar Rapids station KWCR in 1931, and stayed on staff when the station was merged with WMT. His daily program of sacred music, proclaiming him the "Gospel Baritone," was a popular feature on WMT in the 1930s. Along with accompanist Eleanor Gough, Grant made regular Sunday evening appearances at churches throughout Iowa. He later would be a news anchor and program director for the WMT stations.

During the less "politically correct" era of the 1930s, bands such as the "Bohemian Orchestra" and the "German Band" were favorites on WMT. Other variety programs included bands named for their sponsors.

For more than 45 years, when eastern Iowans—and listeners around the Midwest, for that matter—heard the song "Stardust" on the air at noon, it meant one thing to them: WSUI's "Rhythm Rambles" program. It became the station's oldest and best known program, playing the most popular music of the day.

That alone made it unique. In an era before radio disc jockeys became popular, when virtually all music on the air was performed live, Rhythm Rambles played the same records found in music stores, which was uncommon for radio at the time. Station founder Carl Menzer, in a 1979 interview, recalled one of the more surprising bits of praise for the show:

"There were grade and elementary schools all over the country where the kids were pretty well confined during the morning and afternoon, and during the noon period they had an hour off. They would eat their lunch in a hurry and form clubs to listen to Rhythm Rambles. And all the superintendents of schools wrote to us and told us what a good service we were doing because we kept the kids off the streets and out of mischief," Menzer said.

The producer and host of Rhythm Rambles during its final 15 years on the air was Jim Dougherty, who has played jazz and big band records on the Iowa City station for more than 30 years and hosts the nightly "Jazz and Jim" program. As a boy growing up in Muscatine, he was a fan of Rhythm Rambles and dreamed of one day becoming its host; he wound up hosting the program for longer than anyone else in the program's nearly half century.

The show had great appeal for young and old alike. Dougherty recalls as a boy waiting for his older siblings to come home for lunch and wanting to engage in conversation with them; however, they would tell him to be quiet so they could hear the music. After the show was over, he would again try to start a family conversation, only to be told by his parents to be quiet so they could listen to the news that followed Rhythm Rambles each day. "So I always identified the noon hour as the time when I had to shut up and eat," Dougherty said.

For many years in the 1940s and 1950s, the station also featured an afternoon program called "Tea Time," as well as a live piano/vocal program called "Musical Moods—Songs In The Modern Manner," produced in the station's "Studio A" in the old Engineering Building across from the Pentacrest on the Iowa City campus.

Rhythm Rambles was actually a program ahead of its time, as all radio stations would soon conform to the practice of playing various forms of popular music as a way to draw audiences away from television.

WSUI often produced live radio programs in the 1940s in this studio, located in the lower level of the University of Iowa Engineering Building.

"Thank you for turning me on."

The trademark words used by KIOA disc jockey Dic Youngs in ending his Des Moines radio programs for the past 40 years.

9 Spinning the Discs

As television grew in popularity during the 1950s, programs and features popular on radio migrated to the new, visual medium. Traditional radio entertainment fell out of favor; after all, why would anyone listen to a show on the radio when they could see the same show on television? Many predicted radio would simply cease to exist.

To prevent that, radio had to reinvent itself. At the same time, a new form of music called "rock and roll" was catching on, and the marriage between the two was beneficial for both. Soon many radio stations became "jukeboxes of the airwaves."

As part of a 40-year career in broadcasting, Frosty Mitchell began as a disc jockey in 1955, just out of Drake University. He began working for KWWL radio and television in Waterloo, earning $100 a week. The radio programs were broadcast from the mezzanine level of the Russell Lamson Hotel in downtown Waterloo, in full public view. Mitchell would do his afternoon radio program and then travel four miles to the television studio to do the sports report on Channel 7.

After two years, Mitchell left KWWL to do freelance work in the Chicago market, but soon decided to return to Iowa and start a family. He was on his way to a job at KOIL radio in Omaha, and stopped on the way to visit his parents in Des Moines. There he learned that KIOA, where he had worked during college while it was a "farm and home" station, was switching to the new "top 50" popular music format, and he went to work there instead.

The change in KIOA's format "just took Des Moines by storm," Mitchell said, with features such as the "nifty top 50" songs, five minutes of news "alive at 55" minutes past each hour, the "big five" disc jockeys of Des Moines, hosting teen hops at the Val Air

Ballroom, and more.

The station's slogans quoted the relevant Hooper audience ratings, billing it as "The Frosty Mitchell Show, with more audience than all other Des Moines radio stations combined" during the time period. Mitchell was so popular during the late 1950s that for a time he was on the KIOA airwaves during both the morning and afternoon drive times—from 6 to 9 in the morning and 4 to 6 in the afternoon—and his contract included a lifetime non-compete clause, forbidding him from ever working for another radio station within 50 miles of Des Moines.

Mitchell left KIOA in 1960 and bought KGRN radio in Grinnell, just as the rock and roll rivalry in Des Moines radio began to heat up. In the 1960s, KIOA-AM 940 and KSO-AM 1460 each positioned itself as a rock and roll station and pulled out all the stops in trying to be No. 1, leading to an at times bitter rivalry in the pursuit of listeners.

As a teenager growing up in the late 1950s in Des Moines, Dic Youngs was well aware of the rivalry—in fact, he became a key player in the success of each station.

From the time he was a small boy, Youngs knew he wanted to be a broadcaster. He would recreate ball games by talking into a tin can from the privacy of his bedroom. He dreamed of being a sports play-by-play announcer, and gave up offers to play college sports to pursue his goal of being a broadcaster.

His break came in 1957, when at age 16 he won a DJ contest held at the Val Air Ballroom in Des Moines, beating out future Des Moines radio personalities such as Steve Gibbons and Phil Thomas. KIOA's Mitchell invited Youngs to be on his afternoon radio show the next day, and "Youngsie" has been on the

"Frosty" Mitchell as a Des Moines high school student, running the control board at what was then KWDM radio in 1954.

Des Moines airwaves virtually ever since.

He started as a part-time announcer at KSO, and by age 19, was the station's full-time music director. During KSO's glory days as a rock and roll station, Dick Vance was the program director and took the rivalry with KIOA very seriously.

Youngs recalls that Vance once told him, "If I catch you with any one of those guys (from KIOA), you're fired. I don't want you talking to them…if you get a chance, I want you to beat the hell out of them."

"It was bad," Youngs said. "It was a war, man."

The two stations had "storefront" studios on prominent downtown Des Moines streets, which allowed those traveling by car to see the disc jockeys at work as they drove by, adding to the "star status" many personalities of the time enjoyed.

Peter McLane made his way to Des Moines from KWMT in Fort Dodge, which had a powerful daytime signal and was a popular "top 40" station in the late 1950s and early 1960s. When management began to change the format from rock and roll in 1963, McLane decided to try his hand in Des Moines. He interviewed with Vance for a spot at KSO but was turned down; he landed a job at KIOA that proved to be a pivotal step in that station soon becoming the dominant music station in Des Moines.

By the fall of 1963, McLane was KIOA's afternoon drive personality and program director. The station was promoting a "top fifty" music format, which McLane changed to a "Top 9 Plus 40" playlist to capitalize on the station's "AM 940" frequency, and emphasizing airplay of the top nine songs of the week. That move, coupled with a host of KSO personalities moving to KIOA, led to the "good guys" taking the number one spot in the ratings.

One of those who moved from KSO to KIOA was Dic Youngs, who McLane hired away from Dick Vance in 1966. Youngs says it took Vance years to get over it, but that they are close friends today. "I didn't care what shift I worked," Youngs remembers. "I

Peter McLane

wanted to be a KIOA good guy."

After leaving the airwaves in the 1970s to pursue a career in radio sales, Youngs returned with "the original Saturday night oldies show," which quickly became a huge success—so much so that when the station needed a new morning show host, management looked no further than Youngs. He held down KIOA's morning drive spot into the early 1990s when he moved to a longer air shift during afternoon drive time. Now in his 38th consecutive year at the station, he still hosts the important afternoon show, as well as the Saturday night program.

For many listeners—and sometimes, station managers—a radio station's sudden switch to a rock and roll format came without notice.

In Waterloo, after his television station took to the air, R. J. McElroy paid less attention to his AM radio station. At the time, KWWL-AM was playing "middle-of-the-road" music with disc jockeys who for the most part were simply waiting for their chance to be on TV.

To revitalize KWWL-AM in the late 1950s, McElroy brought in Bill Baldwin, who had previous radio experience in Milwaukee. McElroy hired Baldwin to be the radio station's program director, and then left for a vacation in Florida. As McElroy told the story years later, "When I left, we were playing Frank Sinatra. When I came back, the first thing I heard was Witch Doctor!" He called Baldwin immediately and reportedly said, "What in the hell have you done to my radio station?" Baldwin replied that he was trying to make it into a successful radio station and that if McElroy didn't like it, he knew what he could do. McElroy agreed to give Baldwin a chance, and within a few months the station was playing rock music with disc jockeys who did not care about getting on television—and attracting a greater share of the northeast Iowa listening audience.

"Bill had a feel for modern radio," Warren Mead wrote in his history of the Black Hawk Broadcasting Company. "He did it easily and effectively."

Baldwin left KWWL briefly to manage KIOA, but then returned and was with the station at the time of his sudden death in 1970. KWWL-AM would be a popular rock station in northeast Iowa throughout the 1970s.

In that decade, however, a revolution in FM radio started to take place. For years, FM stations had been neglected, serving as nothing but a source for "beautiful music" or merely repeating the signal of a co-owned AM station. But as the greater sound quality of FM came to be appreciated, FM began to develop its own identity.

The situation was right for a "new voice" in eastern Iowa radio, and a group of University of Iowa students thought they were the ones to launch that voice.

Eliot Keller had toyed with the idea of starting a radio station in Iowa City while a college junior, but he lacked the financial resources. The next year, a group of seniors at the university started discussing the idea more seriously. After graduating from Iowa, Keller went to San Diego State University for graduate studies; one of the courses he took there was on broadcast management, and one of the assignments was to write a proposal to put a radio station on the air. Keller made it a practical assignment by sketching out a plan for an FM station in Iowa City, lining up investors, and forming the first corporation for the station they had planned.

On May 13, 1971, Communicators Inc. of Iowa was founded; it later would become KRNA Inc., and is now known as KZIA Inc. Keller moved back to his family home in Moline that summer, and in November, he rented an office on the sixth floor of the Iowa State Bank Building in Iowa City, which would be the station's headquarters for nearly three years. KRNA Inc. went through a long series of legal and financial struggles during that period. Approval for a station was eventually granted by the FCC in July of 1974, and in less than three months, the group had ordered equipment, built a transmitter site, and remodeled studio space in an office building on the south end of Iowa City. Radio station KRNA went on the air at 93.5 FM on Friday, October 4, 1974.

"The goal had been to put together a radio station with a major market sound in what was basically a small-to-medium market. The goal evolved to going on the air 24 hours a day, seven days a week, to do things that were primarily music-driven that would appeal to the young adult and adult market in the Iowa City area," Keller said.

The station began testing its signal a few days before the official sign-on, and started getting requests from eager listeners in the area.

Public Broadcasting In Iowa

While the great majority of broadcasting stations in America are designed to make a profit and serve a mass audience, space has traditionally been reserved on the spectrum for stations that are designed to provide programming for those segments of the audience not being served by commercial broadcasting. Originally known as "educational" stations, these stations now are better known as "non-commercial" or "public" stations.

Much of the experimentation in the early days of radio came from professors and students at Iowa's colleges and universities. The oldest licensed experimental stations in the state are still on the air, known today as WSUI-AM at the University of Iowa in Iowa City, and WOI-AM at Iowa State University in Ames.

Today, they are the only independently programmed AM public radio stations in Iowa—all the others are on the FM band, since Congress mandated that stations operating between 88.1 and 91.9 on the FM band be reserved for non-commercial broadcasting. Even the smallest Iowa colleges and universities provide broadcast services.

Many of the stations serve a small area; the stations are typically operated by college students as a learning tool. The oldest Iowa non-commercial FM station continuously operated by students is Wartburg College's KWAR-FM, which was officially licensed by the FCC at 89.1 FM on October 8, 1951. Others

evolved over time. The University of Iowa's student-run station was formerly a "carrier current" AM station, meaning that the signal could only be heard in dormitories and the immediate campus area; in 1984, however, the station was granted a low-power license at 89.7 FM, where it is known today as KRUI-FM.

The stations known as "public radio" stations are professionally operated, typically housed at colleges and universities. Some community colleges have strong stations that are affiliates of Public Radio International or National Public Radio, such as KCCK-FM at Kirkwood Community College in Cedar Rapids, and KWIT-FM at Western Iowa Tech Community College in Sioux City.

The public radio station at the University of Northern Iowa is unique. KUNI-FM serves a large portion of Iowa from a Cedar Falls-based signal; however, the signal can be heard throughout most of the eastern half of Iowa through a network of stations in cities such as Davenport, Des Moines, and Mason City that repeat KUNI's Cedar Falls signal. A total of six separately licensed stations carry the KUNI signal, including an AM station in Mason City that can be heard well into southern Minnesota.

The non-commercial, or public, stations typically program material not generally heard on commercial stations. Specialized forms of music such as classical, jazz, folk and

blues are often heard on these stations, as well as documentaries and longer-form news stories. While the audience for each of these types of programming may not be large enough to maintain a profitable commercial radio operation, they are a loyal audience that is being served through these specialized stations.

Perhaps the most unique public broadcasting operation is that of the Iowa Public Television network, IPTV. In virtually every other state, a number of separate public television stations operate independently from one another; while they may share certain programs, they are separate and distinct operations. In Iowa, however, all of the public television stations carry the same programming at the same time, creating a true unified network for all Iowans.

The idea of a statewide, educational network first surfaced in the early days of television. In December 1952, Iowa Governor William S. Beardsley told a national governors' conference on educational television of his plans for a 12-station educational network for Iowa, using WOI-TV as the first link. The total cost for the network was estimated to be more than $5 million. Beardsley's plans apparently went nowhere.

The State of Iowa finally got into public television when, in 1969, it purchased the station operated by the Des Moines Public Schools, KDPS-TV 11, for just over a half-million dollars.

Rechristened KDIN-TV, the station would become the first in what was originally known as the Iowa Educational Broadcasting Network (IEBN). Next came an eastern Iowa station, KIIN-TV 12 in Iowa City, in 1970. By the middle of the decade, four more stations were added, extending the network's reach from one end of the state to the other. In areas where there was no room for more full-power TV stations, IPTV utilized translator stations—smaller transmitters that could repeat the original signal on another channel at lower power.

By the spring of 2004, Iowa Public Television network programming was seen on eight licensed stations and an additional eight translator stations, with a coverage map that reached all of Iowa's 99 counties, as well as parts of six adjoining states. Their facilities in Johnston, north of Des Moines, are state-of-the-art and enable Iowa Public Television to produce a variety of programs, from the nationally syndicated "Market to Market" agricultural program, to programs of more local interest, such as "Iowa Press" and "Living in Iowa."

Although Iowa Public Television and the radio stations operated by the public universities receive some state funding, an increasingly larger part of their operating budgets is derived from contributions from members of the audience, giving Iowans a true voice in the success and programming of the stations.

"We felt we would have a huge impact when we started this, but we didn't really know how much impact we would have. We wanted to be financially successful, obviously," Keller said. "It was groundbreaking, and perhaps in some ways we didn't even realize how groundbreaking we were."

In the middle 1970s, many radio stations signed off for a few hours during an overnight time for equipment maintenance; KRNA did not need to sign off because the equipment was new enough to withstand the punishment of 24-hour-a-day broadcasting.

FM had made breakthroughs in major markets in the late 1960s and early 1970s, but not in Iowa. In fact, when KRNA went on the air, many young people had to buy FM radios; they had not needed them before because there was nothing they were interested in listening to on FM.

To hear rock music, consumers had tuned in Iowa AM stations such as KIOA in Des Moines or KWWL in Waterloo, or at night, out-of-state powerhouses such as WLS in Chicago and KAAY in Little Rock. "We came in and just had a tremendous impact," Keller said. By January 1975, after being on the air less than four months, Arbitron telephone surveys indicated KRNA was listened to by nearly half of those who were listening to the radio. "They had never seen those types of numbers in this type of survey," he said.

For the most part, eastern Iowa radio stations at the time rarely used any recorded advertisements; they simply had the announcer read the ad copy. To give the station a "major market sound," Keller and his associates made sure that KRNA pre-recorded all commercial advertisements to enhance the message for advertisers and to deliver a more effective message. It would become a model for others to follow.

"We wanted to do a good job, we wanted to do a professional job, we wanted to have a big impact," Keller said. "We had no idea how big an impact we would have on radio for years in the state of Iowa."

This is not to say, however, that the station was a financial success from the start. In order to generate enough money to put the station on the air, Keller and his partners went into the community to raise investment capital, accepting investments of $1,000 and greater. But the station was grossly undercapitalized, and after four months, the accountant said the corporation was bankrupt. "We told them as long as there was sound coming from that radio, we were in business," Keller said.

In 1996, KRNA Inc. bought rival station KQCR-FM in Cedar Rapids, creating the first duopoly in the Cedar Rapids/Iowa City market. The station's music format was changed from top 40 to country, and it became known on-air as MAX 102.9. Then in 1998, after a 24-year run, Keller and his partners sold KRNA to what is now known as Cumulus Media, and retained ownership of the station at 102.9 FM, changing its call letters to KZIA-FM and creating Z-102.9, playing contemporary hit music. KZIA is now the only locally owned commercial FM radio station in the Iowa City/Cedar Rapids area.

At the same time KRNA began to breathe life into eastern Iowa FM radio, another FM station in Des Moines began to challenge KIOA-AM's dominance of the rock and roll market—and it came from someone who knew KIOA very well.

Peter McLane left KIOA in 1977 after a decade and a half at the station. He worked for a time in major markets, including Dallas and Minneapolis, but returned to Des Moines in the early 1980s as a vice president for Stoner Broadcasting, which at the time owned KSO-AM and KGGO-FM. By this time, KSO had switched

KIOA was a powerhouse rock station in the 1970s.

Radio stations maintained full libraries of vinyl records before today's age of compact discs and digitized music on computer. Pauline Van Pelt Smith is seen in the late 1950s in the KFJB record library.

to a country music format, with solid ratings.

The itch to program and manage a local station struck again, and McLane took over KSO-AM and KGGO-FM when Bill Wells left to manage Stoner properties in Louisville. KGGO used a tried and true formula—a consistent air staff, personalities who got involved in the community, and a great deal of fun—and helped build KGGO into the top-rated station in Des Moines by the 1990s. Capitalizing on its studio location in the small town of Berwick, the station parlayed such fictional entities as the "University of Berwick" into promotional campaigns and merchandise sales for charity, along the way building great listener loyalty.

"I'm very lucky that the people of Iowa rewarded me with three number one radio stations," McLane said—KWMT in the 1960s, KIOA in the 1970s, and KGGO in the 1990s.

While music is predominantly a radio-only phenomenon, the early days of television in Iowa saw several television programs aimed at the new teenage rock and roll audience, long before the age of MTV and music videos.

On Saturday nights in the 1950s, WOI-TV presented a 90-minute teen dance program called "Seventeen," which featured four hosts and dozens of central Iowa teenagers dancing to popular music, similar to the network's daily "American Bandstand." Surveys showed that "Seventeen" was Iowa's most popular teenage dance show, and as was the case with its national counterpart, viewers would tune in to watch their favorite couples dance on the show each week. Among the regular hosts was a young Betty Lou McVay, who became better known for her more than 40 years hosting the "Magic Window" children's program.

Not to be outdone, WHO-TV aired the "Harris Hop" program on Saturday afternoons. And in eastern Iowa, while he was at KWWL, Frosty Mitchell also hosted a television disc jockey show for high school students on Saturday afternoons —"Frosty's Swing Club."

The changing technology of the 21st century means many stations now use computers to run the entire on-air operation. Instead of disc jockeys playing records on a turntable, they simply program a computer that has the music preloaded on it. This allows the station to run without benefit of a board operator on duty. Many stations operate with voices that sound live, but have been pre-recorded into the computer (known in the industry as "voice tracking"). Some stations use pre-recorded voices all the time, while others use them only during overnight and weekend hours.

As with all new technology, glitches sometimes occur. Many stations operating in an automated mode find strange sounds coming over the radio, thanks to a computer server used by several stations in the same building sending the wrong type of music (such as a hard rock song airing on an easy listening station), or no sounds at all, thanks to a hard drive crashing at an inopportune time.

One station bucking this trend is KFMW-FM in Waterloo, known as "Rock 108." All of its programming is live from its downtown studio—every song is played from a CD, every disc jockey speaks live into a microphone, 24 hours a day, 365 days a year.

Listeners may be able to tell the difference—it may be only a coincidence, but the Arbitron ratings for the spring of 2002 showed KFMW with the highest ratings of any station in the Waterloo/Cedar Falls market.

The personal connection listeners have with radio personalities takes on a variety of forms. Dic Youngs once tried to make a phone call when the operator interrupted him, asking if he was

KRNA was a major force during the 1980s, when FM radio come to prominence.

"The Old
Youngster"—
KIOA's Dic
Youngs

Dic Youngs. A somewhat startled Youngs told her he was, and asked how she knew; she quickly told him that she recognized his voice from the radio.

Not all of the contacts with listeners are happy ones. Longtime Des Moines personality Steve Gibbons, who started at KSO and has been the morning personality at KRNT for more than a quarter century, remembers one incident as the saddest thing that has ever happened to him.

A young woman came to the KSO "fishbowl" studio on Ingersoll Avenue in Des Moines late one evening and asked Gibbons to play a song for her husband, who had recently been killed in the Vietnam War. Gibbons said he played the song with "the reverence I could give to something that I didn't really know a lot about," and did not think much more about it.

He learned the next morning from Des Moines police that the woman drove to a gravel road outside of town and waited for the song she dedicated to come on the radio. She wrote a note, including thanks to Gibbons for playing her song request—and in her grief over her husband's death, committed suicide. Nearly four decades later, he still calls it the lowest moment in his career.

Those who came of age during the rock and roll era can now often hear the music they grew up with on the same stations they listened to as young people; the formats of the stations have evolved, whether it's KGGO playing what is now termed classic rock, to KIOA playing the music of its heyday and calling itself "Oldies 93.3." Disc jockeys who in some cases weren't even born when the songs were released are now the on air hosts, and most understand the responsibility that carries with it.

"The fact that we're still playing a lot of the music that baby boomers really loved back then, it's just really fun to be a part of that," said Maxwell Schaeffer, co-host of KIOA's "Maxwell and Polly" morning show. It may be the 21st century, "but we still can relive some of those great days of radio which is rare now, and KIOA still has that feeling." It's not just the music—KIOA still has a "reverb" echo on its microphones, to further relive the older days.

Schaeffer credits Dic Youngs and other KIOA alums for telling stories of the "good guy" era and instilling in him and other younger personalities the importance that KIOA—and other "heritage" radio stations like it—has had in the lives of hundreds of thousands of Iowans. The huge success of the "Rock and Roll Reunion" concerts at the Iowa State Fair is evidence of that. Youngs has hosted the concerts since their beginning, and has only missed one of the 24 years they have been held to sold out audiences at the State Fairgrounds in Des Moines.

Whether broadcasting from a Rambler station wagon suspended above the street for 14 days, as Youngs once did, or from storefront studios, those who were there at the time recognize what a special time the "rock and roll" era of radio was, for both them and their audience.

"I love it. I still love it," Youngs said. "I love the prestige it gives you, and the notoriety it gives you. I'd be a fool to say I didn't, because I would be lying."

"I'd like to be remembered for playing the right music, always running ethical, honest charts at the station, entertaining people and kind of being a fabric of their lives and making the station part of what we were and what we are," Peter McLane said.

"It's been a good life. Knock on wood, I hope I don't die soon, but if I did, I could say I had a hell of a life. Not a lot of guys got to meet to the people I got to meet, do the thing you wanted to do in life the most, and get paid for it," Youngs said.

"There are probably some people who went into their basements in 1962 and are still there because they didn't hear Conrad Johnson say it was safe to come back upstairs."

Former WMT-TV and KWWL-TV news executive Grant Price, on the trust audiences placed in the forecasts of KVTV-TV and WMT-TV meteorologist Conrad Johnson.

10 Watching the Skies

There is an old adage that says if you don't like the weather in Iowa, just wait—it'll change. Those changes are very important in a state like Iowa that sees weather extremes, from blizzards to tornadoes, as part of the normal course of events. The weather is vital for farmers growing crops, those planning leisure activities, and in times of severe weather, for the safety of entire communities.

The founder of television weathercasting as we know it today got into his work as a direct order from his commanding officer in the Navy.

Sioux City television station KVTV was about to go on the air in 1953. Conrad Johnson was in the U.S. Navy, stationed in Sioux City. One day, his commanding officer heard that the new television station was looking for someone to deliver weather information on evening newscasts. He suggested Johnson apply, since he had had meteorological training as part of his work as a Navy pilot—and since it might be a good recruiting tool for young people to see Johnson, in full uniform, on television each night.

Johnson went to the new television station and drew a map on the chalkboard the station provided for the audition, talking for two or three minutes about the current weather. As Johnson later recalled, the director in charge of the auditions did not sound encouraging.

"He said, 'We got a couple three other applicants and we'll get back to you,' and I thought, 'Boy, I got rid of that in a hurry,' because I didn't think I did any good at all," Johnson said. "At four o'clock that afternoon, he called up. The commanding officer came down to where I was sitting. He said, 'You're on, they go on the air next Wednesday. It's Friday, so you've got to get ready.' That's where I got started."

In those early days in Sioux City, Johnson was a part-time television employee. He would finish his duties for the Navy at 4 p.m. each day, drive to the Sioux City airport to review the weather data on their maps, make some notes, and then go to the television station where he would deliver 10 minutes of weather information at the beginning of the 6 p.m. and 10 p.m. Channel 9 news. He would draw a national map on the chalkboard and talk about it for a few minutes, and during the commercial break, erase the national map and create a regional map, all from memory based on the notes he took at the airport a few hours earlier.

Learning the Navy was transferring Johnson to Cedar Rapids in 1957, KVTV management called WMT officials Bill Dutcher and Doug Grant and suggested that they consider hiring Johnson to deliver the weather on Channel 2.

Unbeknownst to Johnson, the two WMT officials came to Sioux City one day and watched his telecasts from a hotel room. The next day, they called and hired him to be the meteorologist for the WMT radio and television stations.

At that time, most weather on television was limited to announcers reading material gathered from wire services; in fact, to that point, Channel 2 relied on the Shell Weather Tower to provide information to the audience.

The "Weather Tower" was a set located in the television studio made to look like a forest ranger's tower, high in the sky; in reality, it was only a few feet off the ground. WMT radio announcers would take turns climbing the "tower" and providing weather information during the news. They were dressed like Shell service

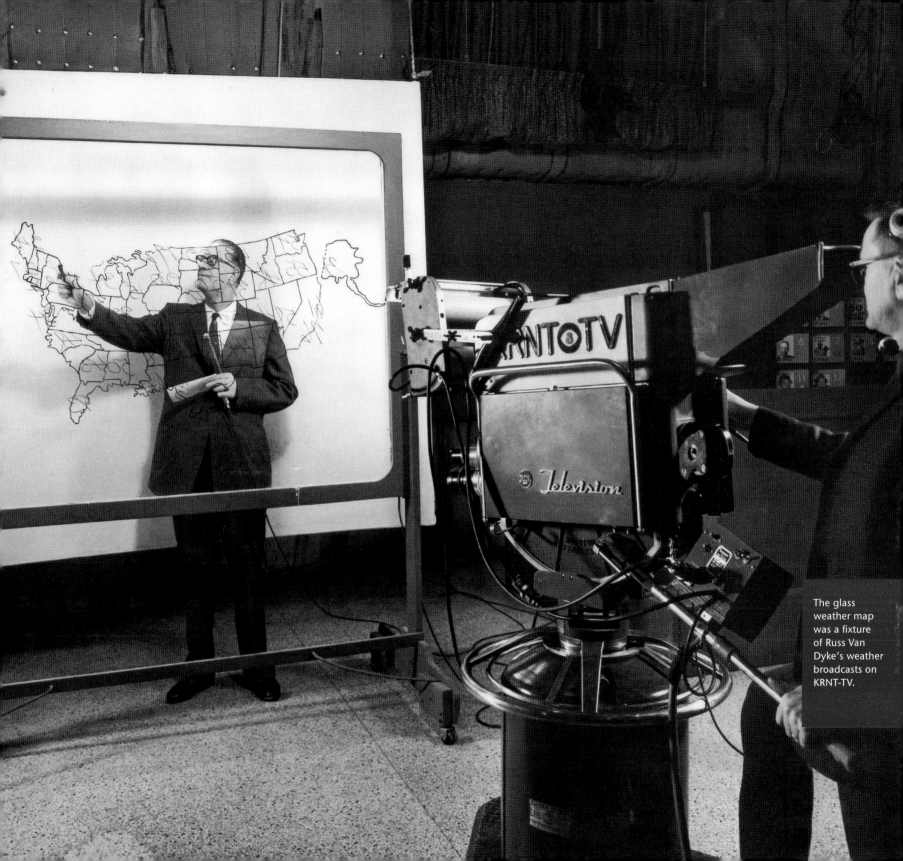

The glass weather map was a fixture of Russ Van Dyke's weather broadcasts on KRNT-TV.

station attendants, in deference to the commercial sponsor of the segment.

Johnson's approach to weather was different. He was one of the first broadcasters in the country to do his own independent forecasting, rather than relying on projections from the National Weather Service. His approach was to deliver a forecast everyone could understand.

"Instead of a scientist talking to a scientist, I wanted to talk to the layman," he said.

At first, Channel 2's weather consisted of Johnson sitting on a stool in front of a drafting table, with a camera looking over his shoulder on the maps he would draw. As technology improved, a wall-sized plastic map was installed, with Johnson using shoe polish to show fronts, temperatures, and data; through experimentation, they learned that white shoe polish usually dripped, but the black would not run. It was all made possible because of WMT's investment in the tools needed for someone of Johnson's skills to do his own forecasting.

"We thought we were on the cutting edge. We were always leading," Johnson said. "Everybody else was trying to follow us, and that's what we wanted to have."

The station soon had a dedicated teletype wire to receive information from the weather bureau and the Federal Aviation Administration, facsimile machines to receive maps to use on air, and in 1959, the first television radar west of Chicago.

"You had more confidence in the forecast if you had access to the basic data," Johnson said.

Someone once said that when Conrad Johnson forecast rain, people all across eastern Iowa shut their windows. He was on Channel 2 for 23 years until his retirement in 1980.

"They still say that we had the best weather system of anybody in the Midwest, and they really appreciated that because they could depend on the forecast being accurate enough that they could make plans based on it, and that to me was the biggest accomplishment that we had," Johnson said. "We tried to tailor our broadcasts and our newscasts to where you would be doing the most good for the most people, where they could understand and relate it to their own operation to the point where they maintained a lot of reliability on our forecast. I think that's the biggest legacy that we had."

Surveys showed that during severe weather in the 1960s, as many as 94 percent of the television sets in eastern Iowa were tuned to Johnson and WMT-TV, which for many years was the only station to have an in-studio radar to track the path of storms.

Before the Conrad Johnson era began in eastern Iowa, other stations in the market tried different approaches to weathercasting.

The first weatherman at KWWL-TV in Waterloo was Duane Hunting, who was at the station for nearly two years. The only maps Hunting had to use were from noon that day, anywhere from 6 to 10 hours old by the time the evening news aired. In the mid-1950s, there was no National Weather Service office in Waterloo, so what little information he was able to get came from the teletype. Despite that, he had five minutes in which to deliver the weather each night. So Hunting spent much time demonstrating weather phenomena; for example, how a hailstone was created.

Hunting completed some meteorology training in college, and worked at the Waterloo airport for Braniff Airways. KWWL station manager Warren Mead contacted the airport manager to see if anyone there knew enough about the weather to talk about it on the television news. Hunting says he was the only one working for any airline at the time to have had that kind of training, so he got the job. "It was a barrel of fun, I must say. I totally enjoyed it," he said.

During his television career, Hunting still worked for Braniff, opening their local office at 5 a.m. and working until early afternoon

The first weather forecasts on WMT were delivered from the Shell Weather Tower.

Jym Ganahl began doing the weather on KWWL while still a 17-year-old high school student.

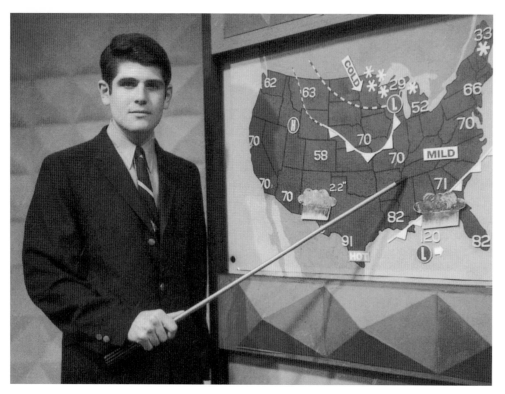

was in northwest Iowa to visit his parents, Hunting would watch Johnson on KVTV-TV 9 in Sioux City and modeled his own Waterloo weathercasts after those of Johnson.

In the late 1960s, a Waterloo teenager who was a regular viewer of Conrad Johnson on Channel 2 decided to try his television forecasting skills. At 17, Jym Ganahl approached KWWL station management and boldly suggested he could do a better job of delivering the weather than their current weathercaster. The station agreed, and he joined the Channel 7 news department.

"Why'd I get into weather? Because of Conrad Johnson," Ganahl said. As a 12-year-old, Ganahl said he "loved watching Conrad on television." Despite not having any experience in public speaking, Ganahl was doing the television weather each

before going to the television station for the 6 p.m. and 10 p.m. newscasts. KWWL owner R. J. McElroy paid Hunting $3.50 per show.

After nearly two years, Hunting thought he deserved a small raise, and tried for two weeks to get an appointment with McElroy. When he finally did get to see the owner, McElroy suggested that for the amount of money they were paying Hunting ($35 per week), "We could have one of our own people do it." Hunting's broadcasting career came to an abrupt end.

The legendary Conrad Johnson had an impact on Duane Hunting before Johnson even came to eastern Iowa. When he

night on Channel 7 while only age 17, one of the youngest television weathercasters in America.

For more than a decade, an increasing number of viewers watched the KWWL news and Ganahl's forecasts until in 1974, the station had the market's top-rated late newscast. Ganahl left KWWL in 1979 for the much larger Columbus, Ohio market, where he still forecasts the weather today for WCMH-TV, the CBS affiliate.

Ganahl's replacement at Channel 7 was another young meteor-ologist whose work was greatly influenced by Conrad Johnson.

WMT's Conrad Johnson set the mold for television weathercasting in America.

Craig Johnson grew up in Fort Dodge, and was able to work with Conrad Johnson for two and one-half years at WMT.

"What Conrad said was law to many people," Craig Johnson said. The two Johnsons are not related, but that didn't stop the Channel 2 promotions department from planting the seed in viewers' minds, with an extensive "Johnson & Johnson" promotional campaign.

Craig Johnson says he knew he wanted to be a meteorologist, but never intended to be on television. After graduating from the University of Utah, he found that the National Weather Service was not hiring, so he took a job in television. He thought it would be a temporary measure; however, he was a regular fixture on eastern Iowa television for more than a quarter-century.

Craig Johnson worked at WMT radio and television from 1977 to 1979 before moving to KWWL and establishing his own reputation for serious, accurate weather forecasting. He left KWWL in 2003 after 24 years to start his own forecasting company and write about meteorology and photography.

"I knew the minute I saw him and the first week he worked for me, that he had what it took," Conrad Johnson said. Grant Price, who worked with both men, calls Craig Johnson the "best television meteorologist who has ever practiced, I say without hesitation."

An Industry With Impact

Today, it is hard to imagine a time before broadcasting, when the only news came from newspapers and entertainment came from live shows or was homemade. The changes in our lives thanks to electronic media have been widespread, and for those who remember when it first came into their lives, the changes have special meaning.

A group of senior citizens gathered at the Bartels Lutheran Retirement Community in Waverly in 1996 as part of the Iowa Broadcasting Oral History Project to share their first memories of broadcasting.

Charlotte Burrack, who was born in 1900, recalled that radio entered her life for the first time in 1925 when her father-in-law built a receiver from a kit. "That was something quite exciting for us," she recalled more than 70 years later.

John Harrington's first memory was as a toddler listening to experimental broadcasts on a crystal set in 1916. By 1927, his family used a radio that ran on a battery, which had to be charged each night. Resembling a car battery of today, it was kept on a charger in the basement, and he remembered that "the last man to go to bed had to turn on the charger each night" so the radio could be used the next day.

While he was a high school senior in 1930, Harrington's family purchased a radio that operated on electricity. "My mother used to be after me to

go to bed, but it was more fun sitting up to see how many different stations I could tune in," he said during the 1996 session. "I sat up there night after night after night. It just fascinated me to know that you could do this. It wasn't to listen to the program, it was just to see how far out you could get stations."

The Reverend Roy Huck, who was 88 years old at the time of the 1996 discussion, remembered that he first heard radio stations like KDKA in Pittsburgh and WLS in Chicago on a set his friend built from a kit mailed from Chicago; it came with two sets of headphones so both of them could listen at the same time. By the 1920s, his parents had purchased an Atwater Kent radio, which sat on a table in a metal case with a "horn" speaker on the top. Growing up in northeast Iowa, he recalled listening to Henry Field give gardening advice over KFNF radio in faraway Shenandoah.

John Harrington recalled that as a boy growing up in Dysart, the local bank had a finished basement, and when there was a special event such as a prizefight on the radio, "We all rushed to the bank to get a free seat because their radio was better than the ones we all had at home."

"I wouldn't have wanted to live without it, radio or television either one," Roy Huck said. "It's been that important in my life. And it adds so much to what we think and believe. I wouldn't want to do without it."

Craig Johnson is an example of what television stations look for in their weathercasters today: people who have a strong background in the science of meteorology who take their jobs seriously and can clearly convey information to the audience.

Now, stations across the country spend hundreds of thousands of dollars for in-house radar systems to help their staff accurately predict weather changes. In Iowa, weathercasting tops viewer surveys as the main reason they watch television news.

Weather at Des Moines' Channel 8 has always been an important part of the news product, but in the earliest days, viewers not only watched for the information, but for the unique way in which it was presented.

Russ Van Dyke would deliver the weather as part of his 10 o'clock newscast each night, using a large glass weather map as his visual aid, with Van Dyke standing behind the map and writing temperatures and other information on it. To the audience, it looked like Van Dyke knew how to write backwards in order for the image to properly appear on screen; however, the map itself was backwards, a mirror image from what the public would see, and thanks to the image being reversed in the camera lens itself, the audience got the desired effect and saw the map and graphics clearly.

The idea for Van Dyke's famous glass weather map originated at a television station in Oklahoma City. According to Paul Rhoades, who anchored the KRNT-TV 6 p.m. news at the time, it was primarily a gimmick, but "it generated a lot of talk about the station." Van Dyke would deliver five minutes of weather using the glass map during the 10 o'clock news, but at 6 o'clock when the glass weather map was not used, Rhoades would present a more basic weather forecast.

When the glass weather map made its debut in 1955, KRNT's general manager told the staff to get rid of it, calling it the stupidest thing he had ever seen. In only a few days, however, viewers made it clear that they liked the concept, so the see-through weather map remained a staple of TV-8 news for more than two decades. The map is now frequently on display at the State Historical Society Building in Des Moines, with Van Dyke's handwriting still on it.

A see-through weather map was one way for a station to deliver weather information on television in the 1950s. Other gimmicks were also tried, with various degrees of success. On occasion, a puppet who hosted a children's show was used to deliver the weather on KCRG-TV in Cedar Rapids, and Iowa's first television station, WOC-TV, originated a weather forecast with a puppet called "Mr. Weatherwise." At times, KWWL featured "weather girls" who would dress differently depending on the forecast—wearing a raincoat and carrying an umbrella if rain was forecast, for example. But times have changed, and the science of meteorology—and its importance to the Iowa audience—has increased in ways no one could have predicted.

"Going into the weather lab today is just mind boggling with what's available," Conrad Johnson said in a 1996 interview. "I just want to get my hands on it."

The National Weather Service's system of issuing watches and warnings was instituted in the late 1960s after a number of devastating tornadoes killed hundreds of people across the Midwest. Now, Doppler radar technology allows weather professionals to predict the presence of tornadoes before they are seen on the ground, and many television stations will pre-empt large blocks of programming to broadcast "wall to wall" when severe weather threatens an area.

Many of today's weather professionals, such as eastern Iowa's Craig Johnson and John McLaughlin of KCCI, are recognized nationally for their work as scientists in using radar and forecasting weather. But the founder of television weathercasting, Conrad Johnson, who died in 2002, was disturbed by some of the trends

Craig Johnson was a fixture on KWWL and WMT for more than a quarter century.

he saw at many stations.

"We used to relate the information. Now we've got to make a show of it to make money," Conrad Johnson said. "The cosmetics are there, but there's no depth to it." He was particularly troubled by stations that send their meteorologists out in the field as feature reporters, delivering forecasts from community events and the like; he believed it sends the wrong signal to audiences.

With the new technology, those audiences are able to get more information more quickly. Thanks to the Internet, many television stations post radar images live on the World Wide Web for people to review at their convenience. New computer programs also

tv **8** *Weather*

8:51

5:40

64°
.06
83°

E - 5

63%

77   78
         73
      78
59
H   L S T O R M
   76   80
88   80

81

98   1971
45 IN 1926

DES MOINES   COUNCIL BLUFFS   MARSHALL TOWN   UQUE

74
78

Connie McBurney was the weathercaster at Des Moines' Channel 8 during the 1970s and 1980s.

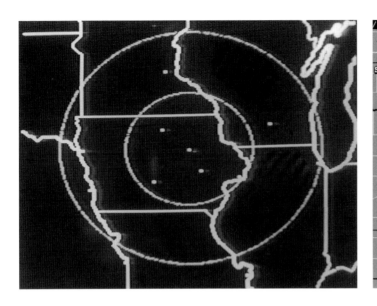

The look of television weathercasting has changed with technology over time, as seen through these views of radar used by KWWL-TV in the 1960s (left) and KCCI-TV today (right).

allow many stations to send updated forecasts to viewers via electronic mail, tailored to their specific community.

But while technology now allows the audience to watch detailed weather radar "loops" on their home computers, it still takes someone who knows the topic to put it into perspective. The field has progressed from early television stations using weathercasters who knew a little about the topic, to today's highly trained meteorologists who carry certifications from groups such as the American Meteorological Society and the National Weather Alliance.

Viewership surveys consistently show that the audience expects those who deliver the forecast to know and understand the science of weather, be accurate and reliable in forecasting, and

demonstrate their experience in a professional manner.

Prior to television, most radio stations simply repeated the forecasts provided by the weather bureau, and since there was not the system of watches and warnings we have today, there were no "weather departments" at radio stations. Even today, most radio stations simply rely upon forecasts provided by the National Weather Service, or by a television station's meteorologist.

A few, however, have had their own staff meteorologists. The last remaining radio station in Iowa to have a full-time meteorologist on staff is KICD in Spencer—Mark Bruggom. The station has had a working radar in place since Collins Radio installed one in 1957.

"I've never believed that a newsman should try to foist his views upon the audience. I've always believed that if the people of this country are given good information, they'll make the right decision, and it doesn't take somebody sitting in front of a camera telling them what it should be."

Longtime KRNT/KCCI anchor Russ Van Dyke, during an interview the day after he announced his retirement in January 1983.

11 | Keeping Iowa Informed

The excitement of being able to hear far-off sounds led to the quick growth of entertainment programming in the early days of broadcasting. But before long, more practical applications, such as the delivery of news and farm information, took hold. The benefits of being able to hear current information live, rather than waiting days or even weeks for newspaper accounts, were evident. And the fact that the audience was hearing the information read to them by another human voice—an announcer behind a microphone—created a personal connection. From the earliest days, news and information has been an important part of broadcasting.

The growth of WHO's information service—providing extensive news, farm, and sports broadcasts—was due in great part to the foresight of station manager Joe Maland. Maland had operated a general store in southern Minnesota, and bought one of the first radios in the area. He played the radio in his store as a draw to attract business. He saw that farmers were entranced by hearing markets from Chicago in real time, rather than waiting for printed versions the next day. Maland decided to go into radio as a career, starting at WCCO in Minneapolis and later moving to WLS in Chicago. It was from WLS that B. J. Palmer hired Maland to run his new radio property in Des Moines, WHO, in 1931.

"I still think it's such a crying shame that his name is almost unknown to the people of the Middle West, when he did so much to bring to people—not only in Iowa but in a vast radius around Iowa in daytime and in much of the country at night—a kind of information service they had never known before," Jack Shelley said.

It was in early 1935 that Maland decided to get serious about news on WHO, and hired the station's first full-time newsman, wire service reporter H. R. "Charlie" Gross. Later that year, Gross got permission to add a second person to his staff. He called the University of Missouri for a recommendation—the first request the school ever had received for a broadcaster—and learned of Shelley, a Boone native who had been working for the newspaper in Clinton since his graduation that year.

Shelley started work at WHO in October 1935. He spent three days following Gross around, learning the broadcast news business, and then began anchoring the "breakfast time news." That first day as the regular morning anchor was the first live broadcasting Jack Shelley ever did.

When the first radio newsrooms were being set up, the logical source for obtaining news was to subscribe to one of the wire services, just as newspapers did. However, newspapers were afraid they would be forced out of business if radio stations started broadcasting news; after all, why would the audience wait for an outdated print version when they could hear fresh updates on the radio? The newspapers put pressure on the wire services to deny radio stations access to their material. National "radio only" news services began, and many traditional wire services then began to sell their product to radio stations.

"Newspapers were extremely belligerent and negative about the idea that the public could get information off that box and did everything in the world they could to frustrate our efforts to become legitimate purveyors of information to the public," veteran broadcast journalist Grant Price said.

The "7 Desk" used by KWWL during its ratings rise in the 1970s, with Tom Peterson (news), Jym Ganahl (weather), and Mike O'Connor (sports).

By the late 1930s, Gross—a former United Press bureau chief—had convinced the wire service to provide WHO with news copy, making it the first radio station to subscribe to the UP. However, the *Des Moines Register* threatened to quit subscribing to United Press if the service sold its material to the radio station; the service did not take the threat seriously, and the *Register*, true to its word, did cancel its subscription, remaining an Associated Press-only newspaper to this day.

In 1940, Gross left WHO to pursue a political career, and Shelley became news director, a position he would hold for the next 25 years. In addition to supervising his staff, Shelley inherited the 12:30 p.m. radio newscast, which had become a fixture under Gross.

"It was a great newscast, and that voice, of course, of Jack Shelley coming on the radio at 12:30, that was one huge PA system, covering the whole state of Iowa," Price said.

Surveys of the time support that view. The Iowa Radio Audience Survey in 1940 showed that WHO was named as the station "heard regularly" in daytime by nearly 80 percent of Iowans. In that same survey, WHO's news broadcasts placed second in a list of "the fifty best-liked programs," ahead of the Jack Benny program and just behind Fibber McGee. WHO's dominance in daytime programming was even more pronounced—almost 32 percent of listeners named WHO news as their "best-liked program" during the daytime; no other program, local or network, got as much as 5 percent.

Jack Shelley was once told that one Iowa family used his newscast as a way to help their little girl find her way home from school. In the days before air-conditioning, one could walk along the sidewalk and hear the sound of the 12:30 p.m. radio news coming through the open windows of each house. The family told Shelley that the little girl was not scared as long as she could hear the sound of Jack Shelley's familiar voice as she made her way down the street.

While WHO covered the entire state with Iowa's largest signal, across town the *Register & Tribune's* station, KRNT, operated with a much more limited range. Their philosophy, therefore, was to focus on the city of Des Moines and the immediate area in its news coverage, a tactic that would yield great dividends in the television age.

In the post-World War II period, KRNT radio's 6 p.m. news was delivered by famous *Register & Tribune* reporter and columnist Gordon Gammack. Paul Rhoades arrived in 1949, and handled the 6:30 a.m.—and later the 6 p.m.—news on radio for five years until KRNT-TV went on the air; he was then primary anchor of the 6 p.m. television news on Channel 8 for the next 38 years.

"Television news, in itself, was not a big deal other than, 'Oh, my. Look at what you can do,' but today it's the profit center of the station," Rhoades said.

The partnership between Russ Van Dyke and Paul Rhoades was unique. Van Dyke was the news director, but because he anchored the 10 p.m. news, first on radio and then on television, much of the day-to-day administrative duties of the newsroom fell to Rhoades. The sharing of newsroom responsibilities in this way allowed the station to maximize each man's abilities.

WHO-TV took to the air in April of 1954; KRNT-TV would not begin broadcasting until July of the following year. Despite being on the air for more than a year before KRNT's sign on, WHO was unable to capitalize on that advantage.

KRNT put their best known talent—Van Dyke—on television at 10 p.m., the same time his radio newscast had aired for years. From the start, KRNT had 20 minutes of news at 10 p.m., while WHO only did 10 minutes of news, so it made KRNT look like they were doing much more. But KRNT's 20-minute news block included the weather, while WHO's was broken out in a separate segment; so while it was not a fair comparison, it is what the public perceived. In addition, WHO-TV originally chose not to do a news

Jack Shelley

Gordon Gammack

H. R. Gross

program on Sunday nights. Then-news director Jack Shelley said Channel 8 "just killed us" by being there for viewers seven nights a week.

In order to compete with the popular Van Dyke, WHO tried a number of men in the anchor chair at 10 p.m. The first late news anchor was Henry Magnusson, who was followed by Clay Rusk. When they did not deliver high enough ratings, the station moved popular sportscaster Jim Zabel into the news anchor chair for a time, before moving respected broadcaster Len Howe into the job.

Shelley wanted to stay off the night shift as long as possible to allow him to act as news director and set story assignments during the day. From the late 1950s, Shelley did the noon news on television and the 12:30 p.m. news on radio. The station finally forced him to anchor on television during the evenings, including a stint at 10 p.m. "For a brief time—not very long—we beat Russ Van Dyke at 10:00, and we were so happy about that," Shelley said.

Ultimately, Bob Wilbanks did the 10 p.m. news on Channel 13, while Shelley did the noon TV, 12:30 p.m. radio, and 6 p.m. TV news. Wilbanks remained the late news anchor and became news director after Shelley left to begin teaching at Iowa State University in 1965.

In the end, KRNT's consistency of on air talent no doubt helped in attracting a larger audience. In fact, during the time that Rhoades anchored the 6 p.m. news and Van Dyke anchored the 10 p.m. news on Channel 8, from the mid-1950s into the early 1980s, WHO went through 14 different news anchors compared to just the two on KRNT.

But viewing habits are hard to change, and to this day, WHO-TV has rarely topped KRNT, now KCCI, in the news ratings. Adding a co-anchor system in the late 1970s allowed the "next generation" of anchors, such as Rick Fredericksen, Dave Busiek and Kevin Cooney, to sit alongside Rhoades and Van Dyke and gain audience acceptance while continuing the station's news tradition.

While WOI-TV produced the first televised newscasts in the Des Moines market, the station has found it difficult to find a large news audience. However, the station's commitment to public affairs programming was evident even when it was the only television station in the market. For example, in the fall of 1951, WOI-TV produced 16 different news and entertainment programs locally. One of the station's most ambitious efforts was a series called "The Whole Town's Talking," which was produced with more than a quarter million dollars of funding from the Ford Foundation. The program provided a forum for discussion of community issues and focused on cities all over the viewing area.

Even in the television age, Des Moines radio listeners have been well served when it comes to providing news and information. For many years in the 1970s and 1980s, KRNT, WHO, and KIOA each had at least a half-dozen journalists in their newsrooms, with hourly updates and feature programs. Names such as Dale Woolery, Jackie King, Jim Vogelaar, Julie Rutz, George Davison, and Ev Hickman were familiar to central Iowa audiences.

His interest in radio cultivated by living in rural Nebraska and growing up listening to, among others, Russ Van Dyke on WNAX in Yankton, South Dakota, Grant Price first worked in broadcasting while a student at Morningside College in Sioux City. Gene Flaherty, the manager of KSCJ radio there, kept the station budget under control by hiring college students who would work for next to nothing. "It just seemed to be a fit for me," Price said.

After serving in the Navy in World War II, Price returned to Sioux City as the night announcer at radio station KTRI. When station manager Diedrich Dierks decided to start a news department at KTRI, Dierks offered him the job. Price left college and decided to become a broadcast journalist.

"I've been an on-the-job trainee ever since. And that was the fit for me," he said. "It was more challenging than introducing Frank Sinatra and Dick Haynes records."

From KTRI, Price went to KXEL radio in Waterloo in 1948 and spent more than a decade running the news department there. In 1959, he moved to the WMT stations in Cedar Rapids, staying until 1972. During that time, he oversaw WMT-TV's virtual monopoly on eastern Iowa television news, yet Price credits others with building the foundation for the WMT news operation.

"It was a successful time," he said. "If foundations are important in construction, they are very, very important in journalism, and a guy named Jim Bormann laid the foundation for that newsroom."

Bormann was news director at WMT from 1947 until 1951, when he left to run the news department at WCCO in Minneapolis. Expanded on-the-scenes news coverage and statehouse reporting from Des Moines were among the advances Bormann introduced to Cedar Rapids audiences.

WMT radio partnered with other Midwest radio stations to support a news reporter in a bureau in Washington, D.C. The correspondent was to give a local slant to national stories, and provide two stories per week exclusively for each affiliate. The Washington bureau reporter was Walter Cronkite, who in his memoirs credited Bormann's WMT news operation with being the only one of those he served that knew how to properly use the services of a correspondent in the nation's capital. After a distinguished career as the CBS television anchorman, Cronkite still has ties to Iowa broadcasting in retirement, recently narrating two radio documentaries for the Stanley Foundation of Muscatine.

"One of the things that impressed me from the first days I was there was the feeling people had in eastern Iowa for the WMT

PEOPLE'S PRESS CONFERENCE

Senate candidates Roger Jepsen and Dick Clark during a 1978 "People's Press Conference" program hosted by Paul Rhoades on Channel 8 in Des Moines.

Dick Cheverton

news department in the country by the Radio-Television News Directors Association. Cheverton has been described as "determined" and a "hard bitten guy." "He was all news, all the time," former WMT-TV anchor Henry Lippold said.

Cheverton wrote a manual for local correspondents, non-journalists in small towns around the state who would call WMT with news stories and were paid 50 cents per story used on the air. The manual was a checklist for matters ranging from burglary to murder, and helped to build not only the WMT news operation itself, but also foster strong loyalty through use of the regional correspondent system.

That "loyalty" worked both ways. In the early 1950s, Robert Johnson was a government reporter for the *Waterloo Daily Courier.* His wife, Edna Mae, had been a stringer for WMT radio for years. This was not a problem until Johnson's boss, Gene Thorn, talked with R. J. McElroy, who was by then in competition with his former employer, WMT. Johnson believes McElroy encouraged Thorn to end the "conflict of interest;" so Thorn fired Johnson with only two weeks notice in front of the entire newsroom. When Edna Mae Johnson told WMT news director Dick Cheverton what had happened, Cheverton asked Bob Johnson to come to the station for an interview. Cheverton offered Johnson a job, but when Johnson said he knew nothing about radio, Cheverton told him, "You know news."

By 1953, Johnson was the first full-time legislative correspondent from an Iowa broadcast station located outside of Des Moines. By the next year, he would be the first late news anchor on Channel 2.

After Cheverton left for a station in Michigan, WMT farm director Chuck Worcester became director of news services until his death in early 1961. Grant Price then held the job for the next eleven years, the longest tenure of any Channel 2 news director to this day.

stations," newsman Bob Bruner said. "If people heard it, they could believe it, and this was their attitude all over eastern Iowa." In fact, when Bruner came to WMT from Indiana in November, 1953, he went to a store to purchase some new furniture on credit. The store owner gladly gave him credit because he worked at WMT, and pointed out that not everyone with a new job in Cedar Rapids got that kind of courtesy from the furniture store.

Dick Cheverton succeeded Bormann in the WMT news director's job, and ushered the station into the television era with great success. In 1955, the station was named the best radio-television

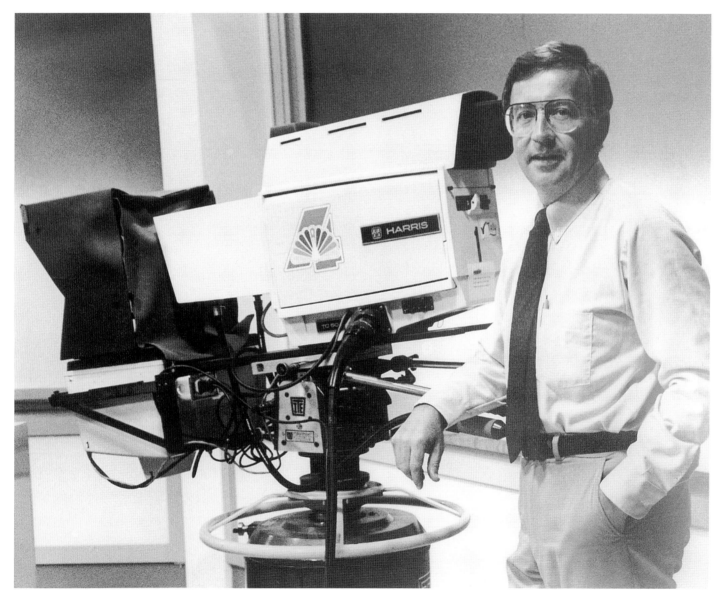

Dave Nixon led two Sioux City stations to the top spot in the ratings over a 30-year television career.

Robert M. L. Johnson

signaling that it was time for people to go to bed.

Many well-known persons came from the WMT newsroom. Bill Roberts was a familiar voice on radio in the 1940s and 1950s, before becoming the first television news anchor at Channel 2. He would later run the Washington, D.C. bureau for the Time-Life-owned stations and serve as president of the international journalists group RTNDA. Iowa native Richard Threlkeld came to WMT radio and television in 1962, and went on to national fame as a correspondent for the CBS and ABC television networks. Dennis Swanson was a news reporter and producer in the 1960s; he went on to a number of important jobs in broadcasting, including managing network-owned television stations in New York, Chicago, and Los Angeles, as well as being named *Broadcasting and Cable* magazine's first national "Broadcaster of the Year" in 2002. To many, however, Swanson might be best known as the man who in 1984 hired Oprah Winfrey to host a local talk show in Chicago, which would soon become a national sensation.

Longevity was a hallmark of WMT-TV's success, as well. With Bob Bruner anchoring the 6 p.m. news and Dave Shay anchoring the 10 p.m. news throughout the 1960s, audiences grew accustomed to the news product; being associated with the long WMT radio news tradition also was a great benefit to Channel 2.

One of the developments in television news in the 1970s was the co-anchor format. The first regular co-anchors in the Cedar Rapids/Waterloo market were Dave Shay and John Bachman, who began sharing WMT-TV's news desk in 1972.

The Waterloo half of the market was home to KWWL-TV, founded by R. J. McElroy in 1953. After McElroy's death in 1965, company attorney Robert Buckmaster became the head of Black Hawk Broadcasting, and stemmed the tide of "revolving anchors" which had plagued the station in earlier years.

Channel 2's dominance of eastern Iowa news during the 1960s and early 1970s was striking. At its high point, more than 80 percent of those watching television at 10 p.m. were watching the late news on WMT-TV. Noted broadcaster Frosty Mitchell says that he was once on a plane flying over eastern Iowa back to Des Moines late at night, when the pilot told the passengers to look out the window and watch as all the lights went out in the houses across that part of the state as the Channel 2 10 o'clock news ended,

Broadcasters as Politicians

More than a few Iowa broadcasters have turned their attention to the political arena. The natural love of people, as well as the base of support many broadcasters have in their communities, made the transition an easy one for many.

While the most famous is obviously former WOC and WHO radio sportscaster Ronald Reagan, who went on to become governor of California and president of the United States, others with Iowa broadcasting ties made their marks in the political arena, as well.

The first person to try to parlay radio popularity into a political career was legendary WHO news director H. R. "Charlie" Gross. After six years on the air in Des Moines, Gross decided to challenge incumbent Gov. George Wilson for the Republican nomination in 1940. Doing virtually all his campaigning by radio (and most of that on WHO), Gross wound up losing the election. An analysis of the voting shows that Gross lost in those areas of the state which were not served by WHO's large signal, but he more than held his own in the other areas of the state.

WHO management did not want a news director who had a connection to politics, so Gross went on to stations in Cincinnati and Indianapolis before returning to Iowa just after World War II to become news director at KXEL radio in Waterloo. He used that station's large signal as a springboard for his run for Congress from Iowa's third district in 1948. This time, he upset incumbent Republican congressman John Gwynne and went on to serve 13 terms as northeast Iowa's representative to Washington.

Jim Wharton, who went by the name Jim Roberts on the air, was news director for KMNS radio in Sioux City before becoming mayor of Sioux City from 1993-1994. In addition, two Iowa television anchors wound up becoming mayors of their respective cities.

Robert M. L. Johnson was a long time *Waterloo Courier* and WMT radio and television reporter who became the first late news anchor on WMT-TV in 1954. In 1957, when the Cedar Rapids safety commissioner died while in office, Johnson was appointed to serve until the next election. He wound up winning election to that position twice, before later serving three terms as mayor of Iowa's second-largest city. He later became a state legislator and a candidate for Congress.

Ken Kew spent his 32-year broadcasting career at KGLO radio and television in Mason City in a variety of capacities, including anchoring news, doing play-by-play of University of Iowa athletic events, and presenting station editorials. His transition from broadcasting to politics occurred in 1974, when he became mayor of Mason City, a job he held until 1986. An enthusiastic backer of north central Iowa, Kew—who died in 1988—had no regrets about spending his entire career there.

"Usually the people in the business are nomads," he once said. "I liked the community, and I liked the work I was doing. I liked the people that I had to deal with, and I saw no reason to leave."

A Des Moines lawyer and radio station owner would go on to serve more terms as Iowa's governor than any man in history. Robert Ray first got into the business as a part owner of Grinnell radio station KGRN; his ownership interest was given as compensation for the legal work he did to start the company. He and his wife later bought a radio station in Estherville, and after his 14-year tenure as governor, he was a major partner in the group that owned WMT radio in Cedar Rapids from 1986 to 1995. The Iowa Broadcasters Association named him to its Hall of Fame in 1982.

Many Iowa broadcasters made a transition to politics in the form of government service.

WHO farm director Herb Plambeck left the station in 1970 to become an assistant secretary of agriculture in Washington.

WMT-TV reporter Martin Jensen was a legislative correspondent in the 1960s who later became a press aide to Iowa governor, and later U.S. senator, Harold Hughes.

And when Robert Ray needed a new press spokesman, he turned to a young KWWL-TV reporter/anchor named David Oman. Oman would later become chief of staff to both Ray and Governor Terry Branstad before himself running in the Republican primary for governor in 1998.

While most Iowans are well aware that Herbert Hoover is the only native Iowan to ever become president of the United States, many are not aware of his ties to broadcasting. Hoover served as Secretary of Commerce during the Harding and Coolidge Administrations, from 1921-1928. Part of his job included overseeing government regulation of radio broadcasting.

This would, at times, put him at odds with Iowa broadcasters, who did not want to share their frequencies with others and did not want to limit their stations' power. But as Secretary of Commerce, he hosted a series of four now-famous Radio Conferences, where station owners and interested parties met to discuss how best to administer the growing number of stations.

Without specific congressional authority, it was difficult for Secretary Hoover to mandate change. The voluntary regulatory scheme he drafted as a result of the radio conference in 1924 was thrown out by a federal court in 1926, and once the Radio Act of 1927 was enacted, establishing the Federal Radio Commission, Hoover's responsibility for the broadcast industry came to an end.

However, much of the groundwork for today's regulation of American broadcasting was laid during the Radio Conferences Hoover oversaw. One of the first acts of the new Federal Radio Commission was to order stations to resume broadcasting on the frequencies and at the power limits assigned by Hoover in 1924—the very same regulations that were deemed inappropriate by the federal court just a year before.

Grant Price

"What was a dismally unsuccessful news operation gradually started to build a base in Waterloo," Price said. "They became the station that Waterloo really depended on for news." The station gradually began to draw viewers from the Waterloo metropolitan area, and by the late 1960s, a consistent on-air presence of Tom Peterson anchoring the news, Jym Ganahl doing the weather,

and Mike O'Connor reporting sports began paying dividends in ratings. Channel 7 had begun to cut into Channel 2's ratings lead. In 1972, Price left WMT and joined KWWL as vice president for news. Within two years, the station became eastern Iowa's top-rated newscast at 10 p.m., a position Channel 7 has now held consistently for 30 straight years.

"Maybe I invented synergy without knowing what it was, but if you look at anything that I've had a hand in, it was definitely the result of the synergy of very, very talented people coming together and producing something that really was larger than all of us," Price said.

"We've always been a team-oriented station here," said anchor/reporter Ron Steele, who has been at KWWL since 1974. "We have dozens of people behind the scenes that get absolutely no face or name recognition. They are the ones, the nuts and bolts of everything we've done in the years that I've been around this market, and I'm really proud of them. They really do a great job to make us, the on-air people, look good."

At the same time KWWL radio went on the air in Waterloo in 1947, the *Cedar Rapids Gazette* turned to experienced broadcasters in starting the news operation at their new station, KCRG. Pat Patterson was the first radio news director. He had been a very popular on air news person for WMT radio in Cedar Rapids. "He was a simply splendid reader of the news," former station executive Edna Herbst said. "He presented it beautifully."

When KCRG-TV went on the air in 1953, Dick Yoakum came from Jack Shelley's WHO news department to serve as the first news director for the television station. He would later become a distinguished professor of journalism at Indiana University.

One of the early 10 o'clock news anchors at KCRG was Tom Pettit. "He had an idea a minute. I would nearly always find under my door in the morning a 'note from the top of T.P.'s head' that was a suggestion from Tom," Herbst said. Pettit would go on to a distinguished career with NBC News, well-known for his coverage of the shooting of Lee Harvey Oswald in Dallas and the resignation of President Richard Nixon at the height of Watergate.

Familiar names at the KCRG anchor desk in the 1960s and 1970s included Dave Carter and Larry Hightchew. Iowa native Doug Krile was the station's primary anchor and news director for a number of years in the 1970s and 1980s. When Krile left KCRG in 1986, Bruce Aune became the station's lead anchor; Aune had previously spent five years as anchor and news director at KIMT-TV 3 in Mason City.

Despite the advent of television, northeast Iowans quickly grew to trust the reporting carried on the local radio station in Oelwein. In 1952, barely two years on the air, KOEL-AM hired a young journalist away from KSCJ in Sioux City to run their news operation. But Dick Petrik's job was not easy—the station's primary coverage area was 16 rural counties in northeast Iowa. In his 40 years at the station, he became known for doing virtually all of his reporting by telephone, relying on law enforcement officials and telephone operators in every county.

"All I would say is, 'This is Dick,' and 'KOEL,' and everybody knew me," Petrik said.

Under Petrik's leadership, the KOEL news department was a dominant force in its area. National ratings surveys showed that in the immediate counties around Oelwein, KOEL consistently garnered up to an 80-90 percent audience share. Whether covering the regional police beat, following bicyclists on RAGBRAI, or reading area birth and death announcements on the air, Petrik used his sources well, making as many as 200 long distance calls a day to gather the news.

Across the state, western Iowans got their television news from a man who had grown up in the area. Coming from a family of farm workers, Dave Nixon, Sr. grew up near Sioux City, in north-

Ron Steele, Jym Ganahl and Tom Peterson of KWWL

east Nebraska. Radio station KMNS was located a few miles from his Dakota City home; the young Nixon could see the station's tower light blinking at night from his bedroom window, and the prospect of broadcasting fascinated him. One day he went to the studio on his bicycle, and was quickly hooked on broadcasting as a career. He later found himself working at the same station along with the idols he listened to while growing up, including "Smiling Sam the Record Man" and "Jolly Roger."

Longtime broadcast executive Bill Turner later invited Nixon to return from the Minneapolis radio station where he had been working to join KCAU-TV as a television anchor. Turner suggested that Nixon go to college and get a four-year degree to enhance his credibility on the air, and even offered to pay the

WMT-TV anchors Bob Bruner, Dave Shay and John Bachman.

BOB BRUNER

DAVE SHAY

tuition. Nixon credits Turner for encouraging his desire for education, which led to his later career as an academic dean at Iowa Lakes Community College.

With Nixon as the primary anchor, the "Major 9," as the station billed itself, became a dominant ratings leader in the market because of its dedication to regional community information. "It was a must watch television station, because it had a real strong local news, weather, and sports product," Nixon said. In fact, KCAU's local news ratings often equaled those of the most popular network programs aired in the market.

Nixon left for Des Moines to anchor the news on WHO-TV for two years, but returned to Sioux City in 1980, this time on his former rival, KTIV-TV. With Nixon at the anchor desk, Channel 4 soon became the top-rated news station in the market, demonstrating the loyalty of his viewers.

Given Iowa's geography, it is difficult to adequately cover all the counties in a television station's signal area. Sioux City stations, for example, reach into parts of Iowa, Minnesota, South Dakota, and Nebraska, while Quad Cities stations serve large populations in Iowa and Illinois. Former WOC anchor Don Rhyne recalled that during his 20 years at the anchor desk, Channel 6 in Davenport covered four counties and a dozen municipalities in two states. "It gets a little frantic once in a while," he said in a 1985 interview. "We've had experienced reporters apply for jobs, come in, be offered the job, take one look at the map, turn around and walk out."

Over the past quarter-century, the role of women on-air has increased greatly. Male/female co-anchor teams are the norm at television stations throughout Iowa; women are the sole anchors for the weekend evening television news on all three stations in the Cedar Rapids/Waterloo market.

The first woman to serve as primary anchor for a television station's weeknight newscasts was Twila Young, who was the sole anchor at WOI-TV 5 for two years in the mid-1970s. The first female co-anchor in the state was at WMT-TV in Cedar Rapids, when Maggie Jensen and Dave Shay co-anchored Channel 2's news in 1974. By 1981, all three Cedar Rapids/Waterloo television stations had male/female co-anchor teams. That was the year Liz Mathis joined Ron Steele at the KWWL anchor desk, the last station in the market to adopt the dual anchor format. They would anchor together at the Waterloo station for 15 years; Mathis has been partnered with Bruce Aune at KCRG in Cedar Rapids since 1998.

The expansion of women into prominent news reporting and management roles is not limited to television. Kay Henderson has been with Learfield's Radio Iowa service based in Des Moines since it was founded in 1982; she has served as news director for the operation since 1986 and is one of only two women to have received the Iowa Broadcast News Association's Jack Shelley Award.

Regardless of who is presenting the information, getting the news on the air first, especially before the stations in larger cities, was important to those who ran radio stations in Iowa's small towns in the days before television.

The late Ben Sanders once recalled getting a phone call at 2 in the morning from an individual at the Mutual network saying a big story was to break early in the morning, and advising him to be sure to be on the air. Between 6 and 7 a.m., thanks to their affiliation with the Mutual network, Sanders' KICD broadcast the story of the end of the war in Germany; he took great pride in the fact that WHO was playing music from a live quartet at the time, only to announce the end of the war nearly three hours later. "That's when we began to prove our worth" as a source for news, Sanders said. "That's what I wanted to do."

It was sometimes difficult, especially in smaller towns, for even those on the air to get used to giving information. Algona station owner George Allen recalled listening to his own station during a local flood to find out if certain highways around the town were closed. When the newscaster failed to provide any information on the topic, Allen called the station and learned from the newscaster that the roads were, in fact, closed. When Allen asked why the information was not on the air, the newscaster replied, "Because everyone knows the roads are closed." Allen said he found a new newscaster shortly after that time.

George Allen's philosophy about local programming was to "find out everything the local paper is doing—then do it better and faster." Longtime Denison broadcaster Don Uker credits Allen with teaching him the secret to running a successful, community-minded station—play music between the things that are really important.

One of the strengths of any station, both in terms of providing a public service but also in building a large audience, is a strong local presence. Frosty Mitchell says he created a personally signed placard that was hung on the Associated Press machine at each of his stations, reading "Does this story have a local angle?" The more local the story, the greater the attachment to the audience.

A number of stations in smaller Iowa cities have established strong reputations for local news coverage. Listeners served by stations such as KGRN in Grinnell, KCOB in Newton, KBUR in Burlington, KGLO in Mason City, KDTH in Dubuque, KICD in Spencer, and KASI in Ames have traditionally enjoyed broadcast journalism with a large market feel. Broadcast journalists such as J. K. Martin, Tim Renshaw, Gordon Kilgore, Larry Huegli, Rich Fellingham and Don Bradley have kept their local audiences well informed for decades.

An independent survey conducted in 1983 concerning audience preferences in the Marshalltown market showed that while a majority of listeners preferred music-intensive FM stations most of the time, more than three-quarters of those surveyed said they turned to KFJB-AM when they wanted news or weather information; that is the sort of loyalty that takes years to build.

Many journalists made the transition from radio to television when the radio stations they worked for started television operations, as well. For even the most successful broadcasters, the transition took some work.

"I never was as comfortable on television as I usually felt on radio," Jack Shelley said. "In radio, you are the show. You're either good or you're not, the newscast worked out well or it didn't. Particularly in the old days when all you did was sit down at a desk in front of a (radio) microphone and read the whole newscast, then you were without any question 'the show.' It all fell on your shoulders. In television, even if everything else was taken care of, you still had this cadre of people out in front which the audience couldn't see, doing all sorts of necessary things to get that program on the air."

"The general rule I've tried to follow is that you're not sitting here talking to 60 or 70 or 80 or 90,000 people. You're sitting here talking to one or two or three, because that's what's in front of each TV set," Russ Van Dyke said at the time of his retirement in 1983. "And I try to imagine that these people have not heard radio newscasts, they haven't had time to read a newspaper, they haven't seen a TV newscast, yet they want to know what's going on in the world today and in the final analysis, whatever went on in the world today has to affect people, because that's the bottom line."

The celebrity status now given to television anchors can sometimes be difficult. "You are forever recognized as you walk down the street or into a restaurant or something like that," Dave Shay said. "This, however, is probably the best place on Earth for that to happen, because Iowans are polite and well mannered."

That close tie between the audience and news broadcasters dates back to the earliest days of radio. "When I got to WHO and was on the air every day for five or six days a week, if I was gone from there, people knew it right away. My voice wasn't there and they would promptly call the station and say, 'Where's Jack Shelley?' or whoever the newscaster was," Shelley said. "Your voice is your trademark and it is absolutely incomparable in terms of identification. The average newspaper reporter never gets that kind of identification, even if he gets a byline."

Broadcasting is not an easy business for those with families. The highest profile shifts are often those in the very early morning or late at night, and stations do not close on holidays, meaning someone has to work.

To lessen the strain on his family, Russ Van Dyke worked a split shift for many years, so he could be there in the late afternoon when his children got home from school, and go to their Little League games. Long-time KGLO farm director Al Heinz spent a lot of time away from his family, given his schedule. On Mondays for many years, he would do the radio markets during the sunrise hours, host a television show for children in the afternoon, broadcast the dinnertime markets on the radio for a half-hour, and then host a television square dance program during the evening, making for a 15-hour work day.

In more recent years, many stations have recognized the need for their on-air personalities to have strong family lives; many television anchors, for example, who work from 2 p.m. to 11 p.m. every day, will take a "dinner break" after the 6 o'clock news and go home to spend time with their families before returning to work to prepare the 10 o'clock news. Managers now are also generally more willing to let their employees take time off to attend school plays and ball games. But the work schedule still takes its toll, and broadcasters—particularly those involved with news—have a high "burn-out" rate when compared with other professions.

Beginning journalism students are taught that every good news

The KCCI news team around the signature "8" desk in the 1970s.

Ralph Childs was associated with the KMA news department from the 1940s to the 1960s.

story includes the 5 W's: who, what, when, where, and why. Most got into the field because of a role model, perhaps someone whose on-air work they had admired. This is what leads the standards of broadcast journalism to be handed down from one generation of journalists to the next.

The experience gained by some of Iowa's veteran broadcasters has been directly passed on to the next generation, as a number of well-known Iowa journalists moved into the classroom. Grant Price retired from KWWL in 1989 and began teaching at Wartburg College, becoming a full-time faculty member in 1992; he continues to teach courses in electronic media today.

Jack Shelley spent 17 years at Iowa State University before his retirement in 1982, building a broadcast curriculum that produced many famous journalists. Dave Nixon left KTIV in 1990 to start the broadcasting program at Iowa Lakes Community College, where he later served as academic dean of the Emmetsburg campus.

Many broadcast journalists saw educating their younger staff members and improving their work as key parts of their jobs. Among the broadcasters most closely associated with KMA's news department was Ralph Childs, who joined the station in 1939. Raised in Waterloo, he started his career at WMT in Waterloo as a writer and producer. He came to KMA, and according to a book on the station's history, "before long his name had become synonymous with news."

In early 1949, Childs wrote *"An Analysis Of KMA News And A Statement Of Policy"* for use by the staff. In addition to a number of overall principles, Childs discussed the difference between "conservative" and "sensational" news coverage. His words still apply today, more than a half century later.

Conservative is not synonymous with dead. A little 'spice' in the news does not go amiss. But it is well to remember that the primary function of spice is to bring out the flavor of the food, not to bury it...Too many of the radio fraternity are fly-by-nights, so interested in their own little egos that they don't light long enough to study the audience they're talking to...Facts are what make the news—not words. A common fault of the budding announcer is infatuation with his own voice. This fault also can be carried over into an infatuation for words instead of facts. Both of these faults can be overcome by thinking in ideas. The newsman's job is first, last and always to impart the news. He is selling facts. If he thinks in facts and ideas, the rest will take care of itself.

A number of today's outstanding radio journalists subscribe to these principles. KBUR news director J. K. Martin leads a staff that frequently wins awards for "overall excellence" for the station's efforts covering the Burlington area. Pennsylvania native Jim Boyd has worked in Iowa broadcasting for nearly 25 years; he spent the first 21 at WMT in Cedar Rapids before moving to WHO in Des Moines in 2001. He is the only person in history to serve as news director of both WMT and WHO, historically the two premiere radio news operations in Iowa.

Iowans also seem to prefer broadcast journalists who stay around long enough to know the area about which they are reporting. It is not uncommon for the most successful stations to have many reporters on staff who have spent 10 or 15 years at the same station, cultivating sources and building trust with the audience. The same is true in the anchor chair—many of those now on the air have anchored news at their current stations for many years, including KWWL's Ron Steele (1979), KCCI's Kevin Cooney (1982), KCRG's Bruce Aune (1986), and WHO-TV's John Bachman (1987). Bachman is the only person to have regularly anchored the main evening newscasts in both of Iowa's largest markets; he began his career at WMT-TV in Cedar Rapids in 1972.

The names of the programs may have changed over time—"Report to Iowa," "Eyewitness News," "Action News," "News Center"—and the slogans or catch phrases may be different—"Live,

Walter Cronkite, WMT's exclusive Washington correspondent during the 1940s.

Local and Latebreaking," "Coverage You Can Count On"—but the commitment of Iowa broadcast journalists to getting the story and presenting it to the audience is just as strong as it was when Charlie Gross hired the young Jack Shelley away from a career in newspapers.

"To develop an entertainment and educational enterprise that blankets Iowa is no small job. I have seen this baby conceived, watched it through pregnancy, nursed it in babyhood; fed it during its swaddling days when it could secure no food for itself; guided it through its struggling boyhood days; fought for it when it was being buffeted here and there as a young man, uncertain where it was headed; and now that it is assuming a man's size job, I am still with it, guiding it through the rapids of hard times."

Col. B. J. Palmer, during the on-air dedication of WHO radio's new 50,000-watt transmitter in 1933.

Covering The Big Stories

Each form of the mass media has its own audience, and does certain things better than others. The immediacy of broadcasting, however, makes it essential in times of crisis, and brings the sights and sounds of the biggest news stories into the homes of millions of Iowans. Being able to convey information quickly and accurately during times of crisis is certainly the "man's size job" B. J. Palmer contemplated some 70 years ago.

The 1968 Oelwein Tornadoes

When a band of strong tornadoes struck northeast Iowa in 1968, officials credited the early warnings broadcast by one radio station with saving dozens of lives.

On May 15, 1968, a series of tornadoes struck Oelwein, Maynard, and Charles City, killing more than a dozen people. At that time, the National Weather Service system of watches and warnings was not as sophisticated as it is today, and storms would often strike before official warnings could be issued.

KOEL's studios were located in downtown Oelwein, but the transmitter and tower were located just south of the city. FCC rules in effect at the time required a licensed engineer to be at the transmitter while the station was broadcasting, so evening and weekend broadcasts often originated from a separate facility at the transmitter site.

As the skies darkened in the late afternoon, engineer Dean Smith saw the devastating tornado approach. He flipped a switch to override the signals coming from the station's downtown studios, interrupting programming to warn citizens of the storm bearing down upon the city. He described the tornado in great detail, ending the announcement by saying simply, "God help us all."

He then escaped from the path of the tornado by hiding in the hollow of a nearby hill; the storm toppled two of KOEL's broadcast towers, narrowly missing the transmitter building itself.

Civil defense officials say Smith's broadcast, providing the citizens of Oelwein with five minutes' advance warning of the tornado, saved as many as 35 lives. Smith himself later left the radio business to become a minister.

Noted KOEL news director Dick Petrik was at home caring for his children after school when he saw the storm destroy a line of houses across the street from his own. After making sure his family was safe, Petrik made his way to the studio to begin broadcasting emergency information. He noticed that the teletype wire had just printed a tornado warning for the area—long after the storm had passed. Shortly after he arrived at the studio, the phone line carrying the KOEL signal to the transmitter went dead. He quickly went to the transmitter site and began a weeklong vigil, broadcasting emergency announcements and information in the aftermath of the devastating storm.

Phone lines were out all across Oelwein for several days, and a network of citizens' band radios was used to get information to Petrik. One CB operator would forward information to another, who would pass the message along through a chain of CB operators until it ultimately reached someone who would take the note down for Petrik to read on the air. Thousands of announcements about cleanup efforts, locating lost persons, and other matters of vital importance were transmitted on the station in this manner.

For a station that began with shares of stock owned by many local business people, this truly was "community radio" providing a vital public service.

President Eisenhower discussing issues with farmers at WMT's National Corn Picking Contest near Marion in 1958.

Central Iowa's Floods of 1993

The spring and summer of 1993 saw heavy rainfall strike most areas of Iowa. Rivers were beginning to rise, but on July 20, 1993, the foremost thought on the mind of KCCI-TV's Kevin Cooney was the celebrity auto race he was to drive in the next day as part of the Des Moines Grand Prix.

Those at the pre-race dinner, however, learned that the race had been canceled and floodwaters were about to strike the heart of downtown Des Moines. One of the guests at the dinner was Governor Terry Branstad. Once the danger to Iowa's capital city was fully known, Cooney got Branstad to go with him to Channel 8 to tell citizens how the state would respond to the impending crisis. Cooney then took to the streets, spending all night covering the efforts of business owners who were furiously sandbagging on Court Avenue.

Before long, the devastation of the flood was becoming apparent. The city's entire water supply was contaminated by floodwaters, and a power outage knocked the station off the air. But in Cooney's mind, the story continued.

"The only thing to do was just go out and cover the news, because we knew sooner or later we'd be back on the air," he said. Shortly before sunrise, station engineers had figured out a way to send a signal from a live truck to the station's transmitter near Alleman so broadcasting could resume. However, it was the crudest of live remote situations. Tapes were being played from the truck, and there was only one microphone. As primary anchor of the coverage early that Sunday morning, Cooney would interview officials by telephone. At first, he would relay what they told him to the audience, but he quickly realized that if he held the microphone to the earpiece on the phone, the audience could hear the officials directly. "It was literally back to 1950s TV," he said.

Conveying information to the citizens of Iowa's largest city during the greatest natural disaster in its history was no small task. "My

Kevin Cooney

wife (KCCI anchor/reporter Mollie Cooney) and I were sitting out here on the set at seven in the morning telling people how to manually flush their toilets. That is not something I thought I'd ever do," he said, but because the city no longer had running water, it was a vital piece of information to provide to an audience. "Things like that stick with you."

Broadcasters at all of Des Moines' radio and television stations distinguished themselves during the crisis, providing continuous news and emergency information updates. It may well have been one of Des Moines' biggest breaking news stories of the television age, but those covering the floods could not let themselves think about its magnitude.

"You don't really think about it at the time you're covering a big story. I'm not sure you really realize how big it is at the time," Cooney said. "It takes more of a retrospective kind of thing. A day, a week, a month, a year later, you realize the information you were putting out was quite vital."

The Crash of Flight 232 in Sioux City

July 15, 1989 looked like an uneventful day for Sioux City television anchor Dave Nixon. Soon after he arrived at KTIV-TV, however, everyone knew the day would be anything but uneventful.

Shortly after three o'clock that afternoon, the newsroom scanner carried a message that the Sioux City airport would be on alert. United Airlines Flight 232 was experiencing difficulty and was being redirected to Sioux City for an emergency landing. All of News Center 4's available crews were dispatched to the area.

The station began breaking into regular programming almost immediately with updates anchored by Nixon in the newsroom. The veteran anchor had been at KTIV for nine years, leading the station to a top position in the market's ratings. Earlier in his career, he spent more than a decade across town at KCAU-TV 9, which had enjoyed ratings dominance while he was its primary anchor.

In 1989 in Sioux City, there were no "live trucks" to send pictures from the scene as the incident was unfolding. Any images carried on the station had to be videotaped, and shuttled back to the station by courier. Updates were coming in by telephone, with messages relayed to the television audience by Nixon. All of the station's employees pitched in; salespeople staffed the telephones to receive information, while members of the weather staff went to the site to serve as reporters.

It is the job of an anchor in that situation to maintain calm and deliver the information in a clear manner; however, the emotion of the situation often breaks through.

"You try to prepare yourself emotionally for the big story," Nixon recalled in a 2002 interview. "After a while, I noticed I was gripping the news desk with both hands, just trying to rein in my emotions."

One runway was designated as the spot where the plane was to land. Scanner traffic indicated that the landing gear was in place, making a fairly routine landing a distinct possibility; therefore, a station reporter and photographer went to that area, and sent a rookie employee, former intern Dave Boxum, to a remote location by the terminal building to shoot video of the plane landing. Boxum was in his first week on the job as a full-time station employee. He had fixed his camera on a tripod, looking toward the south, the direction from which the plane was expected to come. Soon, however, Boxum saw the plane approaching the airport from the north. He took the camera off its steady tripod, shifted it onto his shoulder, and began videotaping.

What resulted was anything but a routine landing, as Captain Al Haynes and his crew struggled mightily to keep the airplane upright. As the now-famous video shot by Boxum showed, the plane hit the ground, cartwheeled, broke apart, and skidded to its eventual landing in a nearby cornfield, with the passenger area remaining upright. Haynes' actions saved 184 of the people on board, and Boxum's video was seen around the world, the only pictures of the crash landing—first shown on the station's six o'clock newscast that evening.

"It may sound cold, but what was racing through my mind was, 'I hope I white-balanced the camera,'" Boxum recalled in a newspaper interview 10 years after the crash. "I was hoping the tape was rolling."

One of the first images onlookers saw after the plane came to rest was of a hospital helicopter rising out of the smoke to a nearby hospital, indicating there were survivors of the fiery crash. "It became a story of hope, because people had survived," Nixon said. Some reporters on the scene, in fact, initially chastised authorities for keeping the journalists behind a fence but allowing sightseers to wander along the crash site; they quickly found out that those were not sightseers—they were survivors of the plane crash, walking toward the airport from the cornfield.

KTIV's special coverage continued with stories about the heroic actions of the crew and the fate of the passengers the next day. Nixon himself went to the airport after the first day of coverage, and found the smell and sight of the debris a traumatic experience. Boxum did not think about the event for many months, but around the time of the first anniversary of the crash, the magnitude of what he had seen began to sink in. "When I was videotaping, I was literally watching people die," he said.

In all the excitement of the breaking story, one phone call from a viewer led to a bit of comic relief that eased the tension somewhat when the plane was still in the air. The viewer had noticed that Nixon—who was anchoring from the newsroom in shirtsleeves, rather than wearing a suit coat—had a small tear along the shoulder seam of his shirt. "Get that hick off the air," the caller said. "He's got a tear in his shirt and somebody in Chicago or New York is going to see this and think we're a bunch of hicks."

But no one in Chicago or New York who saw the coverage produced by KTIV's news team that day, operating as a small station with limited resources, saw it as anything but extraordinary.

A Presidential Press Conference

For the past 30 years, Iowans have become used to presidential candidates crossing the state looking for votes in Iowa's first-in-the-nation presidential precinct caucuses. But the opportunity to interview or ask questions of presidents was not always as common.

The National Association of Broadcasters convention was being held in Dallas during the spring of 1974. As part of the program, President Richard Nixon had agreed to hold a news conference in an auditorium there, with a group of journalists from around the country invited to attend and ask questions. KWWL-TV vice president of news Grant Price took advantage of the opportunity—it was the only presidential press conference he ever attended in his remarkable career, spanning six decades in the field—and the question he asked made headlines.

In the early 1970s, the "fence-row-to-fence-row" policies of Nixon's agriculture department, under the stewardship of Agriculture Secretary Earl Butz, were beginning to cause problems for farmers in Iowa, particularly cattle feeders. When Price asked Nixon how the government was prepared to respond to the crisis, Nixon began with a rather confrontational answer, saying "Farmers never had it so good."

"As he started to work his way through it, he realized he probably had stepped right in it," Price recalled. Nixon attempted to back away from his original statement, but the "farmers never had it so good" remark was carried in a front page banner headline in the next day's edition of the *Des Moines Register.*

Nixon's response to Price's question might have drawn more national attention if it hadn't been for an exchange between CBS News correspondent Dan Rather and Nixon at the same news conference. It was at the height of the Watergate crisis, and after Rather asked a tough question on the subject, some in the audience began to applaud. Nixon, hoping to deflect attention from the question, asked Rather, "Are you running for something?" Rather quickly replied, "No, sir, are you?" The exchange remains a part of the lore of both men.

As far as Iowans were concerned, however, the "farmers never had it so good" remark spoke volumes about the attitude then prevailing in Washington about life on the farm in the Midwest, an attitude that soon led to the formation of groups like the American Agriculture Movement and the tractorcade march on Washington.

The Visit of Pope John Paul II

In the late 1970s, Roman Catholics around the world demonstrated renewed enthusiasm thanks to the leadership of a new, young pope. When Pope John Paul II announced he would tour America, the events took on the aura of stadium rock concerts.

On October 4, 1979, the pope visited Iowa. Iowa's broadcasters were responsible for providing the sounds and images for a worldwide audience and they utilized the newest technology to carry out the job.

Dave Nixon was then the primary anchor for WHO-TV 13 in Des Moines. He successfully lobbied his news director to provide extensive coverage of the papal visit. The station was allowed to send a reporter and photographer to accompany the pope's entourage for four days leading up to the Iowa visit, through appearances in Boston, New York, and Philadelphia. Nixon and his photographer filed reports from the East Coast back to Des Moines, setting the stage for the pope's visit to the heartland.

As a result, Nixon and his photographer, along with an Iowa priest, were included in the pope's official party and were taken by helicopter to Living History Farms, the site of the pope's public appearance before hundreds of thousands. Nixon anchored WHO-TV's live coverage for several hours, with the glorious Iowa autumn on display for the whole world to see.

Des Moines Bishop Maurice Dingman with KRNT's Paul Rhoades during coverage of Pope John Paul II's visit to Iowa on October 4, 1979.

Across town, Paul Rhoades recalls KCCI-TV also having cameras at all the vantage points, shooting many cassettes of videotape, and utilizing a variety of methods for getting the tape back to the station, including helicopters. The live microwave vans and remote satellite trucks, commonplace today, would have changed all that, and made delivery of the images to the audience much easier.

But at the time, those pictures were possible only because of the efforts made by Iowa Public Television, which early on became a state leader in satellite technology. The network's state-of-the-art equipment enabled transmission of the pope's mass to stations around Iowa and the world. Even today, a quarter century later, IPTV's facilities are still utilized by the major broadcast and cable networks when they originate their coverage of events from Des Moines.

Professional Organizations

Iowa's news broadcasters have played a disproportionately large role in regional and national organizations, serving as leaders far more frequently than their brethren from many other, more populous states.

In 1946, a group of broadcasters decided they could improve their work by sharing ideas and information with colleagues from around the country. The National Association of Radio News Directors was formed as a grass-roots organization to help set standards of newsgathering and reporting. The organization, now known as RTNDA, the Radio-Television News Directors Association, is the world's only professional organization exclusively serving electronic newsgathering, with more than 3,000 professional and student members.

Among the 68 broadcasters in attendance at the first RTNDA convention in Cleveland in 1946 were four from Iowa: R. E. "Dick" Burris from KSO, Des Moines; Charles D. Hilton from KGLO, Mason City; Bob Redeen from WOC, Davenport; and Jack Shelley from WHO, Des Moines.

Three years later, the organization asked a University of Iowa professor, Dr. Arthur Barnes, to edit the group's monthly publication. Barnes turned the publication over to his colleague Ernest F. "Joe" Andrews in 1955; Andrews edited the publication until 1970 when RTNDA decided to hire a full-time staff to produce a slicker-looking magazine. Those early ties to the University of Iowa led to the organization deciding to

William Turner

Robert Buckmaster

Keith Kirkpatrick

place its archival materials there in 1962; today, they are located at the University Libraries in Iowa City.

RTNDA has also had a number of leaders with Iowa ties. Among the founders was WHO's Jack Shelley, who served as the organization's third president in 1950. Two years later, Jim Bormann of WCCO in Minneapolis, who was formerly news director at WMT in Cedar Rapids, became president. Shortly after that, in 1955, KRNT's Russ Van Dyke served a term as president. In 1962, former WMT news director Dick Cheverton, then working at WOOD in Grand Rapids, Michigan, held the organization's top post. Not long after that, in 1970, former WMT radio and television reporter Bill Roberts, then the Washington bureau chief for the Time-Life stations, was president. A number of years passed before another person with

ties to Iowa broadcasting headed RTNDA; the 2002 leader of the organization was Dave Busiek of KCCI-TV in Des Moines.

At about the same time, a group of Midwesterners had a similar idea, and in 1948 founded what is now known as the Northwest Broadcast News Association, made up of broadcast journalists in six states: Iowa, Minnesota, North Dakota, South Dakota, Nebraska, and Wisconsin. Jack Shelley was one of the founders of that organization, as well; so was Norm Schrader of WDAY in Fargo, North Dakota, who worked for WSUI radio in Iowa City while a student at the University of Iowa.

A number of broadcasters have served as president of NBNA while working at Iowa stations, including Larry Huegli (KGLO, 1980), Bud Chaldy (KASI, 1977), Gordon Kilgore

(KDTH, 1970), Grant Price (WMT, 1967), Dick Petrik (KOEL, 1963), Jim Schwartz (WOI, 1959), and Dick Cheverton (WMT, 1955). In addition, the organization presents the Mitchell V. Charnley Award, established in 1968 in honor of the noted Iowa State and University of Minnesota broadcast professor. No fewer than seven of the first nine Charnley Award recipients have ties to Iowa and Iowa broadcasting.

Another professional organization with strong ties to Iowa is the National Association of Farm Broadcasters. Older than either RTNDA or NBNA, the NAFB was founded in 1945; attempts to hold an organizing convention earlier were interrupted by World War II. WHO's Herb Plambeck was the second president of NAFB, in 1946. Two years later, in 1948, WMT's Chuck Worcester held the organiza-

Mary Quass

Dave Busiek

tion's top post. The two were among the early inductees into the NAFB's Hall of Fame, which was started in 1986. Plambeck and Worcester were the third and fourth persons inducted, in 1987.

The last person from Iowa to serve as the group's president was Creighton Knau of KMA in Shenandoah, who served in 1983. Others to serve as president included WMT's Bob Nance in 1967, and WHO's Keith Kirkpatrick in 1968.

Within the state, two organizations have strongly supported local broadcasting. The Iowa Broadcasters Association was founded in 1950. The group is made up of member stations "working to promote, protect and enhance free over-the-air broadcasting" and annually holds seminars designed to help all aspects of a station's operation run more effectively, from management to sales, engineering to news. In 1967,

the IBA started a Hall of Fame to honor those who contributed to the growth of broadcasting in Iowa. The most recent inductees bring to 46 the number of persons who have been so honored.

And for more than 40 years, the Iowa Broadcast News Association has focused on helping Iowa's broadcast journalists keep citizens informed about their communities. Since 1972, the organization has annually presented the Jack Shelley Award to an individual who has demonstrated great commitment to the cause of broadcast journalism in Iowa. Shelley, who celebrated his 92th birthday in 2004, has personally presented the award to 32 men and women.

The lists of IBA Hall of Fame winners and IBNA Shelley Award recipients truly read like a "Who's Who" of Iowa broadcasting.

Iowa Broadcasters Association Hall of Fame

2003	Pete Taylor
2003	Sen. Charles Grassley
2003	Ray Johnson
2002	Keith Kirkpatrick
2002	Betty Thomas
2001	Betty Baudler
2000	Peter McLane
1999	Mary Quass
1999	Grant Price
1998	Dean Osmundson
1997	Bob Brooks
1997	Ron Gonder
1996	Forrest "Frosty" Mitchell
1996	Jim Livengood
1995	Don Uker
1994	Jim Zabel
1993	George Carpenter
1993	Dave Steinle
1992	Dale Cowle
1991	Philip Kelly
1990	Bill Sanders
1988	R. J. McElroy
1987	Carl "Andy" Anderson
1986	Paul Olson
1985	E. G. "Red" Faust
1984	Rep. Tom Tauke
1983	Robert H. Harter
1982	Dr. Herbert Strentz
1982	Gov. Robert Ray
1981	Jim Duncan
1980	Jack Shelley
1979	Lew Van Nostrand
1978	Robert Buckmaster
1977	George Dorrington
1976	Herbert Hake
1976	Ralph Olson
1975	Earl May
1975	William Turner
1975	Duane Acker
1974	Roy Carver
1974	Ed Breen
1973	Ben Sanders
1972	Wes Bartlett
1969	Paul Engle
1968	William Quarton
1967	Forest Evashevski

Iowa Broadcast News Association Jack Shelley Award Recipients

2003	Dave Busiek, KCCI
2002	O. Kay Henderson, Radio Iowa
2000	Ron Steele, KWWL
2001	Jim Boyd, WHO and WMT
1999	Kevin Cooney, KCCI
1998	Dick Michels, KSCJ
1997	Dave Nixon, KTIV, KCAU and WHO
1996	J. K. Martin, KBUR/KGRS
1995	Dave Shay, KGAN/WMT
1994	Dennis Sutterer, Radio Iowa
1993	Dale Woolery, KRNT
1992	Ev Hickman, WHO
1991	Dean Navin, KVFD/KUEL
1990	Bill Henry, KBUR/KGRS
1989	Rich Fellingham, KASI/KCCQ
1988	Ned Dermody, KMA
1987	Tim Renshaw, KGLO
1986	Jackie King, KIOA
1985	Paul Rhoades, KCCI
1984	Jim Vogelaar, KIOA
1983	Larry Huegli, KGLO
1982	Cliff Brockman, KCAU
1981	Dan Miller, IPBN
1980	Larry Schmitz, KLEM
1979	Bob Wilbanks, WHO
1978	Bob Bruner, WMT
1977	Russ Van Dyke, KCCI
1976	Bud Chaldy, KASI
1975	Grant Price, KWWL
1974	Gordon Kilgore, KDTH
1973	Jim Bormann, WMT
1972	Dick Petrik, KOEL

A 1960s-era election night broadcast on KRNT, with anchors Don Soliday, Paul Rhoades and Russ Van Dyke. (Note the placement of the Hy-Vee logos on the set, as well as the prominent ash trays.)

Covering Wars

Even if the story was occurring halfway around the world, Iowa's radios and television stations have frequently been there to follow the "Iowa angle" of events.

Radio news came of age during World War II, and no local station in the country had as many fully accredited war correspondents as WHO in Des Moines. No fewer than three members of the WHO staff brought news from the war back home to Midwest listeners.

The first was farm broadcaster Herb Plambeck. Plambeck tried seven different times to enlist in the military during World War II, but due to a spot on his lung, he was rejected each time. Desperate to be of service, he jumped at the chance to be one of only six farm editors in America invited to see London under German fire. His broadcasts from London were aired throughout America. With the help of another correspondent, Walter Cronkite of the United Press, Plambeck became the first Iowan to be fully accredited as a war correspondent.

At the time, the United States military discouraged local radio stations from sending reporters to Europe to cover the war, a situation WHO news director Jack Shelley found discriminatory, since even the smallest local newspaper could easily get a reporter accredited. Finally, in 1944, the military began allowing local radio reporters to cover the war, and Shelley became one of the first to sign up, traveling to Europe in November 1944.

At the time, correspondents were limited to three-month stints overseas, with only one of those months actually being in the field. Shelley chose to take his month in the field right away, a decision that worked to his advantage; the military quickly got caught up in other matters and forgot how long he had been in the field. Finally, on March 1, 1945, the military noticed that he had been there too long and sent him back.

Shelley knew that the network radio correspondents and news-

Dave Nixon (left) with NBC's Tom Brokaw (right) during the 1980 Iowa Caucuses. Both men started their television careers in Sioux City in the 1960s— Nixon at KCAU, Brokaw at KTIV.

papers were giving citizens adequate coverage of the day-by-day events of the war, so he took a different approach. He went to the front lines looking specifically for soldiers from Iowa and adjacent states, collecting lists of names he would then read on the air as part of his regular broadcasts. For many families at home, hearing Shelley read their loved one's name was the only assurance they had that their soldier was still alive.

"That became such an important thing to the families of those kids that we talked to, and we got just deluged with mail at the station, phone calls and so forth, about the references we made to their sons and husbands," Shelley said.

Shelley covered many of the historic events of World War II as one of the few correspondents, local or network, to cover both the European and Pacific Theaters. He reported on the Battle of the Bulge, the dropping of atomic bombs on Japan, and on the final event of the war, the surrender of the Japanese to Gen. Douglas McArthur on the battleship USS Missouri.

For a war correspondent during World War II, getting the story back home was no easy task. Jack Shelley would prepare his script, have it approved by a U.S. government censor, and deliver his report through a military broadcast facility to either New York or San Francisco, which would then pass it along a telephone line to WHO, which would literally cut a phonograph record of the transmission for playback on the air. Because of the rationing of raw materials during the war, the records were made of glass, making them extremely fragile. Some of those rare recordings still exist today in their original form.

Shelley's field equipment was rather crude compared with today's technology. Portable audio tape recorders had not yet been invented. The only way to get a recording in the field was with the use of a bulky wire recorder—a machine that literally recorded voices on a small braid of wire, pulled tightly between the reels. If the delicate wire should break, the strands would unravel and the material would be unusable.

During the time Jack Shelley was stationed on the island of Guam, the first atomic bomb was dropped on Hiroshima in Japan. Within 24 hours, the pilot of the Enola Gay, Colonel Paul Tibbets, was flown to Guam from the air base on Tinian Island for a press conference. "It was the only one of its kind I experienced during the war," Shelley said, as no local government censors

reviewed his copy; rather, special censors in Washington D.C. had to approve every word journalists wrote. Broadcast coverage was limited to scripts read by reporters, rather than hearing the voices of the crew members themselves.

Three days later, another atomic bomb was dropped on the city of Nagasaki, and shortly thereafter, another press conference was held, this one on Tinian Island. Most of the journalists in Guam did not want to make the trip, figuring there would be nothing different from the first press conference. However, Shelley and a radio reporter from Omaha did make the trip. There, they found not only the crew of the plane that dropped the bomb on Nagasaki, but also the crew that had dropped the initial bomb on Hiroshima, along with a number of military officials and scientists. All were available for personal interviews—the only audio of those crews broadcast at that point.

Shelley interviewed eight people, including one of the scientists who, as it turned out, had been a classmate of his at the University of Missouri. He flew back to Guam and went to the armed forces radio facility to have his interviews transmitted to RCA in San Francisco, where they would in turn be relayed to WHO in Des Moines.

"So WHO is sitting there waiting for this, and I'm sitting there waiting for the wire recording. Pretty soon, the technician comes out looking crestfallen and says, 'Jack, the wire broke. I'm afraid we've lost all of it.' And I was about ready to kill him, or myself," Shelley remembered in a 2002 interview. "We looked at it, and it was all frazzled up at the front end, as they always did when the wire broke. Finally, I said, 'Well, there's nothing else to do. Let's just chop off the front end and see what's left.' I was so glad that I had done a lot of talking in advance setting the scene and so forth before I actually started questioning. I don't believe I missed anything Tibbets had to say."

"The only thing we missed was a bunch of hot air from old Jack Shelley," he said.

B - 29 BASE
GUAM, JULY, 1945

WHO's Jack Shelley interviewing U.S. servicemen in Guam.

Ron Steele

provided the hard news details of the event, Shelley had intended to do a "color" report with his impressions of the scene.

Shelley was able to move up to second in line when the reporter for the Armed Forces Radio Network found that his wire recording had broken, leaving him with a tangled snarl of wire and luck much worse than Jack Shelley had with his Tinian Island interviews. To this day, Shelley does not know if the frantic young reporter ever recovered enough recorded wire to broadcast to his audience.

The involvement of broadcasters in covering wars and conflicts continued in the television age. WQAD-TV anchor Jim King traveled to Vietnam to bring Quad Cities viewers a firsthand look at the conflict as it was drawing to its conclusion. Nearly a quarter-century later, KWWL-TV's Ron Steele went to the American military facility in Saudi Arabia after the Iraqi occupation of Kuwait in 1991. In fact, as Steele and reporter Joel Dickman sat on a plane ready to return home, their flight was canceled when Saudi airspace was suddenly closed to all civilian and commercial air traffic. They quickly found out that the "liberation of Kuwait" was underway by American military forces, and they were able to report live via satellite from the scene for several more days.

"For me to be in Saudi Arabia doing a live telecast, interviewing the parents in New Hampton of the teacher we're interviewing in Saudi Arabia, that was really great for a station our size," Steele said. "I think we're pretty proud of that, and I'm really happy to be able to do things like that—even though we are in Iowa, considered to be a small population state where we don't get the kind of respect I think as journalists that we often deserve."

That respect may be lacking from some who live elsewhere, but the Iowa audience has been fortunate since the beginning to experience some of the best broadcast journalism found anywhere.

Soon after, when Shelley covered the surrender of the Japanese, a wire recording again played a major factor. He was chosen by lot to be the third person to feed his story back to the United States, after the commercial network pool reporter and the Armed Forces Radio Network reporter. Since the networks would have

Staff members manually change vote totals during WHO-TV's election coverage in 1974.

> "Any manager of a broadcast station that doesn't realize it isn't going to be very successful. You've got to be part of the community, way up to the hilt—and that sometimes is the difference between success and also ran stations."

Longtime WMT manager William B. Quarton, during an interview for the Iowa Broadcasting Oral History Project in 1994.

13 Giving Something Back To The Community

Broadcasters are licensed to "act in the public interest, convenience and necessity," according to the legislation which established the American system of broadcasting. Recently, the National Association of Broadcasters adopted a campaign to promote this side of broadcasting, called "Broadcasters: Bringing Community Service Home."

A 1928 promotional brochure for WMT, then located in Waterloo, noted that, "It is but natural that such a newspaper as the *Waterloo Morning Tribune*, with its news-gathering and dispensing organization—with its necessarily constant contact with national and local activities—with its wide variety of available talent—with the intimate personal acquaintance of its readers, their families and friends, should operate our radio station that becomes a part of the life of the community it serves and renders a constructive broadcasting service far above the average offered."

While the term "community service" is, to a large extent, in the eye of the beholder, Iowa's broadcasters have traditionally shown that they take their responsibilities seriously.

"Every broadcaster—whether in radio, television or cable—feels a great responsibility to plow back, to help the community," veteran radio and television personality Bill Riley said. "I've always felt that."

"I got a great deal of satisfaction for doing things to help people that make it possible for the small towns to succeed, to offer the kind of services that the public really needs. I've only been able to do that because I had the media to use," said George Allen, who owned and operated KLGA radio in Algona for 30 years, purchasing the station in 1961.

During an unusually harsh winter in 1961-1962, the snow was piled so high at intersections on Algona streets that it was difficult for cars to see each other around the snow mounds. Allen's wife bought red cloth and cut it into 3-foot by 6-inch strips. The station handed them out to area merchants, telling the merchants to give the strips of cloth out for free to any persons who came in asking for them. Then the station promoted their use on the air as a way to enhance safety. Listeners were instructed to pick up the free cloth and tie it to the radio antennas on their cars, allowing them to more easily be seen over the large snow piles.

The merchants quickly ran out of the makeshift safety devices; Allen said this proved to a sometimes skeptical business community that his station was, in fact, reaching its intended audience.

"Instead of running a radio station, you become a community asset. And when you become a community asset, that's when you start being a successful broadcaster," Allen said.

The tradition of service dates back to the earliest days of radio in Iowa. At the dedication of a new 50,000-watt transmitter for WHO in 1933, station owner B. J. Palmer recounted for the audience his goals for the station.

"As long as we have served Iowa, it has been our desire to have this Iowa station known as one that served Iowa for community good. Although privately owned, from the beginning, this company has always taken the position that IT BELONGS TO IOWA; THAT IT IS TO BE USED FOR IOWA'S GOOD, TO BETTER SERVE IOWA INTERESTS," Palmer's script read. "One of the first policies your speaker established when he went on the radio air was that it had to go on with a constructive intent, and had to go on right. That policy has been consistently and conscientiously maintained as the fundamental right for our existence on the air."

KICD's Ben Sanders (left) and Mason Dixon (right) during one of the station's annual "Polio Derby" events to raise money for the March of Dimes.

Those serving in World War II were treated to free cigarettes, courtesy of Clinton radio station KROS and its listeners.

Those stations with a large signal, such as WHO, have the ability to mobilize large numbers of people to action. A few examples from the 1940s are representative of the power of broadcasting.

Following a 1947 flood that ravaged parts of southern Iowa, the station raised nearly $100,000 for flood victims. During World War II, WHO sold war bonds with an aggregate value of $6.1 million. Sales were made to more than 25,000 investors in 46 of the then-48 United States, plus the District of Columbia and three territories. In addition, more than a quarter million packages containing relief items were collected by the station and shipped to those struggling in war-torn Europe.

Some stations supported the war effort in other, more unique ways. KROS in Clinton actually sponsored a program to send cigarettes to servicemen overseas. "Smokes for Servicemen" aired weekdays at 5 p.m., some 20 years before the Surgeon General's first warning about the hazards of smoking and 30 years before the Congressional ban on broadcast advertising of cigarettes.

"Station KROS will send Free Smokes to your favorite soldier, sailor or marine," the promotional poster featuring an image of Uncle Sam read. "Awarded to local men in the service and mailed to them anywhere in the world!"

Even those who originally got into broadcasting as a way to market their products helped out when listeners were in need.

During the Depression, Earl May went on the KMA airwaves to assist farmers who were having cash flow problems during the bank closures. May told farmers to order their seed for the year, even if they didn't have the money; he would agree to hold their checks until the banks reopened. It was a risky gamble. $50,000 in orders came in, but ultimately, more than 98 percent of those checks were good.

During the later national effort to stop polio, many stations were involved in efforts to support the March of Dimes. In Spencer, KICD owner Ben Sanders—himself a polio victim at age 17—and announcer Mason Dixon annually held a "Radio Derby" in the early 1950s to raise money for the cause. The two "old-timers," as they termed themselves, once walked from Spencer to Spirit Lake in the dead of winter to raise funds. In the later 1950s, they sponsored "tractor drives," covering up to 400 miles at a time—and in the process, annually raising $25,000 or more from northwest Iowa listeners in a 24 hour period.

"That's part of it. Serving the public interest to me is a necessity," Sanders said in a 1992 interview, 10 years before his death.

The CBS network encouraged its affiliated stations to raise money for the March of Dimes in 1949. WMT in Cedar Rapids outdid 166 other CBS stations, raising a total of $12,598 that year. The station's activities continued until 1953, climaxing when sports director Tait Cummins tried to match his weight in dimes.

A total of $3,360 was raised—more than six times Cummins' weight in dimes.

Cummins and his wife Dotty were also well known for their efforts on behalf of Camp Courageous near Monticello, a facility for the physically or mentally challenged. They were asked to be temporary and honorary fundraising chairs for the camp when it was founded in 1972; Tait served in that role until his death in 1984, while Dotty continued her association with the camp until her death in 1997. With the strong support of the WMT stations, the facility now serves more than 4,400 children each year.

Another sports broadcaster, KFJB's Dale Smith, sought in 1957 to raise $1,230—in recognition of KFJB's 1230 kHz frequency—for the March of Dimes by collecting pledges to walk a circuitous route from State Center to Marshalltown, through Rhodes and Melbourne—24 miles in all. Smith collected pledges in advance, as well as donations from motorists he came across along the way. By the time all the pledges were counted, Smith had raised more than three times the goal—$4,000.25—despite the coldest temperatures of the winter occurring on the day of the walk.

"The station had a philosophy all the way along, as long as I was associated with it, of becoming involved in community activities. Anything that came along which the station could embellish or become a part of, that was certainly the philosophy," said Al Schrock, who spent more than 40 years at KFJB radio in Marshalltown. Schrock credits Bill White, who served as station manager for 30 years from 1949 to 1979, as setting the tone for the station's active community involvement.

Dale Smith's wintry walk was not the only effort KFJB made to help the March of Dimes. Schrock recalled other station fund-raising activities in the immediate post-World War II period. "All the staff came in, usually during a blizzard, and made ourselves available for any type of talent request a listener might phone in—with a pledge, of course, for the March of Dimes. We sang, we read poetry,

Al Schrock

we did all manner of things," Schrock said.

"The reality is you have to be focused on what you're trying to do. You have to be passionate about what you're trying to do, what you want to do. You have to super serve your listeners, your clients, your prospects. These are the kinds of things that make for success in local radio, and really in most businesses," said Eliot Keller, who was one of the founders of Iowa City station KRNA-FM in the early 1970s, and currently is president of KZIA-FM in Cedar Rapids.

Many station owners and managers not only support community events, they expect their employees to do the same. Sioux City broadcast executive Bill Turner, who played a key role in both Iowa and national broadcasting organizations, believed that a station's

The March of Dimes often benefited from the efforts of Iowa radio stations. Here WMT's Tait Cummins (far right) celebrates raising more than his weight in dimes for the charity.

success was closely tied to its involvement in the community. "He was so adamant about all of us being involved in our community that once a month, we would turn in a report—those of us that were on the air or production or whatever you did—to show what you had done in the community," Dave Nixon recalled of Turner, who managed both KCAU-TV and KTIV-TV during his long career. Many broadcasters agree with this philosophy.

"I don't see how one could be a really good journalist or an asset to his organization or to the state or the nation if he isn't involved, first of all, in the community," the late WHO farm broadcaster Herb Plambeck said in a 1985 interview. "I see no way that you can really be a real contributor if you just keep talking and don't do some giving."

Much of a station's community service efforts focus on programming. Some of the best-known public service programming on KWWL radio was Ed Falk's "School of the Air," which featured Waterloo area schools in special presentations, often from the

classroom. It was a unique concept that won national acclaim, including second-place in Billboard magazine's 1948 local program competition.

In the early 1960s, KTIV-TV in Sioux City produced "Fund 4 All," a quiz program hosted by longtime radio and television personality Don Stone, where local citizens appeared as panelists to raise money for local charities. KWWL-TV in Waterloo aired "Community Quiz" during the 1970s, a competition for high school students with prize money going to support local school efforts.

And when a community is facing a crisis, such as a natural disaster, it is the role of local broadcasters to provide the information needed by citizens.

In 1965, the city of Clinton fought a disastrous Mississippi River flood, but aggressive efforts by volunteers succeeded in keeping water out of the downtown area. Hank Dihlman, who spent 40 years at KROS before retiring in 1986, said the station did nothing but cover the flood 24 hours a day for three weeks.

"The downtown area basically was protected with a temporary dike," he said. "We would put out a call that, for example, there was a problem in one section, and within ten minutes there would be 40 or 50 people there filling sandbags and piling them into place where they had to be. I've always thought it was one of the greatest examples of cooperation that this city has seen."

During the record flooding in central Iowa in 1993 and eastern Iowa in 1999, radio and television stations pre-empted regular programming to provide numerous updates and bulletins for citizens. And during the terrorist attacks on America on September 11, 2001, Iowa's broadcasters complemented national reports with information local communities needed at that time of crisis.

"Usually when there is a disaster in a community, you begin to see radio at its best, TV at its best, because it responds to that. And I hope that the people who are involved in broadcasting in the future will be the kind of people who can understand the positive impact, the force for good, that radio can have and can be," KZIA's Eliot Keller added.

Law enforcement authorities have long counted on broadcasters to help when needed. Within the first few weeks they were on the air in 1922, both WOC and WMT assisted local police in their areas find stolen vehicles by broadcasting the license number, make and model of the missing cars.

The July 3, 1922, program guide for "The Palmer School of Chiropractic Radiophone Studio," broadcasting on radio station WOC, quotes an article from the *Davenport Democrat and Leader* newspaper from June 18, 1922, as follows:

Radio, to catch criminals, is a new law-enforcing weapon put into the hands of the Davenport police department today by B. J. Palmer, who had donated to the city the use of his powerful wireless station at any time the police may call for help...No matter what business it is transacting, The P.S.C. radio will stop and broadcast the crime warning whenever the Davenport police chief calls for this service.

Much of a station's community service programming, however, is able to take a more proactive role in examining local issues of importance. KWWL-TV pre-empted entire evenings of network programming on a number of occasions in the 1980s to present "town meeting" programs focusing on topics such the collapse of the farm economy, education, and politics. The station did a two-hour program on the growing problem of AIDS in Iowa in 1986—long before national attention was focused on the effects of the deadly disease.

"We took a great deal of satisfaction from that. This is the kind of work that television does very well, and it's a great privilege to be able to do it at a local station," said Grant Price, who served as KWWL's vice president for news and public affairs from 1972-1989.

The station was also well known for its "Iowa Illustrated" magazine programs which aired in primetime in the 1970s and 1980s.

Often, Iowa's broadcasters serve when called upon for specific needs in the community. For example, in the mid-1970s, the co-owner of KLEM radio in Le Mars, Paul Olson, co-chaired a "medical manpower committee" to recruit doctors to the northwest Iowa city. Olson cleared the station's log on Saturday, January 24, 1976, for a 12-hour-long radioathon, hoping to raise $20,000 for the effort. In fact, area residents contributed more than $65,000.

Marshalltown radio station KFJB's buy/sell/trade program "Help Your Neighbor" once offered to trade a simple piece of string to a listener, in exchange for something of greater value. As longtime program host Al Schrock recalls, the string was traded for something, which was then traded on the air to a listener for something else, and so on, upping the ante until finally a refrigerator was received. The appliance was then donated to a local charity by the station.

"Things were much simpler at that time. We were not as sophisticated as we are today," Schrock said. "Little things did entertain, and people seemed to respond to that type of thing more than I'm sure they would today. It takes a little more stimulus to get them moving today."

Community service of a different type was practiced by KCCQ-FM in Ames in the fall of 1991. Prior to the start of the academic year, the Iowa State University music department determined it did not have enough money to pay someone to play the carillon in the college's famous campanile. When the school year began, the bells were silent, except for hourly chimes, ending a 93-year tradition.

KCCQ morning disc jockey Kenn McCloud decided to take matters into his own hands, and locked himself in the facility, pledging to stay as long as it took to raise $10,000 to make sure the carillon would again be heard across the Ames campus. Almost five full days later, the "Bucks for Bells" fundraising effort had reached its goal, the disc jockey was "freed" from the

WMT-TV aired one of the first "telethons" in the country, produced in early 1954 to benefit Cerebral Palsy; more recently, the station has annually aired the Muscular Dystrophy Association Labor Day Telethon for the past three decades. Barry Norris hosted the telethon for more than 20 years. Norris is pictured here (left) with Ron Michaelson (right) during one of the first MDA telethons in the early 1970s.

campanile, and music was again heard on campus. Ultimately, $13,000 was raised by the radio station, and a special carillon concert was held the next Sunday, dedicated to McCloud.

The role of Iowa broadcasters in raising awareness of—and funds for—local causes continues to be significant. During the 1980s and 1990s, KIOA's legendary disc jockey Dic Youngs hosted annual 50-hour radioathons to benefit the Variety Club of Iowa. And for the past quarter-century, a number of Iowa television stations, including WOI in Ames/Des Moines and KCRG in Cedar Rapids, have produced telethons each year in support of the Variety Club.

The University of Iowa Hospitals and Clinics benefits from the participation of Iowa television stations in the annual Children's Miracle Network Telethon, which is broadcast nationally. Several Iowa television stations have also been heavily involved with the country's best known telethon—the Jerry Lewis Labor Day Telethon on behalf of the Muscular Dystrophy Association. Stations including WMT/KGAN in Cedar Rapids, KRNT/KCCI in Des Moines, and WQAD in the Quad Cities were part of Lewis' "Love Network" for parts of four decades. The stations forego nearly a full day of regular programming and advertising dollars in favor of putting these telethons on the air.

KFJB was also known for live radio broadcasts of a variety of parades around central Iowa, from events such as the Rose Festival in State Center to the Corn Carnival in Gladbrook. "I have done literally dozens if not hundreds of parades over my lifetime," Al Schrock said. "I hope the listeners enjoyed it. It seems a little trite now to consider that we did that."

"Apparently they were accepted, because we had no trouble sponsoring them," he added.

On one memorable occasion in the early 1980s, Schrock prepared to broadcast the Corn Carnival parade on KFJB-AM when he discovered he could not use the mobile unit as planned because the station was using the two-way communication system to broadcast a baseball game on KFJB's FM station. Undaunted, he pulled the station vehicle into the driveway of a house along the parade route. He asked the homeowners, who were sitting on their porch waiting for the parade, if he could use their phone. They agreed—so Schrock pulled out a pocket knife, unscrewed the phone wires from the wall in the kitchen, and attached a makeshift microphone to bare wires, running the cable back to the station vehicle.

"(The homeowner) was a delightful person, and he accepted the whole procedure with a smile," Schrock remembered. Such resourcefulness was necessary in order to properly serve the listening public.

"It all goes back to the spontaneity and the individuals we had then," he said. "That's the way they thought; that's the way we did things. We didn't think twice, we just did it."

The times may be different today, but responding to the call to serve continues. For example, in the early fall of 2002, Iowa's broadcasters joined with state officials as part of the new Amber Alert Task Force, a voluntary partnership between law-enforcement agencies and local broadcasters to alert the public of child abduction cases. And each year during the holiday season, many radio and television stations partner with local agencies for a food drive. Often this is in conjunction with agencies such as the Salvation Army or the local National Guard; these "Combat Hunger" events annually result in truckloads of food being distributed to needy persons in local communities.

Sometimes, however, it is the seemingly little services, like community calendar programs or lost pet reports, that mean the most—both to listeners and broadcasters.

"I have got a lot of awards," long time broadcaster Frosty Mitchell said, "but I have also got memories of little kids on the phone calling me at KGRN in Grinnell, Iowa, to say, 'Thank you for finding my puppy.' I wouldn't trade that for all those plaques, all those awards."

Collins Radio and Iowa Broadcasting

Like many teenagers in the 1920s, 15-year-old Arthur Collins of Cedar Rapids was fascinated with the new technology of radio. He even had a small radio station on the third floor of the family residence.

Soon after, the young Collins began experiments, particularly in the use of shortwave radio wave lengths. In the mid-1920s, Collins was one of a small group who took a portable transmission outfit to the Pacific Coast, conducting radio experiments in connection with the U.S. Naval Observatory .

One of Iowa's most successful businesses got its storybook start in the basement of a building in downtown Cedar Rapids in 1932. The Collins Radio Company quickly became a producer of broadcast station equipment, as well as radio communication equipment for military and commercial ground stations and airborne applications. Its impact on Iowa broadcasting cannot be understated.

When WMT returned to Cedar Rapids in 1935, Art Collins himself installed what became known as "Collins AM Transmitter No. 1" for the station. It was WMT's first professionally manufactured transmitter; the station previously used a "composite transmitter," a homemade one assembled by station engineers. It was also Collins' first radio transmitter, hence the serial number "1."

For the station's new studios in the Paramount Building, WMT also bought two new audio consoles from Collins. Engineers across the country respected the company's attention to detail and quality. "Art never built anything that wasn't 100 percent," said Ross Wilson, who served as an engineer with the WMT stations for more than 40 years and was there when "Collins No. 1" was installed. "Art was a real gentleman and a real genius in electronics," he added. Collins was also responsible for the first "auto tune" buttons on radios, allowing listeners to preset stations to which they could return with the simple press of a button.

The predecessor of WMT, WJAM, went on the air in 1922 as the first station in Cedar Rapids, funded in large part by the *Cedar Rapids Evening Gazette*. The newspaper soon got out of the broadcasting business, but later returned with the establishment of KCRK-FM and KCRG-AM a quarter century later. With equipment from the Collins Radio Company, KCRK became one of the first FM stations on the air in eastern Iowa, and in fact went on the air a few weeks before the AM station, in late 1947.

Two large studios were constructed on the second floor of the Miller Building on the corner of First Avenue and First Street Southwest in Cedar Rapids. The studios provided space for live audiences, which were utilized during regular audience participation programs. The KCRK/KCRG studios were state-of-the-art, used by Collins Radio as a model

Art Collins

to show visitors and prospective customers.

Collins Radio also outfitted another new eastern Iowa radio station that year. KWWL purchased studio equipment—including a console, turntables, microphones, and tape recorders—as well as a 187-foot tower, for $12,000. With that, and a used transmitter, the station went on the air on November 4, 1947.

By the late 1950s, Collins Radio was developing new radar technologies for use in aircraft. The radar was placed in the nose of planes to help pilots avoid storms. Collins wondered if the same technology might be used in a ground-based system, to assist in weather forecasting. He wanted to test his theory, and turned to the broadcasters across the street from his headquarters.

WMT joined with Collins for the installation of the second such television radar system in the country—the first located west of Chicago—to be used by station meteorologist

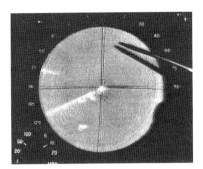

The WP-101 radar used by WMT.

Conrad Johnson. The WP-101 radar had a five-inch screen, and when Johnson wanted to show viewers what was happening, a camera would simply zoom in on his small radar screen. While it may look primitive next to the Doppler radar of today, it quickly proved its accuracy.

Two weeks after the radar was installed, Johnson was learning its many applications. One day, he saw an "echo" on the radar screen near the town of Belmond, at the extreme outer edge of the radar's scope. "I knew at that distance if I could see anything, it had to be tough; it had to be a severe storm," Johnson recalled in an interview more than 25 years later. Soon, reports indicated that a tornado had struck the small Iowa town. "That gave me a lot of confidence in that radar right there," Johnson said, and he soon began to use the radar as part of his nightly forecasts on television.

But some were apprehensive about the new technology, which was mounted on a base outside the station, pointed to the sky. "We were afraid that if it got tilted down, we'd be microwaved or fried," former WMT-TV anchor Henry Lippold remembered. But Lippold added that the radar was so reliable, the news department would send a reporter and photographer to a location once Johnson saw a "hook echo" on the radar, without waiting for reports from the scene—they knew a dangerous storm would be in progress there.

That first Collins radar was not only accurate, but was durable, as well. The estimated life of the radar was 5,000 service hours. By the time Conrad Johnson retired from WMT in 1980, the radar had already logged 120,000 hours of service, and was still being used by the station in the mid-1990s.

The importance of a transmitter—and a friend in the business—was made clear to Ben Sanders when fire destroyed KICD radio in Spencer in the early morning hours of Easter Sunday, 1949.

When Sanders arrived at the station in the middle of the night, the building was "a living torch," but the still-new station owner vowed to be back on the air within 24 hours. Sitting at a card table in the station driveway, Sanders began calling all around the country to get equipment and rebuild the station, even while the fire was still burning.

One of those calls was to Art Collins. Sanders told Collins he needed a new 250-watt transmitter

The KCRG/KCRK transmitter installed by Collins Radio in 1947.

to replace the one lost in the fire. Collins called Sanders back a short time later and said he would give him a transmitter; Collins said another station was expecting it, but given the circumstances, the other station would have to wait.

Thanks to Collins' actions, KICD returned to the air at 6 o'clock Monday morning—missing only one day of broadcasting despite the entire facility burning to the ground. The on-air announcer began simply by saying, "Good morning, Friends—You didn't expect us, but here we are."

Doing the unexpected and meeting challenges, whether in the heat of wartime or in the race to discover new technology, was what the communications world—and Iowa broadcasters—came to expect from Art Collins and the radio company he started in Cedar Rapids nearly 75 years ago.

"The power of television still scares me."

Longtime WMT manager William B. Quarton, during an
interview for the Iowa Broadcasting Oral History Project in 1994.

14 | A Look Toward The Future

The changes that have occurred in broadcasting's first century
have been swift and constant. New technological advances occur
daily, and the ever-increasing consolidation of stations into the
hands of fewer and fewer absentee owners presents new challenges
as the 21st century begins.

"I don't suppose anybody who was born in recent years will
even understand how much our radio and television news for a
long, long period of time was channeled to us by a relatively
small number of information outlets, particularly when it came
to the national networks, which were by and large very responsible
news operations," Jack Shelley said. "They were attempting to
play it right down the middle, not slanting the news in one way
or another, not consciously representing one cause or another.
They had a degree of trust that I find no longer in effect to anything like the same degree.

"One of the reasons is simply that we have so many people
who call themselves journalists, or the equivalent of it today,
practicing some kind of information dispensing and doing it in
many cases without the slightest thought about ethics or credibility,
and I believe this has produced a much, much more nervous
feeling on the part of the general public, of whom to believe and
what sources to trust. That bothers me," Shelley said.

In many ways, the best way to adapt to change is to examine
how those who came through an earlier time handled similar
changes. Many of the current leading broadcast journalists in
Iowa credit those who came before them with establishing a
framework they still closely follow today.

"Under Grant Price, if it moved, we covered it. If it didn't move,
we covered it. We covered everything possible in that community,"

KWWL's Ron Steele said of the man who spent nearly 50 years in
radio and television news in Waterloo and Cedar Rapids.

Veteran journalist Cliff Brockman, whose 30-year career includes
extensive experience in both radio and television, agrees that
broadcasters need to focus on their home areas. "(Local news) is
still the one thing we can provide that people can't get anywhere
else. We can provide the news of their community," Brockman
said, also noting that while local stations air commercials in order
to generate revenue, those commercials from area businesses also
provide a service to the local audience.

The most noted broadcast journalist in Iowa history, Shelley
left WHO after 30 years to begin a teaching career at Iowa State
University. He trained many of today's successful broadcasters. "I
learned more from Jack Shelley than anyone else in this business,
when it comes to really knowing what television news was all
about and understanding how it worked. It's not just throwing
up a camera and a microphone and asking people what they
think; it's knowing the questions to ask, it's being prepared,"
KCCI's Kevin Cooney said.

"I have always felt that we do still probably overemphasize in
some respects the value of the picture. I still think writing is
tremendously important in television journalism, as well as
radio news," Shelley said.

Another broadcaster-turned-educator is Henry Lippold, who
was a late-night news anchor at WMT-TV in the late 1950s before
becoming a distinguished professor of broadcast journalism at
the University of Illinois and the University of Wisconsin-Eau
Claire. Lippold spent more than 40 years in the classroom, and
sees many differences between the broadcast journalism of the

"Satellite farms" have sprouted outside most of today's radio and television stations in order to take advantage of the most current technology.

The author (far right) commenting on the 2004 presidential election for KWWL-TV with anchors Ann Kerian and Ron Steele.

past and that of the present.

"Underlying it all was the fact that we were going for the news, the information, and that I think was historically stronger than it is now," Lippold said shortly after his retirement from teaching in 2001. "We liked to get the news, get it prepared, and get it on right away. We didn't like to sit on it, we didn't tease it, we just put it on." Of course, there were not as many channels then to divert people's attention as is the case today, which some say necessitates change in the presentation of news on television.

One of the greatest changes in television news has been the role of consultants—those who do research and advise stations around the country on how to better present the television news product. The most noted television research and consulting company was founded in Marion, Iowa, in 1957 by former University of Iowa sociology professor Frank Magid. Magid's firm grew, ultimately

staffing offices in New York, Los Angeles, and London—but Marion is still the firm's headquarters.

Some broadcasters view the role of consultants with some concern. When Jack Shelley left WHO in 1965, he could already see the impact consultants would have on the television news product.

"It boiled down in many respects to an attempt to, in my mind, trivialize news and appeal to, if not the sensational, certainly that which was designed to get the most attention, rather than that which was the most efficient and credible information conveyor. And I was worried about that," he said.

"I think anybody in the business has mixed emotions about the role that consultants play—whether they play too much of a role, whether they've become too influential," former WOC-TV anchor Don Rhyne said in a 1985 interview. "I think we weigh what the consultant tells us, and mix that in with our local knowledge of the market, and come up with some kind of accommodation. The very valuable service that they perform is they do a great deal of research and they tell us what the viewers want to see and how we can best serve the community."

It is not easy to constantly be the bearer of bad news, and most of what journalists cover can be termed "bad news." Why continue in a field with notoriously poor pay and long hours?

"It was such a love of my life, the radio and television business. I've always said that if there were some way that I could get some amount of food and a place to live and everything, I'd work for nothing because I loved it so much," the late WMT broadcaster Bob Bruner once said.

"It's new every day," Kevin Cooney said. "It's one of the reasons it makes it a joy to come to work every single day." Another student of Jack Shelley, Cliff Brockman, agreed. "I think it's the opportunity to learn something new every day. It's just always exciting because you never know what's going to happen," Brockman said.

Yet if there is one consistent theme, it is how Iowa's broadcast journalists want to be remembered. Longtime Channel 8 anchor Russ Van Dyke spoke of how he would like to be remembered on January 27, 1983, the day after he announced his retirement after 36 years as a late-news anchor in Des Moines.

"Trustworthy—that the people feel they can depend on what I say. I think integrity is probably the thing I value the most," he said.

Van Dyke's former co-anchor Kevin Cooney, who has anchored both the 6 and 10 p.m. news at KCCI-TV for the past 20 years, has similar thoughts about how he would like to be remembered. "I'd just like them to think, here's a guy who told the story and told it well, and told it so people could understand it," Cooney said.

"When you talk about people like Jack Shelley, Grant Price, Russ Van Dyke, or Dick Petrik, you just think of integrity and that is basically what our business is about. Without the integrity, without the credibility that we have, we have nothing," KWWL-TV's Steele said. "If people do not believe in what we do, we're not going to be in business very long. Those people started what we're doing today."

Like Steele, Brockman would like to be remembered as a journalist who was responsible, honest, and treated subjects fairly.

"We still have to get the story, but we can do that in a certain manner that at least is going to be respectful of those people that we're covering," Brockman said.

"You can say you interviewed famous people, but it still comes down, believe it or not, to the person who is on the street, the average, everyday fellow Iowan from whom we get all our great stories," Steele said.

Today, television programming is rarely produced locally; most stations' local production is limited to the news product, with the remaining broadcast hours filled by either network or syndicated programming. Increasingly, FM radio stations are becoming pre-formatted jukeboxes with music delivered by satellite from far-off locations. Meanwhile, AM radio stations are filled with syndicated news and sports talk programs. Locally produced programming, which was a staple of radio and television stations in Iowa and around the country for decades, has been severely limited.

Despite that, there is still cause for optimism. The local audience appreciates the locally produced programming even more because there is so little of it, which does place greater pressure on broadcasters to live up to the audience's expectations. When major events such as severe weather or breaking news occur in the community, people still turn to their local radio or television stations for information.

And where else can people get the current information important to their daily lives—basic information such as the school hot lunch menu, high school athletic scores, and death notices—than from their hometown radio station?

The audience is still there in great numbers for strong, community-based radio and television stations willing to invest time and effort in serving the local area. There are still great numbers of men and women who love their jobs in broadcasting and work on a daily basis to provide news and entertainment for that audience to the best of their abilities.

Despite the new business pressures in broadcasting, despite those who treat station ownership solely as a business and not as a public trust—in Iowa, at least, the conditions are right to encourage future generations to continue "making waves" in broadcasting, carrying on the long tradition of excellence and high standards.

The Legacy of Quarton and McElroy

They were two men, each working in sales for WMT radio in 1935. Algona native William B. Quarton was sales manager for the station, managed by his brother Sumner. R. J. McElroy was new to the radio sales business, and operated out of the station's offices in Waterloo.

Bill Quarton would later succeed his brother as manager of WMT radio, and build the WMT stations into a dominant force in eastern Iowa broadcasting. "Mac" would parlay his fame as the "Voice of Iowa" into organizing a group of Waterloo businessman to help him found Black Hawk Broadcasting, operators of the KWWL radio and television stations in Waterloo, as well as broadcast properties in other states.

But while the broadcast legacy each man built is significant, perhaps of greater significance are the great numbers of people who have directly benefited as a result of each man's philanthropy.

William B. Quarton

As a young man just out of college in the 1920s, Bill Quarton worked in New York City for Thomas Edison's company. His brother began running the Cowles brothers' Cedar Rapids radio station KWCR; after getting tired of his younger brother telling him how he should do things there, Sumner Quarton suggested that "if you're so good, come on" to Cedar Rapids and work at KWCR. Bill took him up on the offer, and returned to Iowa in November 1931. Not long after, the Cowles family bought WMT and moved the station back to Cedar Rapids. Bill was the sales manager for the station until 1943, when he succeeded his brother as station manager.

Soon after, the Cowles family sold WMT to American Broadcasting Stations, Inc. of Delaware. Bill Quarton became an executive vice president of the company, responsible for the WMT stations. He also became active in a number of professional organizations, including serving as the first president of the Iowa Broadcasters Association in 1950. Nationally, he served on the Television Code Board, the Radio Advertising Bureau, and the Radio Board and Joint Board of the National Association of Broadcasters. He even served a term on the state Board of Regents.

By 1953, the freeze on television licenses was lifted, and Channel 2 signed on as the first station in eastern Iowa on September 30 of that year. Channel 2 capitalized on the reputation previously established by WMT radio, and quickly became a dominant force in television news in Iowa. As a CBS affiliate, the station also enjoyed the successes of the nation's top television network.

In recognition of the geography of the eastern Iowa market, the station began identifying itself as "WMT-TV, Cedar Rapids and Waterloo" —the first television station in the country to use a dual city identification.

Quarton's style and vision was acknowledged by a host of former employees and fellow station owners. "Bill Quarton to me is one of the finest broadcasters I will ever have known," said longtime Spencer radio station owner Ben Sanders. "He was just great." Sanders called Quarton the "grandpappy of radio" in Iowa.

"He was the easiest man to work for," remembers Howdy Roberts, who worked for Quarton at WMT for 40 years.

Former news anchor Robert Johnson, who later became mayor of Cedar Rapids, has the utmost respect for Quarton. "I could never call him Bill. Everyone else did," Johnson said. "I can't call him Bill. It's always Mr. Quarton, to this day."

An official station biography from the mid-1960s credits WMT's popularity to "his tremendous understanding of eastern Iowans and their needs" as well as his willingness to "allot big pieces of budget to two fields: first, promotion and merchandising at the local level;

William B. Quarton

and, secondly, seeking out and building WMT's personalities to a popularity in our area that equals or exceeds that of national celebrities."

"He was maybe the greatest visionary in terms of what the electronic media were capable of doing and being of anyone out of that era," said Grant Price, who worked for the WMT stations for 13 years.

Well known for his promotions, one of Quarton's most successful campaigns won the station listeners, won a small business new customers, and won Quarton himself a wife, all

R. J. McElroy

at the same time.

Elnora Bierkamp owned and managed a store called The Little Flower Shop on a prominent Cedar Rapids corner. The business was too small to afford the ambitious advertising campaign salesman Quarton felt was needed. According to a biographical article from the WMT archives, "Aware of her personal charm and undaunted by the store's puny advertising budget, resourceful Bill concocted an idea which made her flowers as familiar to Iowans as the corn in their fields."

He sold Art Shepard on the idea of hosting his midday "man on the street" program in front of the flower shop, supposedly because of its central location. Listeners tuning in would hear an announcement for the "Man on the Street program, coming to you from in front of The Little Flower Shop." Soon, flower sales increased greatly, and Elnora Bierkamp became Mrs. William B. Quarton.

R. J. McElroy

McElroy was born in Eau Claire, Wisconsin, in 1910; he left home at age 13 to work and help support the family. Returning to Wisconsin, he began work for the F. W. Woolworth store at age 17, working his way up the ladder until by 1933, Woolworth had transferred him to Cedar Rapids as an assistant manager. There he met Art Shepard, the original "Voice of Iowa" on WMT; Shepard soon recommended McElroy for a sales job with the station in Waterloo.

Mac's independent streak was often evident. On occasion, McElroy opted to take the day off to play golf instead of working in the office or on the street, selling advertising. When the Waterloo manager, Don Inman, complained, McElroy would simply say, "OK, fire me and get someone else who can sell as much as I do."

Inman also tried to inspire his sales staff by often rounding up the crew at the end of the day and driving far out into the country; any salesperson who could not produce a new sales contract sold that day would get the privilege of walking back home. To avoid ever making the long walk, Mac had made a deal with Bill Bolster, Sr., the manager of Sweeney's Dress Shop in Waterloo. He always carried a signed contract from Sweeney's in his pocket which he could date and fill in whenever the surprise "ride" was sprung on him.

After serving in the war, McElroy returned to Waterloo to find that the WMT management was going to abandon its Waterloo studios, which had been in operation since 1924, and consolidate its operation in Cedar Rapids. Mac saw the possibility of starting a new Waterloo station to fill the void left by WMT's departure. The only competition was KXEL, a station started in 1942 by former WMT personality Joe Dumond.

On a Sunday night in January of 1947, McElroy had invited a number of business leaders to a dinner at the Russell Lamson Hotel in Waterloo with the idea of selling them stock in his proposed Black Hawk Broadcasting Company. The effort worked, and the company was capitalized with $45,000; $5,000 in common stock, of which Mac owned half, and the rest in preferred stock owned by business leaders in the community. On November 4, 1947, McElroy spoke into the KWWL radio microphone for the first time.

"KWWL is owned by 31 civic minded and public spirited citizens of Waterloo and Cedar Falls. It is their desire that I dedicate the station to the service of all those within hearing of its voice to a better way of life through enlightenment," he said. "It is only because we live in a free country that we are able to keep that freedom alive. KWWL pledges to serve its listeners by presenting all sides of all issues at all times."

"One of the precepts of freedom is the right to worship God as we see fit. As we face the future, we turn to God for inspiration and guidance," McElroy ended, turning to a local minister for an on air prayer for the station.

Just as the upstart KWWL was beginning to make inroads against the more established KXEL, the push for television station licenses heated up, and KWWL and KXEL both filed to go on the air on Channel 7. Their legendary fight led to a lawsuit, with Dumond conceding to McElroy during the trial. Before long, the station McElroy started with $45,000 in 1947 became a company which owned an AM, FM and TV station in Waterloo, as well as stations in Austin, Minnesota.

The Legacy of Quarton And McElroy

But McElroy did not live to see his stations grow into the powerhouses they would become in the 1970s. He died suddenly in 1965, and was succeeded as chairman of Black Hawk Broadcasting by his longtime friend and lawyer, Robert Buckmaster. Through prudent investment in facilities and continued commitment to the community, Buckmaster would preside over tremendous growth in the company.

Lasting Legacies

Quarton retired from the broadcasting business in 1968, and set aside a quarter of a million dollars from the sale of the WMT stations to be given to the Iowa Broadcasters Association for various projects including college scholarships. The donation was made on the condition that IBA members contribute one dollar for every two dollars Quarton donated. The money was quickly raised, and the IBA Quarton Fund was established.

The Black Hawk Broadcasting Company was sold to the AFLAC insurance group of Columbus, Georgia in 1980 for $44 million. McElroy's will provided that the great share of his estate be placed in trust to benefit the children of eastern Iowa. At the time of his death, the trust was not worth very much, but it soon would become a major force in the lives of many eastern Iowa young people. After the sale to AFLAC, the R. J. McElroy Trust found itself worth $40 million.

At that point, Buckmaster and Harry Slife, a longtime Black Hawk official, served on the McElroy Trust Board of Trustees. Knowing of the fund he had established with the Iowa Broadcasters Association, the two men approached Bill Quarton about donating some of the McElroy Trust funds to that effort. They offered to match Quarton's original investment if McElroy's name could be added to the broadcasters' trust; Quarton quickly agreed, and the IBA Quarton-McElroy Trust (or the Q-MAC Fund, as it is known to many) quickly swelled to three-quarters of a million dollars. Soon after, the trust corpus hit $2 million, and the fund was turned over to the Greater Cedar Rapids Community Foundation for administration.

As many as three dozen college students each year receive financial support from the Quarton-McElroy Trust to assist in paying for their educational expenses as they study broadcasting. Millions of dollars annually are awarded by the R. J. McElroy Trust to support scholarships and educational activities throughout northeast Iowa. And the Greater Cedar Rapids Community Foundation makes further investments to benefit eastern Iowa activities, thanks to the direct generosity of Quarton himself.

Today, Bill Quarton is still active in the Cedar Rapids community at the age of 101, and his advice on civic, business and broadcasting matters is eagerly sought. Thanks to the generosity of both men, even some 70 years later, the Quarton and McElroy names will forever be intertwined and remembered with great respect.

Impact on Society

There has been renewed emphasis on the history of broadcasting of late. The oldest radio stations in Iowa are now more than 80 years old, and television stations in every market in the state have celebrated their golden anniversaries.

A decade ago, the Iowa Broadcasting Oral History Project was founded by Grant Price, with support from the Iowa Broadcasters Association among others. Similar efforts to capture the history of radio and television in Iowa had been begun by others around the same time. The tremendous response to the oral history project led to the establishment of the Archives of Iowa Broadcasting, located at Wartburg College in Waverly. Designated by the Iowa Broadcasters Association as a primary repository of materials related to the state's broadcasting history, the collection has grown tremendously in the past five years.

Audio and video recordings, promotional materials, legal files, equipment such as microphones and television cameras, and more are now a part of the collection. This book is only the latest outgrowth of materials from the Archives of Iowa Broadcasting; a number of scholarly articles and a one-hour television documentary have already been produced.

In keeping with the ever-changing technology, greater access to items in the Archives collection—from broadcast audio and video to photos and historical information—is now available through the World Wide Web at *www.IowaBroadcasting.com*.

For many years, analysis of the impact of broadcasting was not taken seriously in social scientific circles, since the medium was still too new. Now, as the centennial of the first experiments in what would become voice broadcasting draws near, scholars have a base upon which to measure the societal impact of the role of mass communication in society.

Judging from the evidence seen to date, the impact has been greater than that of any other invention in the last century. The vision and foresight of industry pioneers like McElroy and Quarton are key reasons why.

A Timeline of Iowa Broadcasting Highlights

1919

The first radio station to be licensed in Iowa, 9YA, began voice transmissions from the State University of Iowa with a transmitter built by SUI student Carl Menzer. The station would later be known as WHAA, and by 1925, as WSUI; Menzer would manage the station until his retirement in 1968.

1922

The first commercial radio station in Iowa was approved for broadcasting on February 18, when the Department of Commerce issued Col. B. J. Palmer a license for WOC in Davenport. It is the oldest radio station in Iowa to broadcast continuously with its original call letters.

Radio station WJAM in Cedar Rapids began broadcasting on July 30, 1922. The first material broadcast was a musical selection titled "Don't Send Me Posies When It's Shoesies That I Need." Station founder Douglas "Tex" Perham installed WJAM in a garage on Cedar Rapids' southwest side, later moving the transmitting antenna and tower to the roof of his home. A few years later, the station would become known as WMT.

In May, KFJB in Marshalltown began live remote broadcasts of local track meets from Franklin Field; later that fall, the station also broadcast football games. These are believed to be the first high school sporting events broadcast live from the field, not only in Iowa but in the entire United States. The presence of radio announcers at the games must have been inspiring to the Bobcats—they won their first ten games that season, including a "double header" on September 23, defeating Belle Plaine 32-0 and Toledo 28-0 in the nation's first live broadcasts of their kind. (The station was officially licensed by the FCC on June 2, 1923, as the 17th radio station then on the air in Iowa.)

1924

WHO in Des Moines began broadcasting on April 11, at a frequency of 570 kHz. Started by the Banker's Life Company, the typical station identification line was "This is WHO. Who? Banker's Life, Des Moines." Later, after Col. B. J. Palmer's company purchased the station in 1930, many claimed the call letters stood for "With Hands Only," in light of Palmer's association with the chiropractic field.

Henry Field's wisdom about gardening and seeds began to be known to thousands as KFNF radio in Shenandoah took to the air on February 22 from makeshift studios on the third floor of the Field Seed Company Building in Shenandoah. The radio and seed competition in Shenandoah heated up in August of 1925, when Earl May's KMA radio signed on from studios in the Earl May Seed & Nursery Company down the street as "the cornbelt station in the heart of the nation."

1926

Earl May receives more than 450,000 votes from listeners across America to win the 1926 Gold Cup from *Radio Digest* magazine. May's crosstown competitor, Henry Field, was the national runner-up in the previous year's contest, but withdrew in 1926 and urged his listeners to vote for May. As a test in the days before formal governmental regulation of stations, May boosted the power of his station and was heard from listeners as far away as Honolulu, Hawaii, and Melbourne, Australia.

The age of the radio homemaker program dawned, when Helen Field Fischer, one of Henry Field's five sisters, began a daily program on Shenandoah radio station KFNF called "The Mother's Hour." Later that year, she invited another sister, Leanna Field Driftmier, to appear on the program. Soon, Leanna would have a program of her own—"Kitchen Klatter," which became the longest-running show in radio history, syndicated to a number of stations.

1927

On April 4 at 6 p.m., KSCJ-AM (for *Sioux City Journal*) signed on the air. Originally found at 670 kHz, the station changed dial position three times in its first decade and a half, until settling at its current 1360 AM dial position in 1941. It is Sioux City's oldest continuously operating station, having also held the same call letters through its entire history.

The first live market reports from a remote location were broadcast on June 6, when KSCJ's Joe Hale began broadcasting the markets three times each day from the Sioux City Stock Exchange Building. Hale did the reports live for more than 35 years; KSCJ did them live on location for more than 50 years, until the early 1980s.

1928

WJAM in Cedar Rapids was sold to Harry Shaw, owner of the *Waterloo Morning Tribune*. Shaw moved the station to Waterloo and changed the call letters to match his newspaper: WMT. The station would remain based in Waterloo until the owners of the *Des Moines Register & Tribune*, "Mike" and John Cowles, purchased it in late 1934 and moved the base of WMT's operations back to Cedar Rapids in 1935. The Cowles brothers merged WMT with the Cedar Rapids station they already owned, KWCR.

Iowa was assigned a single "clear channel" frequency by the new Federal Radio Commission, 1000 kHz. Both WHO and WOC were assigned to share time on the same frequency, beginning on November 11. The stations alternated use of the time, with one station being on during the day one week while the other was on during the evening, and operating on an opposite schedule the next week. Banker's Life sold WHO to B. J. Palmer's Central Broadcasting Company—owners of WOC—in 1930. Within a few years, the Davenport studios are closed and "WHO-WOC" operates from Des Moines until 1933. (WOC returned to the air at a different frequency in 1934.)

1931

On August 28, the State University of Iowa demonstrated mechanical scanning television with home built equipment; the first of its kind in America, the station operated on the air in Iowa City as W9XK with a regular experimental broadcast schedule using audio from WSUI-AM from January 25, 1933, until June 29, 1939. (An electrical scanning system was developed later during the 1930s, which became the basis for the television we know today.)

The first "Iowa Barn Dance Frolic" was broadcast as a half-hour program on WOC radio in Davenport. The program would move to Des Moines one year later for a run on WHO radio and television that would last until 1958.

1935

The first "Yellow Dog Auction" to raise money to provide underprivileged children with Christmas toys was held by KSCJ-AM in Sioux City, sponsored by the station's famous morning "Town Crier" program, hosted by Ray Murphy and Rodney Dean. The effort has continued every year to this day.

WHO radio established its first news department, with H. R. Gross hired as news director. Jack Shelley joins the staff as Gross' assistant later that year. Gross would later move to radio in Ohio and Indiana before returning to Iowa as news director at KXEL in Waterloo, the base from which he would launch his long-time political career as a congressman from Iowa's third district.

1936

On August 26, the WHO Farm Department was founded with the first broadcast by Herb Plambeck, who would be the station's farm director for 33½ years. Plambeck's first remote broadcast was that same afternoon at the first WHO Crystal Studio, located next to the Varied Industries Building at the State Fairgrounds in Des Moines.

1937

KGLO in Mason City took to the air on 100 watts on January 17; in June, the station became affiliated with CBS, the first station of its small size to have the coveted network affiliation.

1938

KTRI (for the *Tribune*) signed on in Sioux City, owned by the daily afternoon newspaper in the market. The newspaper is long gone, but the radio station has broadcast continuously, now bearing the call letters KWSL.

1939

The first WHO Plowing Match was held near Mitchellville. The event would eventually attract hundreds of thousands of attendees each year.

1941

Listeners across America had to hunt for their favorite stations on March 29. This was the day a general realignment of radio stations went into effect as part of the North American Radio Agreement. It was on this date that many stations moved to the AM frequencies they still operate on today.

1943

On December 3, Al Heinz began work at KGLO radio; he would be farm director there beginning in 1947 and was continuing his daily farm broadcasting schedule a half century later.

1944

Fresh from graduation at the State University of Iowa, sports announcer Jim Zabel began work at WHO radio in Des Moines. Zabel still broadcasts sports for the station today, 60 years later.

1946

"Professional" television came to the Iowa State Fair for the first time, as KRNT radio brought a crew from RCA in New York to televise entertainment from a stage to a group of sets outside the tent. An estimated 350,000 persons came through the International Harvester tent next to the Varied Industries Building to watch live television for the first time.

In the fall, the first "Hey, Bob!" show, hosted by Bill Riley, was aired on KRNT radio in Des Moines. The program ran for five years and focused on safety and fun for children. Some 1,300 children attended the live Saturday morning show at the Paramount Theatre in Des Moines each week, with occasional shows filling the KRNT Theater with more than 4,000 persons.

1947

KCRK-FM went on the air, soon followed by sister station KCRG-AM in Cedar Rapids. It was the first FM station in the area, but only lasted a short time before going "dark;" while FM stations are popular today, at that time, there was little interest shown by the public.

KWWL radio went on the air in Waterloo, with owner R. J. McElroy moving his popular midday "man on the street" show from WMT to his new station. "The Voice of Eastern Iowa" aired daily on KWWL radio, and later television, until 1959. McElroy had begun the program on WMT radio in 1935.

1948

The next wave of FM stations came on the air, including the first FM station in Siouxland, KSCJ-FM, and the first broadcasts from University of Iowa-owned KSUI-FM in Iowa City.

1949

WOC-TV in Davenport became Iowa's first television station on October 31. An estimated 400 Quad Cities homes had television sets at the time. The station originally was at Channel 5, but later moved to Channel 6. The station was renamed KWQC-TV in 1986.

Paul Rhoades began his broadcasting career at KRNT radio in Des Moines. He would stay at KRNT radio or television his entire career—43 years—most of which as the primary 6 p.m. news anchor.

1950

The first television station in central Iowa took to the air on February 21 at Channel 4 (the station would later move to Channel 5). The station had no cameras at the time, and viewers saw only slides and film, rather than local persons live. Since there were no other stations in central Iowa, the new WOI-TV could pick and choose between programs from all four major networks existing at the time: ABC, NBC, CBS and the now-defunct Dumont network. The station was located in the former WOI radio building, Exhibit Hall, which actually began its life as a sheep barn on the ISC (now ISU) campus.

The first television station in the state of Illinois outside of Chicago signed on from downtown Rock Island on Saturday, July 1. WHBF-TV served many Iowa residents in the Quad Cities as the local CBS affiliate, and for more than a decade, also aired ABC programs on a delayed basis. The establishment of WHBF-TV at Channel 4 required WOC-TV to move from Channel 5 to Channel 6 as part of a realignment of station channel assignments by the FCC in 1952.

1951

On January 15, the FCC approved a license for KWAR-FM in Waverly. Owned by Wartburg College, the station would be the first student-run, non-commercial FM station in Iowa, and has broadcast at 89.1 FM consistently ever since.

"The Magic Window" premieres on WOI-TV. The program ran for 43 years until March 1, 1994, and stands as the longest continuously running local children's show in U.S. history. For all but the first three years, the program was hosted by Betty Lou Varnum.

Leo Greco and his Pioneers began an early morning radio show on WMT-AM. They would become the first entertainment program presented on WMT-TV when that station was founded in 1953, beginning a 16-year run on television. Both the Greco radio and television programs were sponsored by Kent Feeds, and were syndicated on stations in Iowa and other states.

1952

Dick Petrik began work as news director at KOEL-AM/FM in Oelwein, a job he would have for 41 years until retirement in 1993.

Fulfilling its educational mission as a property owned by Iowa State College (now Iowa State University), WOI-TV became the second station in the nation to develop programming designed for use in the public schools. "TV Schooltime" was one such effort, as was "Landmarks in Iowa History," which for more than 20 years featured an ending cartoon creation by Herb Hake, making that program the most popular of all of WOI's schooltime programming.

1953

On Sunday, March 29, the first television station in Sioux City, and the third overall located in Iowa, signed on. KVTV operated at Channel 9, and the next day, Jim Henry would begin a 32-year run hosting a children's show as the "Canyon Kid." The station became known as KCAU-TV in 1965.

Television came to Eastern Iowa, as William B. Quarton appears on WMT-TV, Channel 2, at 11:35 a.m. on September 30. The first program following Quarton's introduction was the 1953 World Series. The first regular local program was "Sports with Tait," featuring legendary sports journalist Tait Cummins.

After winning a spirited legal contest, on November 29, R. J. McElroy threw the switch to put KWWL-TV, Channel 7, on the air in Waterloo.

1954

Live local children's programming came to eastern Iowa television, with the premiere of "Miss Ruth Anne's School" in January on WMT-TV. While that program lasted only two months, its successor—Marshal J—was on the air for seven years. Both programs predated the long-running national program "Captain Kangaroo," which did not debut on CBS until 1955.

On April 26, WHO-TV 13 in Des Moines signed on as the first VHF television station based in Iowa's capital city.

KGLO-TV 3 in Mason City signed on the air on May 15, owned by the *Mason City Globe-Gazette* newspaper.

The second television station in Sioux City signed on, as KTIV-TV 4 made its broadcasting debut on October 10 as an NBC affiliate.

1955

KRNT-TV 8, the television service of the *Des Moines Register & Tribune*, first signed on the air on July 31 as a CBS affiliate. The license for Channel 8 was contested between KRNT-AM and KSO-AM, which ironically were at one time both owned by the *Register & Tribune*.

One of the first regular programs on KRNT-TV was "Teen Time," which began life as the "Rath Talent Review" on KRNT-AM. The program hosted by Bill Riley, aired on Channel 8 (and later on WHO-TV 13) for a total of 19 years. "The Iowa State Fair Talent Search" debuted at the fair in 1959, tied to the television program; it is estimated that 100,000 Iowa youngsters performed as part of the "State Fair Talent Search" all over Iowa during the past half century.

1957

Dottie Ray began a daily talk and interview program live from her Iowa City home on KXIC-AM 800, which still airs today, 47 years later.

The farm department at WMT radio and television held the first "Iowa's Favorite Farmer's Daughter Contest." The tradition lasted until the late-1970s.

1958

As a child, even future Iowa governor Terry Branstad appeared on "Bart's Clubhouse," which began its 18-year-run on KGLO-TV in Mason City when Bart Curran took over the afternoon children's show on Channel 3 after the previous host of a cowboy serial show there quit.

1959

The Des Moines Technical High School signed on with KDPS-TV, Channel 11. On April 2, 1969, the station was sold to the State of Iowa for $579,000 as the first station in what is now known as the Iowa Public Television network (IPTV).

Dave Shay came to WMT-TV from WOW-TV in Omaha to anchor the late local news, succeeding Henry Lippold. Shay would stay at WMT, later KGAN, until 1993. In April of 1960, the late news was moved to its now familiar 10 p.m. slot, and renamed "Report to Iowa." It became one of the first integrated newscasts in the country, with news, weather and sports all in one show (rather than as their own separate programs, run back-to-back). Shay, meteorologist Conrad Johnson and sports director Tait Cummins served as the late news team for five years, during which time WMT built a ratings dominance—as many as 75 percent of all sets in use at the time were tuned to the late news on Channel 2.

1961

On January 23, eastern Iowa children began seeing their doctor regularly, as Max Hahn began "The Dr. Max Show" on WMT-TV, which ran live Monday through Friday for 20½ years. Thousands of viewers knew to "take it easy, play it safe, and be careful," thanks to Dr. Max's farewell each day, and logged their daily activities in "My Important Book."

Broadcasting legend B. J. Palmer died in May and his son, David D. Palmer, assumes control over the Central Broadcasting Company. David Palmer would oversee the company's interests until his death in 1978.

1963

At 11:30 a.m. on February 27, WMT-FM in Cedar Rapids signed on the air. The first musical selection was "Don't Send Me Posies When It's Shoesies That I Need"—the same musical selection that was played first on what would later be known as WMT-AM on July 30, 1922.

A nearly 40-year eastern Iowa tradition began when Jim Loyd hosts the first "Open Line" program on WMT-AM. Within its first decade on the air, the program generated a monthly bulletin with recipes and homemaker hints reaching a circulation of more than 9,000. The program aired six days a week until the summer of 2000, and lives on today with a Saturday edition.

On August 1, WQAD-TV 8 took to the air from Moline, Illinois, providing Quad Cities viewers with a full ABC schedule. Long time anchor Jim King sat at the sports desk then, but within a year would move to the news anchor position. King anchored news at WQAD-TV until his death in 1998.

1967

WQAD-TV's Jim King made his second month-long trip to Vietnam in September, interviewing more than 100 Quad Cities area servicemen. King's reports from Vietnam the summer before aired during newscasts and as part of three 30 minute specials.

1973

Leo Greco began his Sunday morning show on WMT-AM. The show still continues today, now in its fourth decade.

1974

Ron Steele began work at KWWL-TV on April 1 as sports director. He moved to the news anchor position on July 1, 1979, succeeding Tom Peterson, and now has the longest continuous tenure of any person currently anchoring television news in Iowa. In addition, in the history of Iowa television, no person has anchored both the 6 p.m. and 10 p.m. newscasts for the same station continuously for as long a time as Steele has at Channel 7.

On Friday, October 4 at 6 a.m., KRNA-FM took to the air at 93.5 mHz, the first rock and roll FM station in eastern Iowa, and the first station in the area to operate 24 hours a day, 7 days a week. The first words on the station were, "Hello, am I on?"—the announcer's headphones were not working, and he could not tell if he was actually broadcasting or not. Within four months, an Arbitron telephone survey of listeners showed that nearly 50 percent of the radios in use at the time were tuned to KRNA.

1975

The early part of this year saw the retirement of three long-time WMT radio staffers. In January, Howdy Roberts retired after 40 years at the station, and nearly 31 years of hosting the morning "Musical Clock" program, the most listened to program in eastern Iowa. In February, program manager and former "Voice of Iowa" host Dean Landfear retired after 32 years at the station; he also hosted the late-night "Off the Record" music program. And in March, Ken Hastie retired as station manager after 39 years at the station; he began at WMT in 1936 after having worked at KSO-KRNT as traffic manager.

1979

The visit of Pope John Paul II to Living History Farms near Des Moines allowed Iowa broadcast stations a unique opportunity to produce coverage of the event which is seen by a worldwide audience. Hundreds of thousands of Iowans attended the new pope's mass at an outdoor chapel.

1981

WOI-TV became the first local station in America to originate a live broadcast of an NCAA athletic event via satellite when it brought the Iowa State/San Diego State football game to Iowa viewers from game site in California on October 10.

1982

Des Moines television viewers welcomed back Kevin and Mollie Cooney, who returned to Channel 8 after a two-year stint at a California station. Kevin took over a co-anchor slot at 6 p.m. and 10 p.m., replacing Rick Fredericksen, and in 1985, Mollie began anchoring the midday news; they each hold those same positions at KCCI-TV today.

1983

On March 11, after some 6,600 newscasts on KRNT/KCCI television and another 2,700 before that on KRNT radio, Russ Van Dyke signed off for the last time as the 10 p.m. anchor on Channel 8 in Des Moines. At the time of his retirement, Van Dyke had the longest tenure of any television anchor in the country at the time (28 years). Before spending 36 years in Des Moines broadcasting, Van Dyke was well known for his work on WNAX radio in Yankton, South Dakota.

1984

The Iowa State Fair parade was broadcast live on television for the first time, by WOI-TV. The station had plenty of experience, since it had aired the VEISHEA parade live from the Iowa State campus each year since 1950.

1986

Doug Krile left KCRG-AM/TV after 14½ years at the Cedar Rapids station for KARK-TV in Little Rock. A Sioux Rapids native and University of Iowa graduate, he began his career at WSUI radio while a student, and started full-time work at KCRG immediately after graduation. He had been primary anchor at Channel 9 for many years, and for the last three years had also been news director.

1987

On June 22, the voice of Floppy fell forever silent, as creator Duane Ellett died. "The Floppy Show" was a fixture of afternoon television on WHO-TV for parts of four decades, beginning in the mid-1950s as "Pet Corner," a show designed to find homes for sheltered pets.

1993

The extensive flooding which struck the entire state of Iowa led to a special live prime-time broadcast that aired simultaneously on virtually every Iowa television station. The program was designed to raise funds to help flood victims, and was hosted by Willard Scott of NBC's "The Today Show."

On December 15, Iowa's first television news helicopter made its inaugural live telecast. KCRG in Cedar Rapids was the first to use the technology, designed to help the station cover its 21-county signal area. A decade later, only one other Iowa station (WHO-TV in Des Moines) has its own helicopter for use in live broadcasts.

1994

After more than 44 years of ownership by Iowa State University, the sale of WOI-TV became official on March 1. The sale to Capital Communications came after a bitter legal battle fought by "Iowans for WOI-TV" against the State Board of Regents in an effort to preserve ISU's ownership of the ABC affiliate.

2001

KGAN-TV in Cedar Rapids began producing a newscast that aired on sister-station KDSM-TV in Des Moines. The effort was the first between stations in different markets in Iowa. The newscast is sent from Cedar Rapids to Des Moines by fiber optic connections. The same year, WHO-TV began producing a separate newscast for airing on KFPX-TV in the Des Moines market.

2002

The Salt Lake City Winter Olympics in February provided the incentive for NBC affiliates WHO-TV in Des Moines and KWWL-TV in Waterloo to begin broadcasting a digital television (DTV) signal; each station would begin a regular schedule broadcasting in DTV on May 1, becoming the first commercial stations in their areas to do so. By 2004, 18 Iowa DTV stations were on the air.

2003

KZIA-FM in Cedar Rapids became Iowa's first high-definition (HD) radio station at 3:22 p.m. on May 14. The change in technology will require listeners to obtain new receiving equipment, similar to the conversion needed for digital television. KMRY-AM in Cedar Rapids will become Iowa's first AM high-definition station before the end of 2004. (Interestingly, both stations are independently owned—the only independently-owned commercial radio stations in the Cedar Rapids/Iowa City market.)

Credits

This book is the product of the preservation efforts of a number of people across Iowa, who had the foresight to keep photos, documents and recordings—and most importantly, who were willing to share those items and their memories.

Of greatest help were the videotaped interviews gathered as part of the on-going Iowa Broadcasting Oral History Project. Some of those interviews were conducted specifically for this book, while others have been gathered over the past decade. Information and quotes were used from more than 40 people whose stories were recorded in this way. Noted broadcaster Don Uker conducted interviews with a number of station owners and managers in the early 1990s, and those materials have also been a great source of information.

Thanks go to our friends at Iowa Public Television, who shared videotapes of interviews conducted with noted Iowa broadcasters as part of the network's "Golden Age of Television" series, produced some twenty years ago. Much of the information about children's programming was drawn from segments produced in 1995 for IPTV's "Living in Iowa" series. A series of videotapes commissioned in the early 1990s by the Greater Shenandoah Historical Society on "Pioneer Broadcasters" carefully documented the unique experience of KMA and KFNF in the first part of the century.

Some stations have shared their recent anniversaries with the viewing and listening public, and the programs they produced have helped the author—and countless thousands of audience members—fondly remember milestones in the respective stations' histories. Of particular note were the 60th and 75th anniversary programs prepared by WSUI in Iowa City; the 75th anniversary segments produced by KMA in Shenandoah; a video commemorating the 70th anniversary of KSCJ radio in Sioux City; and videotaped anniversary programs for KGAN-TV in Cedar Rapids, KWWL-TV in Waterloo, and WOI-TV in Ames/Des Moines. A videotape of the luncheon commemorating WHO radio's golden anniversary in 1974 was helpful in providing information concerning Ronald Reagan's time in Iowa radio.

A number of printed sources were also of great help. Some of these materials have never been available to the general public, having been prepared for promotion or internal station distribution. Warren Mead's 1977 history of the Black Hawk Broadcasting Company provided insight from those who were there when R. J. McElroy founded KWWL thirty years before. Robert Neymeyer's biography of McElroy, written in 1997, also provided fresh insight. Neil Harl's book, "Arrogance and Power: The Saga of WOI-TV," includes meticulous research about Iowa State's ownership of Channel 5. The late Herb Plambeck was a prolific writer in his later years; his series of books are full of details previously unknown to listeners. The history of Sioux City radio has been carefully documented by long-time station engineer Sam Seldon, who graciously donated a copy of his work to the Archives of Iowa Broadcasting.

The wonderful photographs contained in this book came from a variety of sources. Specific credit for the WSUI photos goes to the F. W. Kent Collection at the University Archives in Iowa City. Thanks go to the Pottawatamie County Historical Society for the Lee DeForest photo, and to Ben Stearns of Cedar Rapids for the Arthur Collins photo.

Historians who study communication, culture, and the history of Iowa's second-largest city all owe a debt of thanks to Rick Sellers and Rick Plummer for preserving the history of WMT radio in Cedar Rapids; their commitment and diligence has saved many items that otherwise would have been forever lost.

The photos concerning WHO were obtained through the help of radio station chief engineer Raleigh Rubenking, among others. George Davison, co-founder of the "DesMoinesBroadcasting.com" Web site, continues to provide a great service by tirelessly working to maintain the history of radio and television in Iowa's capital city and sharing the wealth of information he and his colleagues have found.

Extensive photographic and research materials concerning KRNT radio and Channel 8 in Des Moines came from KCCI-TV; the author thanks program director Bob Day for allowing access to those materials.

Many of the photos from Shenandoah radio were provided by former radio homemaker Evelyn Birkby, whose son Robert wrote a complete history of KMA in conjunction with the station's 60th anniversary.

The story of the proud history of Channel 2 in Cedar Rapids would not have been nearly as complete without the generous help of program director Melissa Hubbard, who loaned the author many photos from her personal collection of materials.

Writing this book also gave the author an opportunity to reconnect with KFJB's Al Schrock—who hired an unproven 17-year-old as a part-time announcer in 1980 and changed the course of his life forever. In retirement, Schrock compiled scrapbooks that are priceless in telling the story of one of Iowa's most noted regional radio stations; the photos in this book from that era of KFJB's history were generously provided by him.

But none of this—the Archives, the oral history project, this book—would have been possible without the consistent support and dedication of Grant Price, whose vision for preserving the history of this important medium has directly led to all we have achieved so far, and all that we will accomplish in the future. His encouragement and friendship have been a source of inspiration; the role he played in this effort cannot be overstated.

Photo illustration created for holiday cards in the late 1950s showing the Dean Osmundson family of Ottumwa "watching" dad on TV. Broadcasting is the Osmundson family business, as son Mark (seated front) now operates KDAO-AM/FM/TV in central Iowa.

About the Author

Jeff Stein

Jeff Stein is an educator, journalist and attorney. He holds the title of R. J. McElroy Chair and Executive-in-Residence in Communication Arts at Wartburg College, teaching broadcasting and media law and ethics courses. He also serves as executive secretary of the Iowa Broadcast News Association.

Stein is an award-winning broadcaster who has worked for a number of Iowa stations, including KFJB-AM in Marshalltown and WSUI-AM in Iowa City, and has served as political analyst for KWWL-TV in Waterloo and WOI-TV in Des Moines.

He is also the administrator of the Archives of Iowa Broadcasting collection and has spoken around the country on broadcasting, journalism, and mass media topics. Stein is the author of *Covering Iowa Law and Courts: A Guide for Journalists*, published by the Iowa State Bar Association.

He and his wife, Carole Lackey, live in Waverly.